BORN BOTH

BORN BOTH

AN INTERSEX LIFE

HIDA VILORIA

hachette
BOOKS

NEW YORK BOSTON

Hachette Books
Hachette Book Group
1290 Avenue of the Americas
New York, NY 10104
hachettebooks.com
twitter.com/hachettebooks

First Edition: March 2017

Hachette Books is a division of Hachette Book Group, Inc.
The Hachette Books name and logo are trademarks of Hachette Book Group, Inc.

The publisher is not responsible for websites (or their content) that are not owned by the publisher.

The Hachette Speakers Bureau provides a wide range of authors for speaking events. To find out more, go to www.hachettespeakersbureau.com or call (866) 376-6591.

Library of Congress Cataloging-in-Publication Data

Names: Viloria, Hida, author.
Title: Born both : an intersex life / Hida Viloria.
Description: First edition. | New York : Hachette Books, 2017. | Includes
    bibliographical references.
Identifiers: LCCN 2016030284| ISBN 9780316347846 (hardback) | ISBN
    9781478940715 (audio download) | ISBN 9781478969013 (audio cd)
Subjects: LCSH: Viloria, Hida. | Intersex people—United States—Biography. |
    Intersex people—Identity. | Intersexuality. | BISAC: BIOGRAPHY &
    AUTOBIOGRAPHY / Personal Memoirs. | SOCIAL SCIENCE / Gender Studies.
Classification: LCC HQ77.98.V55 A3 2017 | DDC 306.76/85—dc23 LC record
    available at https://lccn.loc.gov/2016030284

ISBNs: 978-0-316-34784-6 (hardcover), 978-0-316-34781-5 (ebook)

Printed in the United States of America

LSC-C

10 9 8 7 6 5 4 3 2 1

To my mother, Doris Matheus-Viloria, who showed me what love is, and to all the intersex people who have had to live, and die, in secret.

Contents

Author's Note

The names of most people I mention in this book have been changed, whether or not I indicate it in the text, and certain events have been condensed.

As someone who respects the importance of preferred pronouns for intersex people, trans people, nonbinary people, and others, I also want to note that some of the people I mention in this book are currently using different pronouns to refer to themselves than they were during the time periods I have written about.

BORN BOTH

THE DARKEST HOUR IS just before the dawn" is an old proverb that's intended to inspire hope in difficult or unfortunate times. The darkest hour is also the hour I was born, on May 29, 1968, seventeen minutes before sunrise. It turns out the saying aptly applies to my birth in more ways than one, but it would take me decades to realize this—decades to learn that my entry into this world was a moment of confusion that would raise questions about both my sex and my gender, the resolution of which was, unexpectedly, a blessing. For the first twenty years of my life I thought I was, physically speaking, an ordinary girl.

CHAPTER 1

The Hazards of Being Female

MANHATTAN, NEW YORK
NOVEMBER 1988

THE TREES ON THE sidewalks of the West Village are in that lovely, colorful state of transition. It's my favorite neighborhood in Manhattan, this enclave of winding cobblestone streets lined with beautiful old brownstones and decades of queer history, like the Stonewall riots of '69 and the infamous Halloween parades down Christopher Street that I'd been lucky enough to attend in high school.

I find the address I'm looking for on Perry Street and ring the buzzer.

"Hey, girl!" I hear Jade say over the intercom. "I'm up on the third floor."

Jade is my good friend from high school. She's a year younger than I am, and the minute she showed up at St. Francis Preparatory School in Queens, she was the girl all the straight boys wanted. I thought she was hot too, but we were in high school in 1985, and "Prep," as we called it, wasn't just Catholic but prided itself on being the *largest* Catholic high school in the United States. In other words, it wasn't exactly okay to make it known at school that I was into another girl.

Jade was more than just a hottie though; she was cool. She was someone who could, like me, hang equally well with the artsy outcasts, the jocks, and everyone in between. She had stayed in New York after high school to go to the prestigious Parsons School of Design and had been trying to convince me to come visit her new place in the city ever since I dropped out of Wesleyan.

Not many folks drop out of Wesleyan, and I certainly hadn't planned on it. When I first arrived there, I had the time of my life. I was away from my parents and living with the largest group of cool people I had ever been around. During freshman year, however, this all changed.

My father, a doctor, lost his medical license after he was accused of sexually abusing a fourteen-year-old patient at gunpoint. Although the charges against him were eventually dropped, the state medical board had been unwilling to reinstate his license to practice medicine.

I knew my father had a gun because my brother, Hugh, had told me about it when we were kids, and he, my younger sister, Eden, and I had taken it out of its hiding spot in my parents' bedroom before. It was a silver handgun, and I remember thinking it was quite heavy. I also remember not wanting to handle or mess with it too much. Fortunately, neither did Hugh or Eden.

Shortly after the sexual abuse charges against my dad were filed, Hugh told me that our father had pulled the gun on him the year before, on the morning after his ex-boyfriend had called the house. I was a senior in high school and Hugh was a senior in college, living at home while going to Pace University in Manhattan, and the call happened late, while we were all asleep. The incessant ringing woke me up. After some time, I heard someone walking downstairs to answer it, followed by my father's voice angrily asking who was calling in the middle of the night. Then I heard him hang up and go back to his room. However, the phone continued to ring, with my dad getting angrier each time he picked it up, raising his voice and cursing at the caller in his thick Spanish accent before the commotion finally ended and I was able to fall back asleep.

Hugh told me that when he woke up the following morning, there was a gun pointed at his head, and my father was holding it, demanding that he tell him whether he was gay. Apparently, Hugh's ex had said something that implied it, and my dad wanted confirmation. Hugh was terrified and had answered that he was bisexual in the hopes of staving off a lethal response.

Although my brother got him to put the gun down, our father promptly kicked him out of the house and even stopped paying for his college tuition. He also took back the car he had bought him as an early college graduation present—and gave it to me to take to Wesleyan.

During the fall of my sophomore year, my family had gone to the proceedings against my father to show support. Everyone but me, that is. I felt bad for not going, but I just couldn't bring myself to do it because deep down, I believed that he was guilty. For some reason, despite the lack of evidence, and the fact that he was my own *father*, I didn't doubt he would do something like that. I didn't like to think about it or talk about it—I still don't—but it had to do with the way I'd seen him looking at and acting around young girls all throughout my childhood. Including me.

So my mother and siblings went to the proceedings without me, and they reported back that there was a tape recording of my father asking the girl to give him a blow job. Even if the act didn't actually happen, he had wanted it to. That was bad enough, in my opinion.

After the trial, things at home only got worse when Hugh outed me as a lesbian during one of Dad's why-can't-you-be-more-like-Hida tirades. Since we were little kids, and long before the gun-to-the-head incident, our father had been reading Hugh the riot act for being a *"maricón"*—which is Spanish for "faggot"—as well as for not being as smart or accomplished as me. Considering all the torment that Hugh had endured, I ultimately couldn't blame him for snapping and telling our dad I'm gay too—even if it did fuck up my life. Unsurprisingly, once my dad knew I was a lesbian, he didn't want to pay for my college tuition either, especially with all the money he had been spending trying to get his medical license back.

Having to drop out of college because I no longer had the funds to pay for it left me in such a state of despair that I didn't even try to convince my father to change his mind. In fact, cutting all ties with him seemed like a great idea to me, despite the problems it would cause.

"I'm so glad you made it!" Jade says when she opens the door, the late afternoon sun streaming in behind her. It catches the red in her long, disheveled hair and makes it glow like fire.

Jade's actually a brunette, but as usual her hair's dyed some more interesting color. It was blond when we first met, which made her mild resemblance to Madonna a lot more obvious. Jade's face was a little longer and tanner but similarly heart shaped, with luminous skin, big eyes (Sicilian brown, in Jade's case), and a prominent beauty mark above her lip.

There are plants on every possible surface of her apartment, a Persian rug over the hardwood floors, a pillow-covered couch, and a big wooden coffee table buried under a stack of art books. Two tall living room windows overlook a tree-filled courtyard, heat steaming up between them from one of those old metal radiators that keep New York apartments so cozy.

"Wow, this is so cute!" I gush.

"*You're* cute," she quips. "The girls are going to be fighting over you tonight!"

"Yeah, I wish!" I laugh.

The plan is to eat here and then go dancing at a club. Jade knows I've been bummed after having to drop out of Wesleyan, and she thinks it'll cheer me up. She's right that I need it, the fun and the potential for romance and sex, but what would *really* cheer me up is a full scholarship to an equally prestigious university.

After we finish eating and getting ready, we walk across town and stop in at The Tunnel, a gay bar where my brother, Hugh, bartends. It's a narrow, dimly lit dive of a bar that lives up to its name.

"Hey, you two!" Hugh yells over the music when Jade and I step up to the bar. "It's so good to see you! What'll it be?"

Jade and I decide to do shots so we can get a good free buzz before making our way over to The World, which is hosting a lesbian night tonight. We have two rounds.

I guess Jade can handle her booze much better than I can though, because I remember only a few moments from the rest of the night, whereas she remembers all of it.

The first thing I remember is getting to the club and realizing that it isn't actually lesbian night but Jade and I going in anyway since we're already there. The next thing I remember is being on the dance floor surrounded by men. The third is being pressed up against a wall while some guy is kissing me. And the last is having some guy—presumably the same one that was kissing me—on top of me, fucking me, before hearing Jade scream at him.

That last image is the first thing I think of when I wake up the next morning in Jade's bed, and it makes me feel nauseous, like something cold and foreign is running through my body, chilling my insides. I lie there, paralyzed.

After she wakes up, Jade finds me in this state and tries to console me.

"You've had sex with guys before, and ones you didn't know very well. Maybe try to think of it like *that*?"

I know what she means but it doesn't help.

"But I *wanted* to have sex with those guys," I say. "It feels so different that I can't remember this and that I didn't want it to happen. I mean, the only reason I even went out last night was because I wanted to meet a girl. And—oh my god—I doubt he used a condom. I might be pregnant!"

"I'm so sorry, girl," Jade says, realizing it's no use trying to minimize what happened. "I wish I'd found you sooner."

She tells me how it went down. Jade and I had been dancing and some guys were hovering, trying to dance with us. Then I said I was going to the bar. When I didn't come back for a while, she started to worry, so she went looking for me. She found me in an empty coat-check room downstairs by the bathroom, with one of the guys from the dance floor on top of me. She yelled at him to get off me, but she had the feeling she was too late to stop him before he had finished.

When I hear this, I'm so upset I can barely speak.

"How the hell did I get so drunk?" I manage to ask.

"Well, we had those two double shots," Jade says. "I guess maybe that's more than you can handle—"

"Doubles?" I interrupt her. "They were doubles?"

"Yeah."

I hadn't realized how much alcohol we were consuming, but I scold myself and think, *I shouldn't have had two shots. I shouldn't have downed them so quickly. I should've known that it would be too much for me. I present myself as a tough chick, but physically, I'm still petite.*

For several weeks after the incident in the club I wait anxiously for my period, which is late, and I'm relieved when the blood finally starts trickling. But that's all it does. Trickle. That isn't normal for me, but I want so badly not to be pregnant that I convince myself it's okay.

BROOKLYN, NEW YORK
JANUARY 1989

A couple of months later, I'm doubled over in pain and can't ignore that something isn't right. I go to the nearest hospital, Downstate Medical Center, and tell the doctor what happened. She's a woman, so I expect her to be sympathetic.

Instead, she stares at me coldly and asks, "What birth control do you use?"

"I'm a lesbian and I don't usually have sex with men, so I'm not on birth control," I begin. "I think I'm pregnant because my period was spotty and I've had these really terrible pains in my stomach. They're so bad I sometimes have to just lie down in the fetal position."

"I'll have some blood work done and I'll call you with the results," she responds.

A week later there's a message from her on my answering machine when I get home from work.

"We got the results and I need you to come in immediately for more tests," she says. "Please come in first thing in the morning, as early as you can. It's urgent, really—you have to come in first thing."

The tone in her voice gives me the feeling that I'm at death's door. I imagine she's going to tell me they've found cancer or something and that I have only a few weeks left to live. So I spend the rest of the night drinking half a bottle of vodka while crying and praying to Jesus that the prognosis isn't horrible.

I gave up on Catholicism when I was about eight and decided that it taught girls and women to think they were inferior, but I always loved Jesus, who didn't seem to share any of Catholicism's judgmental opinions. He was all about love and everyone being equal. He disapproved of the overvaluation of money and hung out with prostitutes and the other dregs of society because he preferred their company and didn't believe there should be a social hierarchy. Basically, he was like a rebel with hippie values, which massively appealed to me.

I pray to him until I pass out.

After I arrive at the hospital the next morning, the doctor runs a sonogram and informs me that I have an ectopic pregnancy, which I've never heard of. She explains that it's the result of an embryo forming in the fallopian tube instead of the uterus.

Then she tells me that the condition can often be fatal, especially if the tube has burst and there's hemorrhaging. After conducting a procedure so that she can evaluate the state of my fallopian tube, she confirms the worst: the tube *has* burst and the hemorrhaging is so dangerous that she'll need to operate immediately.

There's a good chance I won't survive.

She asks if I want to call anyone to tell them what's happening. I try my mother, but she's not home and I don't feel like leaving the information on the answering machine she shares with my dad. Then I try my apartment, but my roommate, Patrick, isn't home either. I leave a message so he'll know what hospital I'm in and ask him to tell my mom.

When I fill out the forms to admit myself into surgery, I'm informed I've been taken off my family's Blue Cross plan. I guess that's another one of the punishments my dad doled out after discovering I'm a lesbian, and I have to spend almost an hour filling out forms for Medicaid before they'll admit me.

When I finally make it to the operating room, my doctor reiterates that I might not come out of the operation alive. It definitely isn't what I want to hear, but strangely, I begin to feel calmer and more peaceful than I ever have.

"I understand," I say.

I can tell my placid response seems odd to her. Maybe that's why she reminds me, once again, how life threatening my situation is.

Although part of me wants to scream, "C'mon! At least say you're going to try to save my life!" I remain in this calm state.

"Yes, I understand," I repeat before another doctor administers the anesthesia. "I may not survive."

I COME TO ON a cot in a large room that's filled with other recovering patients, and I'm screaming. The anesthesia has worn off, and I can't believe that the aftermath of surgery could hurt this much. I frantically try to grab one of the nurses or doctors moving about the room so I can ask them to give me more drugs, but my words are coming out funny and they ignore me.

I pass out, but the next time I wake up I'm in a real bed in a different hospital room. I can hear laughter and Caribbean accents coming from the hallway.

I'm confused, until I remember that this particular part of Brooklyn has a big Jamaican population. I was happy I could get to the hospital pretty easily on the bus from my apartment, which is in Bensonhurst—not exactly a hip, close-to-Manhattan neighborhood, but the apartment was big and dirt cheap.

The faces of two nurses pop into my hospital room doorway.

"Oooh look—she's finally awake," one of them says, looking at me with a big smile.

"We was wondrin' when you'd be wakin' up," the other says, walking over to my bedside. "How're you feelin', my love?"

"I'm okay," I say, still a little out of it.

"Well, you just relax, shuga," she says, propping up my pillow and giving my forearm a gentle squeeze. "We gonna take good cara you."

Her voice and her touch radiate through me, soothing me like nothing has in a long while.

The next day, my mother visits me in the hospital. She's distraught and asks me about what happened. When I tell her, the first thing she says is, "How could you do that?" before telling me that it was my fault for getting drunk.

Her words are like knives.

One strikes my vagina, cutting away at the wound that has barely started healing. The other bores deep into my heart, cutting through its layers like the growth rings in a tree trunk until it gets all the way to the core, what my heart had been like when I was a little girl seeking her protection.

I can't believe another woman—my own mother, no less—can blame me for what happened as I lie here, having almost died. It's almost crueler to me than my rape itself.

The morning after it happened, Jade told me that the guy she found on top of me had been trying really hard to make me laugh and talk to him. So he thought I was hot, I think, and he was probably drinking himself and wanted to have sex. Part of him probably even tried to convince himself that on some level I was into it, or that I wouldn't mind because I looked like I wasn't a virgin. He could just tell his friends he met this hot drunk girl who fucked him right in the club and everyone would believe him.

The thought of this being true reminds me how completely used and violated I feel, but at least I'm able to discern what his motive likely was.

It's harder for me to understand how my mom could criticize me when I'm hurting so much from the experience. Even before I ended up here in this hospital bed, I had been so disturbed by what happened at the club that every time the memory surfaced I felt shaky and sick to my stomach.

Things had been done to my body, literally inserted into my body, while my mind was elsewhere. It was so disturbing to me, and dehumanizing—like I'd been a lab animal, snatched up and used as a tool to fulfill someone else's goals. My own needs, my life, were deemed worthless. Whenever I remembered that night, the feeling it gave me made me want to be dead.

So I tried not to think of it, and I didn't discuss it. Even though I typically tell my friends everything, I hadn't told a soul. Only Jade knew, because she was there, and I'd barely spoken with her about it after that first morning. Part of me hoped that if I didn't talk about it at all, it would feel less real, almost like it had never even happened.

Some women I know would have turned to their parents for comfort, at least their mothers, but I'd had no desire to share what had happened to me with mine. They both come from very Catholic, sexist, old-fashioned South American cultures, where "respectable" women aren't supposed to drink or go to clubs unless they're chaperoned by their husbands or brothers. So I knew they would disapprove of my going out like I did. In their minds it would probably amount to my being responsible for having been raped.

I also know that my mother is freaked out seeing me in this hospital bed and that people can say crazy things when they're upset, but I still wish she could have kept her thoughts about my culpability to herself, at least while I was here.

As much as I love my mother and want to be understanding, her words hurt like hell. In fact, they hurt like hell *because* of how much I love her. They hurt so much it feels like they're going to destroy me. I feel a huge, protective rage welling up, so I ask her to leave, my voice quavering with anger.

Once my mother's gone, I cry like an abandoned baby until one of the nurses comes into the room and comforts me in her warm Caribbean accent. She feels like an angel sent to save me, and she does. She saves me from losing all hope, and comforts me more than my own mother had.

ABOUT A WEEK LATER, during my follow-up visit, my doctor says, "Can I ask you a personal question?"

"I guess so," I answer.

"Has your clitoris always been this large?"

I think back to the first time I remember noticing something was different about my genitalia. I didn't know the word *clitoris* yet, but I *had* noticed my "thing" and that it moved a little whenever I peed. It seemed like the stream was coming from it. In fact, I was convinced it was, until I learned that only boys peed that way.

So I decided to give myself a genital exam to find out what was going on. Of course in an ideal world I would have just asked my mom, but I knew I couldn't talk to her about such things. *Privates are private*, she always said, and would hide hers whenever she changed while my siblings and I were in the room. She even made my little sister, Eden, and me hide ours from each other. I hadn't seen Eden's privates since she got out of diapers.

I also never knew how my mom was going to react to things I told her. One time, when I was about four, I told her about how my best friend, who was a boy, asked me if he could kiss my butt and that I let him. I didn't know it was so different from kissing my hand or my forehead. I just thought it was funny and that she would laugh like I did, but she started yelling at me and then did something I never imagined she would: she told my dad. I never saw the boy again.

That said, it was best for me to figure out the pee thing on my own. I unplugged the desk lamp in my bedroom, grabbed my pink plastic handheld mirror, and set up in the bathroom upstairs.

I angled the lamp to act as a spotlight, stood over the toilet, and held the mirror in a way that I could see my privates in it. Then I let it rip.

It was hard to tell at first, but after a while I could see that the pee was actually coming from a tiny hole somewhere *underneath* my clitoris. I remember feeling disappointed for a moment. For some reason, I liked the way it moved and the idea that I was urinating out of it. But I also knew that it was better this way. I was a girl, after all, and girls were not supposed to pee like boys.

In the examination room, the doctor clears her throat.

"Um, I don't remember any sudden growth spurts," I answer, "so yeah, I guess it's always been large."

"I'd like to do some tests," she says with a strange look on her face.

"Why? Is there anything wrong?"

She pauses, looking down at my chart. "You said on your form that you've had acne problems in the past."

"Yeah, but only briefly when I was in high school, and not more than anyone else..."

"And you also said that you have some facial hair on your upper lip..." she continues, eyeing me closely.

"Well, yeah, but not more than most Latin or Mediterranean women..."

"I just think it's a good idea," she insists.

"But why? Is there some kind of medical issue or something I should know about?" I ask, confused.

"Not necessarily..." she begins.

I can tell that, for some reason, she seems reluctant to answer my question.

"Well," she finally blurts out, "it just isn't normal."

I don't like the tone of her voice, or the thinly veiled look of disgust on her face. She reminds me of the snobby people at the fancy restaurants my parents sometimes took us to when I was a kid. They weren't used to dark-haired Latinos like us having enough money to mingle among them, and their expressions were far from welcoming.

"Well," I say firmly, feeling anger welling up, "since there's no medical issue, then no thanks—I don't want any tests."

The appointment ends soon afterward and I leave, knowing I'll never go back.

Fuck her, I think on my way home. I know my body's different, but she didn't have to make it sound like I'm *abnormal,* in a bad way.

As much as I try to ignore these kinds of thoughts though, her comments begin to fill me with nagging doubts over time, the way certain remarks can.

I begin to think, *She is a doctor, after all. Maybe she knows something I don't.*

A FEW MONTHS LATER, I finally decide to see a gynecologist at The Center, the gay and lesbian community center in Manhattan. They have a medical clinic with a sliding scale, and I figure their doctors will be more accepting.

"Um, you know how I told you about my ectopic pregnancy?" I ask the doctor as she's wrapping up my routine gynecological checkup.

"Yes."

"Well, the doctor who operated on me said, afterward, that she wanted to do tests because my clitoris isn't normal. Like I'm a freak or something because it's as big as it is."

"Well, that wasn't a very nice thing to say, was it?" she says.

I'm relieved and grateful to see that she's a caring person.

"No, it wasn't. But do you think there's anything I should be worried about?" I ask.

"If you want to lie back down, I'll check again," she says, "but your ovaries felt fine to me."

"That'd be great," I say, lying down.

"Yup," she says, as she feels around, "same as I thought the first time—perfectly healthy."

"Thanks for checking again."

"You know," she continues, looking me right in the eyes, "genitals come in all shapes and sizes, and I think your clitoris is beautiful."

Her words are as soothing as the Caribbean nurses' in the hospital, and I feel a tear of relief and gratitude roll down my cheek. I search her face for insincerity, so used to people like my dad who look down on anything outside the status quo, but I can't find any.

In the weeks that pass I'm struck by the contrast in how the two doctors had viewed me. One saw me as I see myself: healthy, with a variance in my genitals that's nothing to be ashamed of.

Part of me wonders if this doctor said those things just to be nice, but it still feels good, especially since the other doctor had found me so strange. The way she had wanted to run tests makes me think of sci-fi movies where unusual beings are whisked off to government labs upon discovery. I have a vague sense of having narrowly avoided something, but I have no idea what.

CHAPTER 2

A Herm Grows in Queens

QUEENS, NEW YORK
FALL 1974

The house is in Flushing, North Flushing," I hear my mother saying on the phone.

My mother had been working for as long as I could remember, but after my dad finally passed the exam that allowed him to be a doctor in the United States, we had enough money to buy a house, and my dad told her to stop.

The house is different from the apartment we had in Jamaica, Queens, where my mom and dad, who are from Valera, Venezuela, and Barranquilla, Colombia, respectively, moved in 1965 with my Colombian-born brother, then named Hugo, in tow. This new place is not as cozy, but it has stairs, three flights of stairs to be exact, which I like running up and jumping down. They go from the basement to the attic, which I think is cool but kind of spooky at the same time.

Last week, I started first grade at a new school, St. Andrew Avellino's. It's Catholic, like my kindergarten in Jamaica was, but in kindergarten there were a lot of kids who looked like me, or had even darker features. A lot of them spoke Spanish too, like I did with my parents at home.

My new classmates don't speak Spanish and they don't look like me. At all. They don't have dark hair and dark eyes, except for Ken. My mom says his family is from Japan.

"Hey, is Ken your brother?" a girl in my class named Beth asks me.

"No," I answer.

"Oh, okay," she says. "I'll tell the other girls."

"What do you mean?"

"We all thought you two were brother and sister," she says.

Ken and I both stick out because of how we look, though my name makes me stick out too. I noticed on the first day of school, when my teacher, who is a nun, called out all our names to make sure we were there.

"Heidi?"

I sat in silence.

"Or, wait . . . Is it *Hilda*? Or Hi . . . da? Vil-or-eee-ah?"

I recognized my last name and realized she was talking about me.

"Here," I said like the other kids had.

"How do you pronounce your name?" my teacher asked.

"Eeda," I answered.

"Eeda? But there's an *H* here, is there not?"

"Yes . . ."

"So how can you pronounce it Eeda? To me it looks like Hilda, but with the *L* missing. I could say Hi-da . . ."

I didn't like the sound of Hi-da, or the other names she called me. "Eeda," the way my family said my name, had a musical sound. Especially when you added my middle name to it, which was what my mom always did.

"Hida Patricia!" she'd call out, which in Spanish sounds like, "Eeda Pa-tree-see-ya!"

My teachers spoke English though, not Spanish. I tried a few times to get them to say my name the way my parents did, but they wouldn't.

By the end of the first week of school I told them to just call me "Heeda." "Eeda," like at home, but with the *H* said out loud, like in America.

With my name worked out, I mostly like going to school. The nuns are strict—some are even mean—but there are plenty of kids my age to play with. We don't have a school yard, but the nuns block off the street at recess so that we can play out front. They separate us though. The boys have to play in the street and the girls get the extra-wide sidewalk.

We play things like tag and jump rope and my favorite school-yard game, Red Rover, which involves charging an opposing team's players and trying to break through their locked arms. I love running as fast and hard as I can during the game, and I get so into it that some of the girls on the opposing team don't even try to stop me, quickly unlinking their arms right before I get to them to spare themselves the blow.

Although I can be a bit of a bruiser, I don't totally fit into the tomboy category. For one, I like girls' clothes. I remember, for example, waking up on the morning of my fifth birthday and happily running to my closet to pick out my favorite dress to celebrate the day, a pink-and-white-checkered number.

I also don't mind my school uniform. The boys wear pants with a button-down shirt, and we wear a kind of dress that's a skirt attached to a jumper top, which we wear with a shirt underneath. I wish the school could've picked better colors than green and yellow, but the skirt part is okay. I'm used to wearing them because of my mom.

She loves to dress me in girly clothes, and I love her. I think she's the most beautiful woman in the world. I remember waiting for her to come home from work when we lived in the apartment. When she'd open the door and walk in, it seemed like the whole room lit up.

My mom has long black hair, glowing skin, and a face that is so nice to look at. And I'm not the only one who thinks so. Everyone thinks my mother is beautiful.

"Wow, your mom is so pretty," my classmates say whenever she comes by school.

It makes me beam with pride.

I play with most of the girls in my class, but there's one that I'm especially drawn to. Her name is Cindy, and for some reason I notice her smile and her face more than anyone else's. I want to be around her all the time.

Cindy and I haven't talked in class, but one day, at recess, I decide to walk over and introduce myself.

"Hi, I'm Hida," I say.

"I know," she responds, looking at me a bit shyly but with that same sweet smile I had noticed.

Soon, we're best friends.

Cindy looks totally different from the girls I knew in kindergarten. Her hair is thin, straight, and yellow like a lemon, instead of black or brown. Her eyes are unlike any I've ever seen. They are shaped like a cat's and are the color of a pale winter sky.

Sometimes I hear the girls in my class talking about one of the boys, saying he's cute. The way they say it reminds me of how I feel about Cindy, but when the girls talk about the boys that way, they say it's a "crush." I'm not sure if that means I have a crush on Cindy, or why it's not okay if I do. All I know is that I like looking at her and being around her as much as possible.

After second grade, Cindy's family moves to Florida. I miss her, but I still have my other friends, like Beth. After figuring out I wasn't our Japanese classmate's sister, we became friends. It was easy—not only because we see each other in class every day, but she lives right around the corner from me too, on 168th Street. Beth's father is also a doctor, like mine. I can tell my dad likes her more than my other friends because of it, which seems weird.

"I like Beth; she comes from a good family," he had said when he found out.

My father is a short, domineering man with light-green eyes and lizardy skin whose moods spill out of him like showers during a rainy season. One minute skies are bright, and the next we're running for cover from one of his outbursts, which often leave me drenched in my own tears.

Luckily, he's at work a lot, but when he's home, he's like a volcano: ready to erupt at any time. My brother and I try our best not to set him off, but it could be something as simple as forgetting to kiss him good morning that did it. Or good night.

"Hida, come down here," I'd heard him call out one night during first grade, after I'd gone upstairs to go to bed.

When I got downstairs, I found him standing by the dining room table with his belt in his hands.

"Did you forget to kiss me good night?" he'd asked.

"I was just putting on my pajamas," I answered.

"And you do that right before going to bed. So you forgot, didn't you?"

"Umm..."

I was hesitant to answer because I could tell he was in one of his moods.

"You forgot. Admit it," he demanded, his voice rising angrily.

"Okay. Yes, I forgot. I'm sorry."

"After I work so hard every day to give you everything you have, you think it's okay to just go to bed without saying good night?"

"I'm sorry, Daddy, I was just tired," I said, feeling scared.

"You're right, it's not okay, and I'm going to teach you a lesson so you don't forget again. Come here and bend over," he said, pointing to the table next to him.

"Dad, please, I just forgot. I'm sorry! I won't do it again!" I pleaded.

"Come over here now or it'll be even worse," he said.

I could tell that he meant it so I walked to the table next to him and bent over it.

"I'm doing this for your own good, so you remember how to be a good girl," he said, before swinging his leather belt back and pelting my bottom with it.

It hurt so much I screamed out loud, but he did it two more times.

It seemed crazy to me, that he would get this angry—and punish me so severely—over a good-night kiss. But he was right: I never forgot to do it again.

The worst part about it all was that my mom couldn't seem to do anything about his outbursts. She'd tell him to stop when she witnessed them, but he never did. Sometimes he'd even threaten to hurt her, for "talking back" to him.

Of course she thought about leaving him, but whenever I heard my mom say this to my dad during one of their arguments, he'd say he would try to get full custody of us if she did. She seemed trapped, having fallen in love with a man who showed her how horrible he was once she was saddled with kids, a continent away from her family and friends. I always felt like it was my job to protect her from my father's mean words. I'd get mad and yell at him to stop whenever he started in on her. Oddly, she didn't always appreciate it.

"Hida Patricia, don't talk that way about your father," she'd say angrily when I called him something awful. "At least he takes care of us and doesn't hit us."

"But he *does* sometimes," I once said. "I don't think my friends at school get hit just for forgetting to kiss their dad good night."

"Oh, that's nothing," she said. "And you better not be telling your friends about that. We don't talk about things that happen at home with strangers. They're private, okay?"

"They're not strangers. They're my friends."

"It doesn't matter. These are private family matters, *okay*? You understand?" she asked.

"Yes, okay," I said, but I didn't, really.

How could she stand up for this guy who was so mean to her? She was so wonderful and beautiful—didn't she see she deserved more than just not being hit?

I didn't get it, especially because, in other ways, she was so smart and strong. She'd landed in New York when she was only twenty-three, with a one-year-old son and barely speaking a word of English, but she'd found a job in a doll factory and then as a file clerk and supported her family of three—which eventually grew to five after Eden and I were born—while my father stayed at home studying. I was proud of my mother, who was so sweet that even animals loved her, like she was a female Saint Francis. However, I couldn't say the same about my father.

FALL 1976

By the time I'm in third grade I'm old enough to realize that I'm not supposed to dislike my dad. Other kids love their parents, and I understand that because I love my mom. But when my classmates speak fondly of their fathers, I just can't relate.

Then again, their fathers probably don't call their mothers "sluts" and "whores," or other terrible names every day. I'll be minding my own business somewhere in the house, and the next thing I know I'll hear him calling my mother something horrible, like "parasite."

That was a favorite of his, as in, "You live off me like a parasite."

It doesn't make sense to me, especially because she *wanted* to keep working, but he wouldn't let her because he thought his wife should do what *he* wanted. Also, even if she didn't work, wasn't he still supposed to love her and want to take care of her?

I hated how mean he could be toward her, and it hurt to hear him speak, not just about my mom but about women in general, in such a vicious way.

"WHERE IS BETH'S FAMILY from?" my father had asked me after meeting her for the first time.

Beth has five brothers and the whole lot of them look alike. They're tall and skinny, with thin hair that varies in color from light straw in the summer to a very light brown in winter.

"I don't know," I'd replied, forgetting. "Ireland...maybe Germany too?"

"They're Scandinavian, I think," he'd said with a notable tinge of respect. "They're very *blond.*"

I think his comment is strange, considering how dark his own sisters are. My brother had pointed it out two years ago, when we came upon a picture of my dad's three sisters while looking through old photo albums.

"Dad, I didn't know your sisters were black," he had innocently stated.

"They're not black!" my father had said, obviously not happy to hear that.

I looked closely at the women in the picture. They weren't super dark but they were definitely *as* dark as some black people, like the funny dad on *Sanford and Son.* Their hair looked different from mine too. Coarser and thicker, just like Sanford's, actually.

"They're Colombian," my father had continued. "Lots of us look like that."

Look black? I'd wondered.

It was confusing. Like many situations in my youth.

I don't know why my dad isn't as dark as his sisters, or why he thinks certain groups of people are better than others. We're all people, and Jesus—who is so important in our religion—says all people are equal. So why does my father feel so differently?

I can tell from the things he says that he thinks lighter skin is better than darker skin, that being "macho" is much better than being a *maricón*—or whatever my brother is—and that my mom doesn't deserve to be treated kindly. The thought of these things begins to make me wish I didn't have to live in the same house with such a judgmental and mean man.

I begin to look forward to going to school even more because of this, though I get in trouble there for things like talking or making my classmates laugh. Somehow, I'm always too loud or too playful, even when I try not to be. A lot of the boys get in trouble for those things too, but not as much as I do because the teachers have this "Boys will be boys" excuse for them. It doesn't seem fair. Between that and my father, I feel mad a lot.

Fortunately, as third grade progresses, I find myself drawn to another classmate, Evy. She has these adorable freckles that remind me of Pippi Longstocking. We have even more fun than I had with Cindy and become best friends.

By fourth grade, most of the girls are talking about having crushes on boys, especially leading up to Valentine's Day. In art class, we make cards for our parents, just like last year, but this year some of the girls want to also give cards to the boys they "like."

"I think Danny's cute," Beth says to a group of us one day. "I'm going to give him a card."

Evy's cute, I think, but I keep it to myself. By now, I know that the word that my father calls my brother, *maricón*, means a boy who likes other boys instead of girls. I also know that it's supposed to be a sin, because that's what I learned from my parents and at school, and I figure it also applies to girls who like girls instead of boys. Like I do.

I had asked my mom why my dad thought my brother was a *maricón*. According to her, it was because of the time when my brother had gotten into her makeup. It happened before I was born, when he was about three. He'd wandered happily into the kitchen where my father was, showing off a face smeared with red lipstick, which greatly upset my dad. He had been on edge about my brother and his "girly-ness" ever since.

Luckily, having already learned how to separate my private and public selves in terms of my language and my culture, it's easy to do the same thing with who I like at school. My inner self knows I like girls, but my outer self never lets on. I don't go so far as to make up crushes on boys, but I let everyone think that I like them—and I certainly don't let on about my crushes on girls at home.

SUMMER 1978

"Let's go to the car," my dad says in Spanish.

It's Sunday morning, my favorite, because my mom is usually in a good mood making arepas, and we have a nice, long breakfast. I don't want to leave the table yet.

"Why?"

"You'll see soon enough."

"Fine."

His car is in the driveway, and when we get to it, he tells me to get into the driver's seat. He gets into the passenger seat and hands me the keys. Then he points toward a spot next to the steering wheel and tells me to slide the biggest key into the slot.

"Really? But..."

"Do it," he says.

When I'm done, he tells me to turn the key. I do it, and the car makes a sound and starts to purr.

"Whoa!" I shout.

About fifteen minutes later, to my delight, I'm parking the car by the curb in front of our house.

"Wow, that was amazing!" I say once I've successfully parked.

My dad smiles.

"And now what?" I ask.

"Turn it off!" he says, laughing.

The next day, it becomes my job to back the car out of the driveway and park it in front of the house for my dad, so he can walk out the front door and get right in. It's a brand-new, metallic-blue Cadillac Sedan de Ville, and my dad is very proud of it because I guess it cost a lot of money. Plus, it's huge. I have to slide way down the seat to reach the pedals, but I make it work.

It seems a little weird that my dad wants *me* to do this job, when I'm only ten, instead of giving it to my brother, who is fourteen, but my dad always reminds me that I'm capable of doing great things—like when he praises me for getting good grades in school; or tells me that I can be anything I want, from a doctor, like he is, to president; or brags about my good grades to anyone who will listen. It's clear that my dad has very high expectations for me and my siblings, but my brother never seems to get the praise that I do. It makes me think my dad has kind of given up on him. He wanted his son to be the "little man of the house," like a little version of him. He even named him Hugo after himself! But my brother's never been anything like my dad.

In fact, he's so unlike him that he's going to legally change his name. He researched the process, got all the forms prepared, and Mom and Dad agreed to sign them, so he's changing his name from

Hugo to Hugh. It's just one letter, but it seems to make him into his own person.

At the end of fourth grade, my best friend and secret crush, Evy, tells me that her family bought a new house. She has to switch to a different school district next year. I'm devastated.

I've never noticed how sad so many songs are, but now I do, and the words seem to be speaking to me. Like when I hear Barry Manilow's, "Can't Smile Without You."

I feel like this with Evy gone, and music takes on a new role. Listening to music has always been one of the best things in my life: the activity we do as a family during which my parents tend to be happiest and rarely fight. It's also a means of escape for me when they do fight.

Now I use music to wallow in my sadness.

One day, in the midst of my mopey summer, my mother says, "When you were born, they thought you were a boy."

She chuckles to herself and looks a little guilty, like she's let the cat out of the bag. I had been asking her about childbirth, because one of the characters in the book I'm reading is pregnant, but I never expected her to say *that*.

When I ask her what she means, she just chuckles again, like she can't believe she just told me that, and says, "Nothing."

I am so struck by her comment that I stop reading. I feel confused, curious, and mainly, fascinated, because I've noticed that most girls don't act like I do. My friends pointed it out.

We were marching silently down the hall in single file, as we often did at Catholic school, and Beth and Evy had started miming something to me. I'd quickly made out, "You are a..." something. They'd waved their arms big and wide, giving away the next word: *big*. "You are a big..." Then they'd held their hands up like a gun and pretended to shoot. Shoot? Shot?

You are a big shot? I'd mouthed.

They'd nodded, giggling quietly. I'd been surprised, because I was used to people saying that about boys—boys who are kind of full of themselves. I didn't think I was like that, but I couldn't really deny that I felt pretty happy with myself.

I figured it couldn't be *too* bad, since they still liked me, but now I wonder: Does being a big shot make me boyish? That's not the only way that I act more like the boys than the girls either. I speak out more and fight more and get in trouble more...

I think about things like this as I mull over my mom's comment. I don't know that there are actually people with bodies that are not clearly male or female, so I imagine she must be talking about the ways that I *behave* more like a boy sometimes. I assume that, in the end, they must have figured out that I'm a girl, just like I had when I'd given myself that examination in my bathroom.

I go back to my book and don't question being female.

I know how difficult it is to get straight answers out of my mother. Every Sunday at Mass, for example, when the big kids and adults go up for communion, she stays seated next to us. She's the only adult in the whole church who doesn't go up. Even the really old people make the effort to hobble their way up the aisle.

But every time I've asked her why she doesn't take communion, she just says, "I can't." When I ask her why not, she always says, "Ask your father." Something about the way she looks when she says it, though, makes me not want to. It seems like something best left unknown, like the evils that I'd read about escaping from Pandora's box.

There are also less cryptic things that she refuses to explain, like why her last name is Matheus, even though she's from Venezuela. Everyone at school is always talking about what they "are," and you can usually tell from their last names. The Doluccis are Italian, the Murphys are Irish, the Pulaskis are Polish, etcetera.

Matheus doesn't sound Spanish though. But when I ask my mom where it comes from, she insists it's Venezuelan.

"But Mom, Matheus isn't a Spanish name; it has to be from some other country."

"What other country? I'm Venezuelan."

"I know you're Venezuelan, but what country was your dad from?" I ask.

"He was born in Venezuela too," she replies.

"But what about *his* dad? He had to be from somewhere else."

"I don't know! Everybody is from some other country. Why do you care?"

"Because all the kids are talking about what they are and Matheus doesn't sound like a Spanish name, so…"

"Look, you just tell those kids your mother's Venezuelan. That's what my father told us. That's it."

I've often thought my mom's responses to things are weird—like the way she'd reacted the first time I'd cut my hair. I was five or maybe six, and I'd wanted bangs. I did a pretty good job, except one side was just a little shorter than the other. So I cut a little off to even it out, but then *that* side was shorter than the other. Within a few minutes I had overly short bangs across the front of my face.

I wasn't that happy with my new look, but my mother's response was shocking. She screamed the moment she saw me and yelled, "What have you done!" as if I'd just set my room on fire. She was absolutely furious and I didn't get why. I was the one, after all, who had to live with my butcher job. I had done it after dinner and *The Carol Burnett Show,* my favorite, was coming on soon. My brother and I were usually allowed to have dessert and watch it, but that night I was sent to bed early, without dessert or *Carol.* I cried at the incomprehensible injustice of it all.

What had I done? Why did it upset my mother so much? I fell asleep without knowing why. What I *did* know was that I wasn't supposed to cut my hair. My lessons in girlhood, and the consequences of not following its rules, had begun.

FALL 1979

"That one looks just like Hida!" one of the boys in my class shouts.

I'm in sixth grade, and we're studying evolution and primates in science class. Some of the other boys laugh and snicker.

I'm embarrassed and annoyed. I think it's a stupid comparison, and I tell him so, but somehow, it catches on. First it's just him and a few of his friends, but within a few days, almost all of the boys in my class have joined in. Within a few *weeks*, it's almost all the boys in my whole grade, which consists of three classes.

"Oo-oo, ah-ah!" they call out, making monkey sounds.

"Go back to the jungle!"

"Monkey wanna banana?"

"Hida wanna banana?"

It's not long before my nickname becomes Hida Banana. I'm mortified. I don't know what to do to make them stop. My first reaction is to yell at them, like I yell at my dad when he's mean to my mom.

"Just ignore them, Hida Patricia," my mom says when I tell her about the teasing. "They'll stop if you don't pay them any attention."

I try that approach for a week, but she's wrong: they don't stop. Plus, it feels even worse to just stand there, powerless, while these idiots insult me.

I decide to retaliate by yelling at them whenever they start in on me. Soon, I develop quite the horrible mouth, especially for a sixth grader.

On one particularly bad day of teasing, I yell, "Shut the fuck up, assholes!" As I say this, I approach the boys menacingly with waving fists, temporarily making them scatter.

My anger isn't enough to make them stop though. If it were a one-on-one situation, each of the boys would be too afraid to continue, but once the boys get into a group, as they often do, they feel brave enough to do anything, like forming a circle around me every morning when I walk into the school yard and imitating jumping, screeching monkeys.

"Hey, it's Hida Banana!"

"Oo-oo, ah-ah!"

"Hey, ape face!"

"Monkey wanna banana?"

"Oo-oo, ah-ah!"

At the time, I don't realize that racism is behind the boys' teasing. I just know that, to most of them, my darker skin and black eyes and hair make me look like an ugly animal.

On these kinds of mornings, there are so many of them surrounding me that I don't bother yelling back. Instead, I do my best to imagine an invisible, impenetrable wall around me. They are on the other side, barely audible.

Still, protective wall notwithstanding, their actions make me hate them. Between their cruelty and my dad's at home, I feel so angry I want to break things—sometimes even hit the boys who tease me so much.

But beneath my self-protective anger lies a pit of sorrow and pain. I don't know why my father has to constantly be hurtful toward my mother, or my brother, but it fills the house with fear and pain. I long to escape it, lest I drown—drown in the sorrow of having a father like him.

Now, the pain and sorrow have followed me here, to school, where I'd previously been safe. I don't know why the boys enjoy being so cruel. I tell myself they're mean and stupid and that one day I'll be so gorgeous that they'll eat their hearts out.

I pretend they can't hurt me, but the truth is, they do. I'm scared every single day I have to go to school, dreading the moment that they'll be calling me an animal and I won't be able to stop them. It feels alternatingly sad, humiliating, and infuriating—enough to make me feel crazy sometimes. Or like disappearing so it will all end.

One afternoon, I realize that it can. I'm down in the basement, seeking cover while my parents fight upstairs, and I spot a big plastic bottle of blue liquid. It has a picture of a skull and crossbones on the label, with the words "Danger: fatal if swallowed" underneath it.

"You're a parasite," I hear my father yelling. "I don't even know why I married you."

I could chug at least a third of this bottle down, I think as I sit down cross-legged in the middle of the floor. I rock gently back and forth, clutching the bottle in my lap.

"Tell me about it," I hear my mom yell back. "I must have been crazy to marry *you!*"

I'm sure it'd be enough to kill me before they even realized what I'd done, I think.

I twist the cap off the bottle. My hands are shaking.

"Oh yeah? You should *thank* me!" my father yells.

Why does he have to be so mean? I think, the tears racing down my cheeks.

I bring the bottle slowly up toward my mouth. My hands are shaking so much that some of the blue liquid spills out over the top.

There's never going to be anyone to love me, I think, *because all the girls will always love boys, not me.*

"No one else would have married a whore like you."

The bottle top is in front of my lips, and they are quivering I am shaking so hard.

I just want it all to be over, I think, as I take a deep breath and prepare to chug down the liquid.

But what if there is someone, Hida?

The voice seems to originate from outside of me, but here it is, in my head.

What if somehow, someday, there was a girl who could love you, love you in that way, but you never found her because you were dead?

Damn it! I think, lowering the bottle to the floor. *I can't do it. I can't.*

I collapse onto the floor, its hard weight holding me up, and sob. I sob so loud that I drown out all the yelling above and all the monkey sounds I've ever heard. I sob until my sobs are the only sound in the Universe, enveloping me in their warm embrace.

TO HER CREDIT, BETH never leaves my side when the boys make fun of me. She never makes up excuses not to walk to school together. I would certainly understand, as I'd do anything to escape the circle of torment myself. I'm glad she doesn't though, because having her next to me means I have a comrade and a witness. I can't be obliterated.

Then, at the end of sixth grade, something happens that makes me feel better: I start bleeding, and to my girl classmates, that's like winning a trophy. It's because of the Judy Blume book *Are You There God? It's Me, Margaret*. It's wildly popular among all the middle-school girls, and in the book, a group of young girls have a competition over who will get their period first.

We didn't stage an actual *competition*, but we did agree that the first girl to get hers had to tell everyone. Then she'd have the important role of sharing details to let us all know what to expect. As luck would have it, that first girl was me.

"Does it hurt?" someone asks.

"Not at all," I'm happy to report. "It's just messy."

"Well, you're officially a woman now!" everyone chimes in.

I like to excel at things, and this is another one to add to the list, along with academics and sports. My parents are proud of those things, but when they find out I've gotten my period, my father takes me to see some doctors who poke and prod at me down there, which is how I describe the visits to Beth.

Soon after these visits to the doctors, my father tells me I'll need to start taking pills every day.

"What are they for?" I ask.

"To help you grow taller," he answers.

I'm above average height for the girls in my class, so I find it strange that he thinks I need that. Then later that night, I overhear him and my mom fighting about it.

"We don't know what those pills will do," my mother says.

I can't make out my father's response—he's whispering—but I hear my mother say, "But it's experimental," and, "She doesn't need that."

Surprisingly, given his "I am the master" routine, my mother must have won. He never mentions it again and I don't end up taking the pills.

This year, for the first time, it's a relief when the school year finally ends and summer rolls around. Beth and I are old enough to do fun things on our own now. Like going to Whitestone Pool.

That's how I finally see another girl's privates up close. Beth and I are changing into our bathing suits one hot summer day when I drop something and reach down to pick it up. When I glance up, I am staring directly at her privates. To my surprise, the area is completely flat, with the exception of several grooves that I can't make out very well in the brief glimpse.

She's missing something, I think. *Why is her area flat?*

I remain silent though, not knowing what to say. I don't want to make her feel bad or anything, after all.

FALL 1980

Summer ends way too soon, and my teasing resumes in seventh grade. I've been switched into a different class, away from Beth, and I'm afraid that maybe the new girls in my class will join in the "Hida Banana" crap. To my immense relief, they don't.

As the months go by, several of them even start sticking up for me. I've become friends with the popular clique, the pretty girls that all the popular boys want to date, and they're not afraid to stand up to the boys.

Like many things in my life, my bullying is dualistic: Boys do it; girls don't. Boys are mean to me; girls are kind. It mirrors what I experience at home with my mother and father.

Getting support from a whole group of girls makes things much better. Even if the boys think I'm ugly, the *girls* don't, and their opinion matters much more to me.

"She doesn't look like a monkey at all! Shut up!" my new friend Laura yells at them.

Laura is considered a "cool" girl, and she's also smart, funny, and kind, which makes me like her right away. She thinks most of the boys are idiots and that their teasing me is just another example of this fact. Fortunately for me, the boys seem to respect Laura because they desire her, and they listen to what she says. Within a few months, the teasing has abated, and I'm popular again.

Although we're in different classes, Beth and I still hang out after school. One afternoon, we find my brother Hugh's porn magazines, and we look at dozens of pictures of women spreading their legs for the camera. Even after seeing this larger sampling of women's privates, I don't think there's necessarily anything *that* unusual about me. Probably because the women in the pictures don't seem real.

First of all, they either have *no* pubic hair or just one skinny line of it. Then there are their breasts—which are all abnormally huge. These women are obviously modifying themselves, and who knows how far they have gone to do so. The fact that my privates look different than theirs doesn't seem like anything to worry about.

On most fronts, other than home, things are peachy. I'm at the top of my class academically, which my dad is very proud of, and the same people who used to make fun of me now want to be friends. I'm also an all-star basketball player, which I love, and a cheerleader, which I did just because it's a way for me to hang out after school with my girlfriends without my parents having an issue with it.

I'm not *totally* sure that my genitals are different from other girls' until the end of seventh grade, when I overhear some of the boys in my class talking about me. They're standing just outside the school's front doors, which are propped open, and they don't notice that I'm standing inside within earshot.

The week before we had a day off for some kind of teachers' retreat, and my friend Laura and I were hanging out at my place, alone. We found my parents' alcohol supply and, being clueless about how much to drink, poured ourselves each a tall glass of vodka—no mixer—and gulped it down. Then we wandered over to the house of one of our classmates, who was a boy. He had said yesterday that he'd be having a party.

By the time we got there, we were completely wasted, and the party itself was a blur. But I remember that the rooms were filled with boys and no other girls. There wasn't an adult in sight.

I also remember waking up with my pants around my ankles and a boy's face in my privates, my shirt up around my neck.

Across the room, I heard another boy's voice saying, "Get her pants off." When I turned my head, I saw Laura there, totally passed out.

"Hey," I managed to call out. "HEY!"

The boys scrambled off of us.

I pulled my pants up and my shirt down, lifted Laura up, and made a beeline for the door. We barely made it to my place before passing out again in my room.

The boys hadn't said anything to us about it since then, and we hadn't breathed a word about it either, to anyone. Pissed off as we were about it, we knew we were supposed to be home. *They're assholes*, I think to myself. *Total assholes, and I know it.* But I feel kind of guilty too, like we shouldn't have gone over there.

A week later I overhear them talking about what they saw of my body.

"She doesn't have much going on in the boob department," one of the boys says.

"Yeah, but she makes up for it in other places," the boy I'd seen with his head down by my privates replies.

My heart is beating so loudly I feel like everyone must be able to hear it.

So he noticed that I'm different, I think. *And it didn't bother him.*

The realization is nice; however, the comment makes me aware that my privates are different. Nevertheless, I don't know that anything other than male or female exists. So I continue growing up oblivious to the true nature of myself.

FALL 1982–SPRING 1986

My obliviousness about what my body's difference means continues into and throughout high school, but I do know that I'm "gay"—or, to be specific, a "lesbian"—and it's terrible at times. What saves me is my love of experiencing new things. There are many of those to keep me busy.

Like sex, for starters. I've been crushing on girls for years, but in the fall of my sophomore year, I start fooling around with men, because they're the only available option. Even here, in New York, I don't know anyone who's out as gay or lesbian—especially not high schoolers.

Despite that, I meet a girl I like, in that special way. This time, however, I tell her how I feel. To my utter shock and surprise, she says she feels the same way. We know we can never be together though, not openly, the way boys and girls are. So our feelings are thwarted, triggering a constant, nagging depression within me. Honestly, between that and my dad's constant raging at home, life feels awful.

Fortunately, high school is also where I meet and befriend Jade. It happens by the keg at one of the parties in the park near our high school, which is known as a hangout for the cool, bad kids.

"Hey, I like your hat," she says as she pours herself a cup. "Where'd you get it?"

It's a black leather cap that I've customized myself.

"I made it," I answer proudly. "Well, to be specific, I got the main hat at a shop in the Village, but I took off the brim and added the silver studs."

Everyone knows that "the Village" means Greenwich Village in Manhattan.

"Cool!" she responds. "I like hanging out in the Village too."

Jade's soul is alternative, and so is mine, even though I sometimes hang out with the popular, mainstream kids at school too.

Jade and I both love bands like the Cure, and she's the first person I've ever met that's into androgyny.

"Oh my god, I love the way he's a man but he's so *not*, you know?"

she says one afternoon as we listen to *Let's Dance,* her new David Bowie album.

"Yeah, that's super cool," I agree. "Grace Jones is like that too."

Hugh had turned me on to Grace—her music is popular in the gay dance club scene. She's also unapologetically androgynous, with a short, cropped haircut and a flat chest that she shows off like a medal of honor. Yet despite her masculinity, there's also a fierce femininity to her too. Like if she were an animal she'd be a black panther, with lipstick.

I *love* her and Bowie—and Prince too, with his eyeliner, tight pants, and heels. I like him so much that I even hung the poster that came with his *Dirty Mind* album up in my locker. It shows him standing in a shower, wet, and practically naked except for a small pair of black leather underwear.

"Who's the sleazy guy in your locker?" one of my fellow cheerleaders asks when she sees it. "I hate his skinny mustache, and why is he wearing eyeliner?"

"That's Prince," I answer. "He's awesome."

At the end of sophomore year, in June, *Purple Rain* comes out. By fall of my junior year, nobody says Prince is sleazy or asks me who he is anymore.

Junior year is also the year I decide to lose my virginity. I've been doing "everything but" until now, and no one has said anything about my body being unusual.

Then the man I lose my virginity with tells me my body is beautiful, and we continue to see each other after the fact. He's a pretty good catch, I suppose: a handsome, twenty-four-year-old graduate student in engineering. We met on one of my Saturday nights out with Beth—the ones where our parents drop us off at the movie theater and we ditch as soon as they're out of sight to walk along the strip of blocks on Bell Boulevard where guys cruise around trying to pick up girls.

Losing my virginity is a somewhat pleasant, and thankfully pain-less, experience. Still, even after doing it a few more times, in all different positions, I find sex mostly boring. The man, however, does not—he eventually asks me to marry him.

Although I think it's flattering that he wants to make an honest woman out of me, as a sixteen-year-old lesbian, I find the notion of spending the rest of my life with a guy—especially one I barely know—comically ridiculous.

Nevertheless, being proposed to sends a strong message that I'm acceptable and desirable as a woman in straight society.

It also doesn't hurt that I've developed a huge love of makeup. My classmates in high school are more ethnically diverse than they'd been in elementary school, and I'm suddenly considered attractive, especially with makeup and feminine clothing. So I deck myself out to the nines every day. It's probably in part to make up for feeling so ugly in middle school, but I really do like putting on makeup.

Then again, so do lots of the male musicians I look up to. Prince even sings about not being a woman but not being a man either in his *Purple Rain* hit "I Would Die 4 U."

Is he saying that just because he wears makeup and high heels, or is it something more? I don't know, and I don't know why, but hear-ing that makes me feel happy. Something about it makes me feel less alone. And hopeful.

Despite my budding attraction to androgyny, however, I'm per-ceived as a girl, and a straight one, in the eyes of all my teachers and classmates. Unbeknownst to them, I am actually a lesbian, albeit a nonpracticing one as of yet. Unbeknownst to *me*, as well as them, I am not only a lesbian, but an intersex one.

CHAPTER 3

A Hermaphrodite by Any Other Name

MANHATTAN, NEW YORK
SPRING 1990

HEY, GIRL," JADE SAYS when I pick up the phone, "I think we should move to San Francisco."

I'd lived in San Francisco for six weeks last summer, not long after my ectopic pregnancy ordeal, and I'd loved it. So had my girlfriend, Linda, who had visited me during my last week there.

Linda is butch, the opposite of the type of woman I've always been attracted to, but I'd fallen in love with her anyway. She's funny and caring and very authentic; she has to be in order to dress the way that she does in our society. Looking so masculine automatically makes her an outcast and a rebel, and I respect that.

Linda's feeling fed up with New York, and so am I. We've had some great times, the city and I, especially when I'd go out in its gay club scene. My favorite place to frequent is Rock 'n' Roll Fag Bar, on Tuesdays. They play all the goth punk music I love to dance to, like New Order and Siouxsie and the Banshees.

Our old roommate, Nicolas, took us for the first time last year and introduced us to a bunch of the regulars, like one of the DJs he was dating, Larry Tee, and Larry's drag queen friend RuPaul. I had just turned twenty-one, and being there made me feel like I was part of something new and raw and edgy and *queer*, in a way I'd never seen.

Linda and I had also moved to the East Village this past winter. It's the home of The World and other cool New York institutions like St. Mark's Place and another popular queer club, The Pyramid. Our new place also meant I could walk to work now, instead of sitting on the D train for an hour. But even all that convenience and queer punk-rock coolness can't make up for the stresses of my limited college-dropout income and tiny apartment, not to mention a lifetime's worth of hauntingly bad memories, from my dad's abuse to my near-death experience.

That said, moving to San Francisco sounds very appealing. Besides being a fun place to live, UC Berkeley is right across the bridge, and it's actually affordable—for California residents—even though it's considered one of the top universities in the country. It's a viable means for me to get as good of an education as I would have at Wesleyan but without my parents' financial help or a mountain of student loans. Between that and Jade and Linda chomping at the bit to move, the decision's pretty easy.

On a hot July day in 1990, my mother drops the three of us off at Penn Station for the sixty-dollar Greyhound bus trip to San Francisco. Three days later, we're there.

SAN FRANCISCO, CALIFORNIA
JANUARY 1, 1991

Ray opens the door with a grin. "Hey, you," he says in a slow drawl. "Happy New Year." There's a kind of lazy mischief in his eyes—he knows exactly why I'm here. I hope it's not obvious that I spent the morning sobbing.

I step into his apartment. It's exactly what I should have expected from the bachelor who makes my sandwiches in a South of Market deli and wears his hair in a dreaded Mohawk. The place is a mess, first of all, with mismatched furniture, dishes in the sink, and sweaty clothes strewn all over the floor.

"Want a beer?" he asks. It's early afternoon, too early for beer, but I shrug.

"Sure."

He opens his refrigerator, buries his head in the door for a moment, and comes out with two Stellas. He cracks both open and hands me one with a wink.

I'm guessing my straight girlfriends would swoon at the sight of him. Unfortunately, his looks are wasted on me. It's not that I don't think he's handsome—I wouldn't be here otherwise—but even the handsomest guys don't do what women do for me.

I laughed on the inside when he first gave me his number. "We should hang out," he said. I'd taken it, thinking, *Can't fault you for trying, but you're sniffing up the wrong tree.*

But that was before my girlfriend, Linda, and I broke up, and everything fell apart. Jade has done everything she can to make me feel better.

"Just get up," she said this morning, shaking me as I lay in bed. I responded by putting the pillow over my head.

"Come on," she said, her thick reddish-brown mane swaying over me. "Take a shower. Get dressed."

I groaned.

"You can't keep wallowing in your sadness, girl. It's a new year, a fresh start. Just get out and do something, anything."

Okay, then. I'll do something. I'll fuck my way out of my misery.

I called Ray and said, "Hey, let's hang out." Simple as that. A few hours later, here I am, and we both know why.

I watch him down his beer in a few huge gulps. He wipes his lips with the back of his hand. He sees me watching and shrugs. "I'm nursing a raging hangover," he says.

I take a big swig of my own beer, knowing the faster I get a buzz, the more I'll want to do this.

We make small talk for a while, even though neither of us seems to especially care what the other is saying. The only time the conversation gets interesting is when I mention my ex.

He grins. "A girl, right?"

"How'd you guess?"

"Oh, I don't know. The buzz cut? The combat boots?" He laughs and shakes his empty bottle. "I'm getting another. You want one?"

"Sure," I say casually. And I do. I want another and another and another. I want to drown the ache in my gut that I've had since I realized Linda had found someone else.

"Well, I don't mind a girl who likes a girl," he says suggestively, as he takes two more bottles out of the fridge.

I reach out my hand, but he doesn't let go of the bottle right away. We hold eye contact and grin at each other.

A few minutes later, he gestures toward the tequila on his coffee table. "You want some?"

"Sure," I say. "We can still celebrate the New Year, right?"

"Hell yeah." He rinses out some shot glasses that were sitting in the sink, cuts up a lime, and hands me a lime wedge and a glass.

We do a couple of shots, and I'm already feeling better. Maybe 1991 will turn out all right after all.

After the tequila, we move on to weed, which we inhale from a giant glass bong. I'm starting to feel pretty numb, but it beats everything else I've been feeling. And it doesn't take long before he moves his chair over toward me and kisses me. We exchange deep, wet, weed-and-tequila-tasting kisses. Sometimes, when I close my eyes,

I think kissing a man isn't that different from kissing a woman, save for the scratchy cheeks and the muskier smell.

I relax into his kisses in the same way I relaxed into the alcohol and pot. I can push everything away if I just let other forces—booze, drugs, sex—take over. I can make the questions, disappointment, and loneliness just disappear.

Inside my jeans, I feel myself getting hard.

Ray's hands move up and down my back, over the round of my backside, and then over the top of my thighs. Soon, just a few minutes after the kissing started, he's on his knees, working his way down my stomach with kisses.

He fumbles with my belt and I start getting nervous. He's heading right for my genitals before we've even rubbed up against each other.

I should warn him, I think. I'm already so hard that I know my clitoris will look unusual: its most dick-like. But I can't think of exactly what to say or do to steer things differently. How do you warn a straight guy that your clitoris is so big it resembles a penis?

I can't think of an easy way, so I try to just relax and concentrate on the sweet buzz from the beer-tequila-pot combination. I can hear my own breathing, deep and urgent.

He undoes my jeans and slips them off. Then he buries his face into my underwear.

"Whoa," he says, pulling away.

He looks at me, stunned. Then he pulls my panties off before I can say anything.

"Jesus Christ," he half shouts, "is that a dick?"

I'm twenty-two years old, and by this point in my life, I've had a lot of sex. So I've seen plenty of reactions to my clitoris. Most guys had just appreciated my body without mentioning it, like the guy I lost my virginity to, who had looked me up and down and said I had a beautiful body. Later, the first girl I made love with, and several others who followed, gasped in delighted surprise. And Linda, the girl who just broke my heart, had even given my clitoris a nickname: toys (yes, "toys," plural, even though I've got only one; guess she meant the whole area).

The most common reaction I've had, though, is a kind of hunger. Sure, there might be an initial moment of surprise, but I've discovered that people tend to love surprises in bed. They make them ravenous.

Ray does not look ravenous though. In fact, he's staring at my genitals with something like shock.

Still, there's a part of me that's relieved. After all these years, someone has finally asked me the question: Is that a dick?

"Well, it's kind of different," I start, "but…"

I'm certain the answer is no. If it were a penis, I'd ejaculate and pee out of it, right? But the truth is that when I have sex with women, sometimes I feel like it is, because I like to penetrate them with it. I can't do it deeply like a regular guy, just barely, but enough to know what it feels like.

"No, it's a clitoris," I blurt back.

Apparently, that explanation is not sufficient to wipe the look off his face, so I keep talking. "They come in all shapes and sizes."

He eyes my crotch warily, so I continue. "And you know, the bigger they are, the more sensitive they are too."

He looks at me, still not completely trusting my explanation of what he is seeing. "You sure it's not a penis?" he asks.

I don't know. Am I sure?

"Yeah," I say softly, consciously making my voice sultry, the way I imagine he likes women to sound. "I'm a woman. Feel."

I place his hand on my wetness, and I can feel him relax.

"Okay," he says slowly. "I guess you do *feel* like a girl." He slides a couple of fingers inside of me just to make sure.

I feel a sense of relief that I can prove it, but the whole thing just adds to my general sense of confusion. I think to myself, *How many people who menstruate and have been pregnant have to "prove" their femaleness?*

"You had me worried there," he says. "I thought you were a guy."

"Nope, not a guy," I respond.

It's a crazy thing to have to say, especially in this context. What's even crazier, though, is that rather than feeling offended, what I really feel is relieved to have it confirmed that there is a substantial way in which I'm like a man rather than a woman. Or *male* as well as *female*. Although I can see it with my own eyes, the fact that no one knows besides the people I've slept with has made it feel kind of like it's been in my head all these years.

"Wow, I could use another beer right about now. How about you?" he asks.

"Yeah," I say. "That sounds great."

We guzzle down some more beer and do a few more bong hits—both of us trying to push that uncomfortable moment away—until we're relaxed enough to resume.

Later, when we're finished, we sit together, me on his lap, both of us drinking more beer. He picks up the remote control, turns the television on, and flips through the channels until he finds a football game.

God, what is it with men and their sports games? I wonder. As I sit there in his lap, I feel like I'm beginning to be transported to a place my mind won't normally let me go.

My dad used to zone out in front of the TV too, I remember, during baseball season. I always found it so annoying because the game got priority over anything else we might want to watch.

"You know," he says, snapping me out of my daze, "I'm a little wiped after that."

I move into the nearest chair and wait for some conversation. None comes.

"So," I say, getting up and stepping into my clothes, "I'm gonna go."

"Oh yeah?" he asks absentmindedly. "You got stuff to do?"

"Yeah, kind of," I lie. I stumble putting my jeans on. The combination of booze, pot, and sex has left me clumsy.

"Okay," he says, glancing up from the game. "Hey, that was fun."

He pauses, then adds, "Different, but fun."

I walk toward the door, and, still naked, he gets up and follows me.

"Thanks for the beer and the smoke," I say.

"Totally," he answers. He gives me a quick hug. "See you at the deli."

I decide not to wait for the bus and walk home instead.

It's a good call because not one bus passes as I walk past each deserted stop. *Maybe all the Bay Area bus drivers take New Year's Day off,* I think. The streets are quiet, and all I hear are the sounds of my boots slapping the pavement.

At the third bus stop I pass, I see a skinny black man in a puffy 49ers jacket seated on the bench and slouched against the Plexiglas wall. In his lap, there's a forty-ounce bottle of malt liquor peeking out of a paper bag. His head is drooping down, chin to his chest, and every now and then it bobs. I watch him as I walk and realize I'm probably almost as drunk as he is right now.

I wonder where he'll end up later, when the temperature really drops.

When I finally get home, Jade isn't there. But she's left me a note:

Hey, girl—went out with some friends from my yoga class but I left you some of that pasta dish that you love in the fridge, in case you're hungry. See you tonight! Xoxo

I wish Jade were here to talk. I need to cry, to let my heartbreak pour out in a torrent of satisfying, salty tears, but I can't. The sobs won't come, and only a few drops run down my cheek. Even my tears are lonely.

Then I remember Ray's shock upon seeing my genitals for the first time.

Bet he wasn't expecting that! I think.

Slowly, I crack a smile.

The next morning, I'm reminded of a book I read at Wesleyan, the memoirs of a nineteenth-century French hermaphrodite named Herculine Barbin. I'd come across it in a box of free books at the end of my freshman year and immediately snagged it. I read the myth of Hermaphroditus as a kid in a Greek mythology book my parents had lying around, and I found the concept of someone being both male and female pretty cool.

Herculine's life, however, had been tragic. After a childhood and adolescence spent living secretly—and blissfully—with her body's difference (like me), doctors had discovered the large size of her clitoris and forced her to undergo a battery of medical exams. Eventually, she was tried in court for "gender fraud," where she was deemed to be more male than female and sentenced to change her legal gender and live as a man. She committed suicide shortly thereafter.

I related to the first part of Herculine's memoirs—particularly how she fell in love with one of the other girls in the convent they lived in—and couldn't wait to tell my friends about it. But when I finished the book, I felt scared. I suppose I didn't want to imagine that I could be in her situation, that my existence and identity could be the subject of such questioning and punishment.

I never spoke about the book, and my fear of being persecuted as a potential hermaphrodite had quickly subsided. That is, until now.

FEBRUARY 1995

I'm on the corner of Sixteenth and Dolores Streets in San Francisco, waiting for the 22 bus, and as it pulls up I grab a copy of the
SF Weekly. On the cover is a picture of a person's face that looks
half-male, half-female. The features seem pasted together, like a
collage I might have created as a kid. The resulting visage is smiling, with huge eyes that seem all-knowing yet, at the same time,
confused.

The headline reads "Both and Neither." The words jump out at
me from the cover. I walk to the back of the bus, take my place next
to an old Chinese woman with a bag of groceries on her lap, and
open to the article.

It's about *intersex*, a term I've never heard before that refers to
people who are born with both male and female traits—what some
would call hermaphrodites.

Both male and female traits.

The bus lurches forward, and I sit there, completely frozen. For
a few moments—the time it takes to get to Market Street—the world
disappears. Although I've heard of hermaphrodites, they seemed
so rare that you'd never actually meet one. Like those yogis in the
Himalayas that are rumored to be two hundred years old.

This article, however, tells me that one in two thousand people
are born with genitals like mine, which they call "ambiguous." That
means intersex people are a lot more common than I thought—
they are everywhere, in fact. And sometimes, they don't even know
they're intersex.

They don't even know they're intersex.

Jesus. Is this the word I've always lacked? Is this the word to
describe my very private, secret difference—the difference that has
become more and more confusing over the years?

There are two women interviewed in the article. One is about my age and looks smart and pretty, in a slightly rebellious sort of way. She reminds me of the women with whom I went to Wesleyan. But that's where the similarity ends, because both she and the other woman in the piece endured something the likes of which I've never heard: their clitorises were surgically removed. Their doctors had decided that they were too big and recommended cosmetic genital surgeries to their parents to help them "fit in" as women. But the women in the article said the result was just the opposite, because the surgeries made them unable to orgasm. The thought of those little girls having forced operations gives me the heebie-jeebies, but the article says it's the standard treatment in the United States and other parts of the first world for babies born with "ambiguous genitalia."

I look up from the paper, shocked. The old lady next to me has nodded off peacefully. Her head bobs back and forth as the bus bounces over the pavement. She wakes up whenever there's a particularly bumpy patch, then drifts off again just as quickly. Her presence calms me. Life goes on, despite the craziness that has just unleashed itself from the pages of this newspaper.

The women in the article sound a lot like me, and they're intersex.

You could have put an article in front of me about aliens being discovered working in the White House and it would have been less shocking to me than this information. I mean, I've known that my body is different for a while, but to possibly be a *hermaphrodite*? And to learn there is a worldwide medical effort to eliminate intersex people? It sounds like a frightening science-fiction movie.

There's a part of me going, *Na-na-na, can't hear you*, because it's so much to take in. I've been getting my period since I was eleven. I *must* be a woman, right? And I've never had one of these surgeries.

But at the same time there's also a quiet, persistent voice in my head going, *Aha! I knew it!*

I remember several incidents in a flash. My mom's strange they-thought-you-were-a-boy comment, thinking I peed out of my clit, being asked if I have a dick . . .

I didn't know there was even a word to describe someone who wasn't a typical woman, but now I do.

When I get home, I run into the kitchen to tell Jade what I've read.

"Girl, I told you I thought you were a hermaphrodite years ago!" she says.

"You did?"

"Yeah, back when you first went away to college, and I was still a senior in high school. I was doing my graduation project on male, female, and androgynous archetypes—remember?"

"No!"

"Yes!" she continues. "You told me about sleeping with a woman and that your clitoris was way larger than normal, and I said it sounded like you're a hermaphrodite."

"Oh wait—*that* I remember!" I say.

"*Girl,*" I had told Jade, "now I know why guys are such freaks about getting laid—it felt *amazing!*"

"More amazing than getting penetrated yourself?" Jade had asked.

"They're so different it's hard to compare, but I guess I'd have to say yes. It was the most incredible sensation I've ever felt—like flying but underwater and then up in the air, above the clouds, and back again in warm, delicious waves . . ."

"Hey," I ask Jade now. "Are you *sure* you used the word *hermaphrodite*? The article said there's also another word: *intersex.* Have you heard that word?"

"No, I haven't. In my research the word *hermaphrodite* was always used to describe people that have bodies that are kind of a combination of male and female."

Huh, I guess intersex *is a newer label,* I think. *That's probably why I've never heard it before.*

"Remember how I told you about that five-sexes article," Jade continues, "and that I didn't know exactly which one you were but that it definitely wasn't the 'regular' female one?"

"Oh my god!" I exclaim, laughing. "That's right! I remember now!"

"Jesus, your denial runs deep!" Jade says, laughing too.

CHAPTER 4

Metamorphosis

SAN FRANCISCO, CALIFORNIA
JANUARY 1996

Do you want to come by the salon after closing for a makeover?"
Tabitha asks one afternoon.

She's one of the "info girls" whose job it is to sit at the kiosk on
the first level of the Westfield San Francisco Centre and dispense
information to the throngs of people who walk in from Market
Street. The Centre is an urban mall on the corner of Fifth and Market Streets in downtown San Francisco, and I'm working here as a
security guard so I can put myself through UC Berkeley. It features
spiraling escalators going up nine flights, surrounding a round, open
courtyard topped by a glass dome. When you stand in the middle of
the first floor and look up, it's kind of like being in a giant donut.

Tabitha's supposedly straight, but she doesn't seem like it when
I'm around. I can feel it every time our bodies come near each other,
which I facilitate as often as possible by taking breaks to go visit her. I
don't care if I'm misreading the vibe, because I like talking to her, and
if I'm not, then even better, because she's hot.

She also works as a receptionist at the mall's hair salon.

"A makeover?" I ask, laughing.

I do wear makeup sometimes, especially when I go out to parties or clubs, but I'm not into it like I used to be in high school and my early twenties, when I was practically never seen without heavy eye makeup and lipstick on. These days I usually have more of a natural look going on, with some eyeliner or mascara but that's about it.

"I know it's not exactly your thing," she says back, laughing, "but I think it'd be fun."

She's right; it is fun. She has to lean in so close to put on the makeup that I can smell her—and she smells really good.

"So, what do you think?" she asks when she's done.

"Wow, I look really different," I say. "I'm not sure. What do you think?"

"Well," she muses, looking me over, "I think you look beautiful—stunning, in fact. But I actually think you look better without it."

"Huh...That's cool," I reply.

I find it interesting because I tend to think most women look better with a little makeup on. I even think a lot of men look better with a little on too, come to think of it. Like when they wear eyeliner.

"Hey, do you want to go out sometime?" she asks suddenly.

"Sure," I say. "Did you have anything in particular in mind?"

"Well, I've been wanting to go dancing. Maybe you could take me to some place in the Castro or something..."

The Castro is famous for being a gay mecca, so I take her proposition as a big hint. A few nights later, after a few drinks and some sexy dancing, we're in my bed.

She sighs and moans and says things like, "Take me, take me," which should turn me on but don't because they seem fake. They feel like they're a part of her fantasy of sleeping with a butch woman, not a response to my actual presence or skills in bed. I go through the motions of pleasing her, wondering if she's as bored as I am.

Still, not one to fuck and run, I pop into her store the next day during my break. When she sees me, she walks over and gives me a big, unexpected, very sexy, full kiss on the mouth. It's sexier than everything we did last night.

I'm impressed by the very public gesture and take it to mean that she's having feelings for me. This makes me start to have feelings too—feelings that evaporate when her boyfriend comes in a minute later and she kisses him right in front of me.

She had mentioned she had a boyfriend when we were out dancing, before going back to my place, but I didn't want to see them kissing. I use an incoming call over my walkie-talkie as an excuse to leave the store immediately.

"What is the big deal?" she asks when she finds me outside, smoking a cigarette. "You knew I had a boyfriend."

"Yeah, but you didn't have to flaunt it in front of me," I reply.

"What was I supposed to do, pretend he was my friend?" she asks. "That's how we greet each other."

"You know what? It doesn't even matter; we are so through!" I shout.

I'm so pissed I'm shaking.

"I can't see why you're so upset about it," she sighs, exasperated.

Then her lip curls up as a look of amusement sweeps over her face.

"God, you really are such a girl, aren't you?" she asks, half laughing.

The sound of her laugh is torturous. I stand there, silenced.

"Hey, c'mon—I was just joking…" she says.

"It's not funny," I blurt out angrily. "If you didn't want to deal with a girl, you should've just stuck to your boyfriend."

"Oh Hida, stop being so sensitive."

"Sensitive? You know what? Fuck you."

I storm off before she can see me getting upset. I *am* sensitive, but I don't want to admit it. I don't want to admit that even though I should've known she was just experimenting, I'd started hoping it was more. Even worse, that it isn't the first time I've done this.

Most of the women I've slept with or gone out with since Linda have been bisexual, and it's usually ended in tears—mine—when they've gone back to their socially approved lives with men. The problem is, even though I know it's risky to date bisexual women for that very reason, they seem to be the only women I'm attracted to that are also attracted to me.

In high school I'd watched the vampire movie *The Hunger* more times than I can count, in which the gorgeous French movie star Catherine Deneuve seduces a young Susan Sarandon. That's what I'd imagined lesbians looked like: two feminine, pretty women together. But much to my disappointment, in the real world it seems like all the pretty lesbians want women who look and/or act like men: the butches.

It's partly a result of how popular the butch/femme dynamic has now become in the lesbian world. Every time I approach a feminine lesbian, she says something like, "Thanks, honey, but you're not my type"—usually with an amused look on her face, like I should have known she dates only women with crew cuts.

As much as I want a pretty girlfriend, I haven't wanted to have to change who I am to get one, and until this moment I didn't feel like I needed to, because there have been plenty of bi women interested in me. They always say something about my being strong or tough but also appreciate my pretty, sensitive side.

But now Tabitha has come along and broken the bi girl etiquette: she expected me to be strictly masculine. She obviously misread me, because my emotions came as a surprise to her. And it's even more annoying because guys get jealous too, all the time, but when they do, no one says they're being "such girls."

I can't stop thinking about those words; they're like a bad song that gets stuck in your head. They stir up the hundreds of ways of putting women down that I've been hearing since I was a kid. It started at home with my father and continued with Catholicism, like when the little boys in my class began chanting, "Girls are just ribs," after we were taught the brilliantly sexist story of Adam and Eve.

I've been hearing shit from men about being a woman all my life, but now it's coming from another woman too? I can't take it. Can't take being told I'm less than, or less attractive, because I'm a girl.

JANUARY 21, 1996

The minute I sit up in bed I know with certainty what I want to do: I want to stop looking like a girl. By that I mean I want to stop wearing and doing all the things that I've been taught to as a woman: makeup, hairstyling, tweezing my eyebrows—even shaving my legs and armpits. All of it.

It's hard to tell exactly what has made this desire so strong and this decision so clear. I guess it's the combination of recently learning that I might be a hermaphrodite and being really, really fed up with being devalued as a woman.

Ironically, it's my mother's birthday—the woman who's told me, since high school, that I look better with a little lipstick on. *She'd hate this*, I think, as I pick up the phone to make the birthday call.

Why have I bothered wearing makeup at all since I came out as a lesbian? I wonder. It only lessens my chances of meeting someone, because people incorrectly assume I'm into men. Have I done it because it felt right, or just because it's what I've been taught to do? It's hard to figure out because, either way, I'd taken to it like a fish to water.

But now, like hundreds of feminists before me, I decide that I shouldn't have to alter my appearance with makeup and revealing clothes and uncomfortable shoes for people to find me attractive. Men, after all, don't have to do any of that stuff. In fact, the less they do, the more attractive most women seem to find them.

Besides, a little voice in the back of my mind adds, *you might not even really be a woman anyway. You might be intersex, like you read about in that article last year.* I'm not sure, because I haven't reached out to anyone, or done any research, but the possibility looms large.

When I take to the streets with my naked face and comfy clothes and sneakers, I immediately notice something new. Men are staring at me: gay men. I live in the Castro, the gayest neighborhood on earth, and these guys usually look right through me like I'm invisible.

Suddenly, beautiful gay men are staring at me with open, unabashed smiles. Instead of people finally knowing I'm a lesbian, it seems they suddenly think I'm a boy. My hair happens to be short, a cute pixie cut that looks super feminine with product and a made-up face, but without all that it seems to look like a guy's haircut, because all the people at the shops I visit on my errand run are calling me "he" or "sir," despite my voice, my short height, and my personality, which I've often been told isn't very masculine. I find it almost hard to believe, given my past of being called a "beautiful woman."

A guy in a gorgeous sweater who looks like a less rugged Hugh Jackman walks toward me on Market Street. As he passes he stares right at me with a look that evokes something I've never felt. There's something about his lust that's less predatory than when straight men have lusted after me. I turn around to get another look at him and catch him doing the same thing. Interestingly, getting cruised by this handsome gay man is kind of hot, but it's not what I expected.

The weirdest thing about my change in appearance, though, is that I'd barely had to do anything. In fact, it's kind of the opposite. I've *stopped* doing things.

I didn't need to put on a costume to become this new person. In fact, I'd taken one off, one I hadn't even realized I was wearing. It turns out once the girl costume came off, there was a boy underneath.

Has he been here all along? I wonder. *Have I just been covering him up with makeup?*

The fact that I'm able to convince everyone around me that I'm male starts to feel like a cool kind of challenge, a nonstop acting gig, and I quickly realize that I am expected to act, in a lot of ways, just the opposite of how I had as a girl. "Excuse me, could I possibly trouble you for…" is no longer necessary. In fact, it isn't cool to be *too* polite or nice as a guy. It comes off as weak.

"Hey, man, you got the time?" I yell to some guy across the street, and instead of giving me a why-the-hell-are-you-talking-to-me-in-that-unladylike-way look, he just hollers the time back with a nod.

I enjoy trying out all sorts of new things, like walking with a scowl on my face, thinking about situations that piss me off. And instead of being told to "smile," I get a positive reaction. Guys show me more respect and girly girls seem to find it sexy. They stare at me from under long eyelashes with coy, inviting eyes.

I haven't only stopped grooming myself as a woman; I've also stopped wearing women's clothing. I basically switched from typically female to typically male grooming *and* garb, wearing my loose, unisex jeans and tee shirts to go with my new au naturel appearance.

Since I don't have that much gender-neutral clothing in my closet, I go shopping and discover that men's clothes actually fit me pretty well, with my small hips and breasts. They're not sexy in the slinky way that women's clothes are, but they give me an "I don't give a shit" feeling that's sexy in its own cocky way.

It's a sturdy, uninhibited sexiness. Nothing hugging my body, constricting my movements and making me worry about having an ounce of fat. I guess a loose sundress would be the same, but I'd never been into those, and I always felt vulnerable to the wind blowing them up. There is no vulnerability with men's clothes: the fabrics are thicker and the cuts less revealing, providing a protective barrier against the outside world.

My change in wardrobe reminds me of how some parents dress their babies in gender-specific clothing because, if they don't, people might not know what sex they are. Oftentimes, parents need clothing to define their children as boys or girls.

It's pretty much the same with me, except if someone got a good look at *me* naked, it might confuse, rather than clarify, the situation. As long as I remain dressed though, I can pass just as easily for a boy as a girl, depending on the clothes I wear.

I'm not sure which I prefer. I'm not even entirely clear on why I'm doing this or if it will last. Only one thing is clear: my life of being "such a girl" is, at least for the moment, a thing of the past.

MARCH 1996

"Holy shit!" my friend Eric shouts. "I didn't realize that was you, Hida! I thought you were Marina's new boyfriend."

Eric and Marina are good friends of mine. I first met Eric years ago at Wesleyan, and Marina was the first roommate I'd found in San Francisco, after moving here almost six years ago. I'd picked her out of a group of strangers to fill Jade's room when Jade moved back to New York to finish art school. It was fun, but we'd both found new apartments when the lease ran out.

A couple of years later, I had convinced Beth, who's remained a good friend since elementary school, to move out here from New York. Then, when Beth needed two roommates, I introduced her to Eric and Marina, who happened to be looking for places, and now they all live together in an apartment on Haight Street, where we're headed now.

"Whoa, you are *really* starting to look like a guy," Beth says to me when we walk in. "Are you getting mistaken everywhere you go now?"

"Yup," I answer. "Even Eric here didn't recognize me just now!"

"Yeah, I saw her walking with Marina and thought she was her new boy toy," he says.

"So what's it like being a guy? Gimme the lowdown!" Beth demands.

"Well, for one thing," I answer, "guys don't treat me the way they used to."

"Really? How so?" Eric asks between clenched teeth as he holds in a bong hit.

"Well, like today, when I went to the hardware store, no one asked me if I needed any help, like they always used to. It actually took me awhile to find a guy to help me, and he just showed me where the stuff I needed was and walked away before I could ask him how to use it."

"Yep, just as I suspected," Beth says. "They assume you're more competent as a guy."

"Yeah, and they're not as helpful when they're not hot for you," I add.

"Oh c'mon," Marina says. "There are some nice guys out there!"

Marina looks like a dirty-blond Betty Boop, and she isn't as cynical as Beth and I.

"All I know is that the minute I went from looking like a cute girl to looking like a guy, all the 'niceness' went with it," I share, "and the assumptions that I can do all sorts of things increased."

"So are you saying they're all just assholes who wanna get in girls' pants?" Marina asks.

"No, I'm just saying it's different now that they think I'm a guy. They might nod or say, 'Hey, buddy,' or something, but there's none of that warm friendliness they used to have when I was a pretty girl."

"Wow..." she says, taking it in.

"Except gay guys," I add. "Now they're friendlier than ever!"

"YOU BEEN WAITING LONG?" an older man with a kind face and boyish smile asks while I'm waiting for the Muni train the next morning.

He has a wealthy, retiree-going-yachting kind of look: baby-blue cardigan, cream-colored slacks, and loafers.

"No. About five minutes."

He's smiling like he has all the time in the world.

"Are you heading out to San Francisco State?" he asks.

"No, Berkeley."

"Oh, Berkeley," he says, his smile widening. "That's a very good school."

"Thanks. I like it."

Five years ago, just as planned, I had established California residency after living in the state for a year and then transferred into UC Berkeley, getting a full scholarship. The students were so mainstream, though, that I had hated it and left. Now, I was giving my bachelor's degree another go. This time, since I knew what to expect, I had been liking it more.

The train stops and we get on.

"What are you studying there?" he continues.

"Anthropology, for right now," I respond.

"Oh, the study of man," he says, grinning. "What a good choice."

"Yeah, I guess." I laugh, catching his drift.

I always appreciate a good joke. Even if it's coming from someone I'm not interested in who is hitting on me.

"Well, you seem like a very intelligent young man," he says, extending a hand. "My name's Walter. I'm a professional photographer."

"Oh, that's cool," I say, shaking his hand.

"You know, you've got a really interesting face. Maybe I could photograph you sometime?" he asks.

"Yeah, maybe…Hey, I don't mean to be rude but my stop's coming up."

"Oh, of course. Here's my card. Give me a call—maybe we can get together sometime," he says, with a telling twinkle in his eye.

I'M NOT SURE WHAT the enormous student body at Berkeley thinks of me, but whatever it is, no one has said anything. I figure most people just think I'm a guy. I'm almost twenty-eight, but I look like a teenage boy, so it's easy for me to blend in with all these guys just out of high school.

Only the people in my classes who have met me know for sure that I'm legally female. And regardless of their views, we're at Berkeley, a beacon for civil rights and diversity. No one is going to give me shit for looking like a boy, even if they want to.

At work, sliding into the new me is a piece of cake. My security uniform at the San Francisco Centre is a navy blue men's suit, complete with the tie. When I first started working here, I looked like a woman, so now some of the same people who work in the retail stores and know me keep asking my coworkers who the new guy is.

"So when I told them that you were actually a girl," Eddie, my supervisor, tells me, "they said, 'No, the *guy*. You know—the short, clean-shaven one.'"

APRIL 1996

"Hey, you wanna go to Litterbox tonight?" my friend Tom asks me one day after class.

Tom is my new gay friend from Berkeley. We'd met at the

beginning of the spring semester a few months ago, on our first day in Intro to Queer Studies. As hip as Tom is about queer folks and gender diversity, even *he'd* been fooled by my appearance.

"I have to tell you," he'd confessed as we walked out of the second class, "when I saw you walk in, I thought you were a guy, and I was thinking, 'Ooh, he's just my type.'"

A few hours later we're entering Litterbox, the newest, thus hippest, queer club in San Francisco. The crowd's about 50 percent fags, 30 percent dykes, and 20 percent who the hell knows. It's a pretty good mix, in my opinion: enough girls to scope out and gay boys to keep things upbeat, while the straights and bis keep things from feeling too insular.

"You Spin Me Round (Like a Record)" is blaring and a multitude of queens are camping it up under the multicolored strobe lights. Tom wants to see if any of his friends are in the back room, and as I glance over the unknown faces one stands out.

My body twitches at the sight of her. Her red hair is glowing under the lights like a small fire flickering at her table, and beneath it is a dazzling smile and eyes like the Mediterranean at midday. I'm not necessarily that crazy about blue eyes, but hers are possibly the brightest I've ever seen.

Tom, it turns out, knows everyone at her table. He makes the rounds, introducing me.

"Hi, I'm Christina," she says.

Christina. I memorize it and let my eyes linger on hers for a moment before running off with Tom, who's dragging me toward the dance floor.

The next weekend I see her again, at Muffdive. The club bills itself as "a dive just for dykes" and it lives up to its name: dark and reeking of beer and cigarettes. It reminds me a little of CBGB's without the stage in the back. A lot of the women even look like the teenage punk boys that packed the NYC club when I went in the late eighties.

Christina's stunning, with glowing, smooth skin and cool bone structure a lot like Uma Thurman's. Plus, she dresses cool. It's a killer combination.

Before I realize what I'm doing, I walk right up to her. She sees me walking over but acts surprised when I reach her and looks down after saying hello. I like her shyness, particularly in contrast with the flashy, red sports jersey shirt she's wearing.

"So do you come here a lot?" I ask, not caring how cliché my question is.

"Yeah, or sometimes I go to Red or Litterbox."

"Yeah, that's where I met you," I say, giving her an unmistakable look.

She catches it and looks down again, smiling. Coquettishness, in its natural form, always arouses the seducer in me. In certain cases, it's enough to provoke an immediate advance. No planning, no hesitation, no thought involved at all.

"Do you wanna dance?" I ask.

"Sure," she says happily. We start off stiff but quickly loosen up as our bodies greet each other. The dancing is clearly foreplay, our movements intimating other possibilities. By the time we're ready to stop, it's last call.

We move to the other side of the room, away from her friends. Then we're just standing there, sweaty and happy, waiting for our breathing to regulate and wondering what to do next. I know we'll end up in an ocean of awkwardness if I don't do something fast.

"Can I kiss you?" I ask her in a low, husky whisper.

We look each other in the eyes.

"Yeah..." she answers slowly. "I'd like that."

Sometimes kissing is so much more than the delicious wetness of two wanting mouths finally introducing themselves. It's more than the exciting possibility of greater physical pleasure to come. Sometimes it's the simultaneous merging of two formerly separate souls into one perfectly balanced entity. This is one of those times.

I can tell the minute I pick her up for our first date the following weekend that Christina is gaga for me. We go to dinner and by dessert we're making out across the table. Then we kiss at every stoplight on the motorcycle drive home, thanks to my open-faced helmets. We kiss as she fumbles wildly with her keys. We even kiss on the way up the stairs.

Once in her bedroom we can't get naked soon enough, tearing off each other's clothes. Her body seems to feed mine. We push into each other desperately. Her voice gets higher with delicious-sounding moans, her eyelashes fluttering in submission. It fills me with an almost angry need to push into every inch of her flesh, to fill her completely.

When it feels as though every cell in my body has fought its way to the end of my amazingly mysterious organ, I too begin to gasp. Deep, uncontrollable sounds escape as a great force begins to unleash itself. Then, in a sudden flash it flies through me, exploding into Christina. She screams with me as her body receives it.

I lie on top of her, holding her head in my hands and kissing her as tremors upon tremors run through us. Then I roll onto my back, cradle her into my torso, and look around her room for the first time. She has a dream catcher on the wall over her bed, some books on a shelf, some candles, a feather.

"Wow, that was amazing," she says in her lovely, breathy voice. "I've never met anyone like you before. I mean, whose clitoris is so . . . large."

"Yeah, neither have I," I respond jokingly.

"Did you take testosterone to make it grow that big?" she asks.

"No," I answer, surprised by the idea.

"Really? It's just always been that way?"

"Yeah, as long as I can remember."

"And you never wondered about it? Nobody ever said anything?"

"Well..." I say, thinking back, "there *was* this one gynecologist who wanted to run some tests."

"And did you?"

"No. She was looking at me like I was something freaky she wanted to get under a microscope, so I told her I didn't want them."

We see each other again a few days later.

"You're such a boy," Christina whispers in my ear when we're having sex.

It's almost frightening how much it turns me on. I don't understand it and I never expected it. I had always thought of myself as a girl, and as far as my personality was concerned, no one had thought otherwise.

But now, without changing my behavior all *that* much, I'm also "such a boy."

They're both me, though, so which is it? Boy or girl?

The reality suddenly, finally smacks me like never before: women aren't supposed to be able to penetrate other women with their own erections. They're not even supposed to *have* erections! It's tiny but it's still something: something that likes to part women's lips and push inside them. How can I really call myself a woman when I can do that?

"I always thought of you as both anyway," Marina says when I tell her about my date later that weekend, "like a girl/boy or a boy/girl or something."

"I guess I would be a boy/girl, since I'm really a girl."

"I actually see you more as a girl/boy," Marina says, "but whatever you call it, this new look is hot."

On Monday, it's back to work as usual.

"Hey, can I get a signature?" a delivery guy asks me.

I'm at the dispatch desk in the security office, hanging with my supervisor, Eddie.

"Sure," I answer, moving my motorcycle helmet off the counter and out of the way.

"Is that your bike in the garage?" the delivery guy asks as I sign the receipt.

Only the mall's corporate higher-ups are allowed to park in the building's basement-level garage, as it's used for all the deliveries that come in, but they make an exception for me since my motorcycle doesn't take up much space.

"Yeah," I answer.

I always wanted a motorcycle, but my mom had been terrified by the idea. Now that she's three thousand miles away though, I had finally gotten one to make it easier to get to Berkeley.

"Wow, I don't know if I could handle a big bike like that," he says to Eddie. "This guy's small but he's strong, huh?"

"Yeah, he sure is," Eddie says, sneaking me a wink.

"And you've got a new hot girl on your bike almost every day!" the guy continues.

"No, it's the same girl," I correct him.

"Oh, really? Is she your girlfriend?"

"Yeah."

"Man, I wish I could have a nice bike and a beautiful girlfriend like that to ride on the back. You're a stud, dude!"

"Yeah, he's the man," Eddie chimes in.

"Yeah, whatever," I say, laughing.

I wait for him to leave before turning to Eddie.

"Oh my god, I thought he knew I was a girl by now! He's been coming in for months."

"I'm telling you, they all think you're a guy," Eddie says, cracking up, "and not just any guy—a superstud!"

I'd never wanted to be a man, but I had sometimes wanted to be as obliviously confident as some of them. Now, with Christina, I had gotten there. I had made it to the land of male arrogance and it was fucking delicious.

Being with Christina provided the comforting assurance that I could fuck a beautiful girl whenever I wanted to. I'd be walking down the street and get a flashback of her full lips on my clit, and next thing I knew, I was hard. And the girls I passed on the street seemed to sense it.

It was like my hard-on gave off a magnetic, magical force, an undetectable frequency that only babes could feel.

The whole thing was eye-opening, an insight into a whole other world I'd glimpsed only from the outside, a world I'd read about, seen movies about, but never understood and *would* have never understood if I hadn't felt it for myself.

"OH DEAR," THE ELDERLY woman who's just walked into the restroom says, looking at me, "I guess I didn't look at the sign."

"No, you did," I say.

"But…"

"I'm a woman," I say. "Don't worry."

She stares at me in disbelief as I walk past her on my way out, and I decide that that's the last time I'm using a women's restroom. I've been using men's public restrooms about 90 percent of the time, and it's been a lot easier than I imagined, since men don't stare at each other the way women do when they're in the bathroom. The only challenge is when there are *only* urinals, in which case I bail.

It works, but it is pretty weird for someone who has been female all her life and *isn't* taking testosterone. It's been three months since I stopped dressing like a girl, and I don't bother correcting people when they call me "he" or "sir" anymore. I did it every time at first because I felt compelled to broaden their idea of what women can look like. But now that it's starting to sink in that I might not be a regular woman anyway, it seems a little strange to force people to say "she." Especially when even my own girlfriend doesn't see me that way.

Christina and I are officially an item by now, and I'm heading over to her place tonight, as usual. When I get there, her gay roommate, Jeremy, answers the door. He's wearing magenta stretch pants and a striped tank top.

"Hey, do you guys wanna go to Litterbox tonight?" he asks me. "Suzy can drive."

Suzy is his straight raver friend, and she pops out of his bedroom a second later. She's wearing a turquoise jumpsuit and a gigantic sunflower necklace.

"Hey, you!" she shouts when she sees me, popping a bubblegum bubble and handing me a giant balloon. "You wanna whippit?"

"Sure," I answer.

"Where's Christina?" I ask as I exhale.

He points my head toward the kitchen and runs off. I hear him talk her into going out tonight as I float off to giggle land with Suzy. A half hour later we all head to Litterbox in Suzy's car.

After we arrive, and as we're squeezing our way past dozens of glittery, sweaty bodies to get to the back bar, I notice an unusually straight-looking woman eyeing me. She's wearing a little black dress, stockings, heels, and full makeup under a well-groomed blond bob. She stands out like a nun at a strip club in this place, and I register the look in her eyes as one of total intoxication.

We finally get to the bar, and Christina and Suzy handle the drink orders, leaving Jeremy and me to our own devices. We've scarcely made our first catty observation when the woman comes over.

"Hi. Are you two gay?" she asks.

"Yes…" we answer hesitantly, surprised to be asked this question at a gay club.

Then she leans her face in close to mine and says, "Does that mean you've *never* been attracted to a woman?"

For a moment I don't understand what she means. Then it hits me: she thinks *I'm* a gay man too. For years I've had straight men trying to convert me into a straight woman, but I've never had a straight woman try to convert me into a straight man.

I look over at Jeremy, who seems equally amused.

"Well," I say, deciding to get it over with, "I actually *am* a woman."

"Ha!" she says, bursting out laughing. "You are not!"

"Yeah, I am," I assert.

I notice another woman hovering behind her.

"No, you're not. *I'm* a woman," she continues. "I have breasts."

"I have breasts too," I say. "They're just small."

"Oh my god, you do not!" she says loudly. She reaches her hand out and runs it up and down my chest to check.

I'm taken aback that she just felt me up. If she were a guy, or a more intimidating woman, I might even feel violated.

"*These* are breasts," she then says, grabbing her own and pushing them together for maximum impact.

Apparently feeling me up hadn't changed her perception.

"Look, I don't really care what you think," I tell her, "and I don't even know why you're here. In case you hadn't noticed, this is a gay club."

"I *am* gay. I'm a lesbian and that's my girlfriend," she says, pointing at the woman lurking in the background.

We've both been fooled because I would never have thought she was a lesbian. But if she is such a lesbian, why is she hitting on someone she thinks is a gay man? I presume it's one of those weird acting-different-when-you're-drunk things.

"Okay, you're a lesbian, whatever," I sigh, my patience wearing thin.

"Yeah, I'm a lesbian and *I'm* a real woman. I can have babies."

"I can have babies too," I respond, hoping to burst her bubble of self-righteous ignorance.

"Oh, please!"

She's yelling now, just inches away from my face. I catch a few choice words as I watch her unravel before me.

"I have a womb . . ."

"Real breasts . . ."

"*Real* women can . . ."

Her arms are flailing on either side of me as she rants on furiously. She's too close and too angry and it's freaking me out. Before I realize what's happening, my hands fly up to her throat, clasp around it, and I hear myself yelling, "Back off, bitch! You're starting to *really* annoy me!"

In an instant the color drains from her face. I didn't squeeze her throat—I just held it—but I quickly let it go and allow my hands to drop to my sides. My words hang in the air like a bubble before it pops and disappears.

I suddenly remember where I am when I see Jeremy's face, and her girlfriend's, frozen in expressions I can't quite place. Shock? Fear? Concern? A combination of all three?

Other faces are staring as well. I realize how bad this must look to someone who didn't see the buildup, regardless of whether I look like a man or not.

"Okaaay…" she says, backing away slowly toward her girlfriend.

I turn to Jeremy and we stare at each other in wide-eyed amazement.

"Are you okay?" he asks.

"I can't believe I did that. I put my hands around her neck. And I called her a bitch. I hate that word."

"I know, but she was in your face freaking out on you. I think it was just a reflex to make it stop."

"Yeah, I guess, but *I'm* freaked out now. I didn't even realize it was happening until I heard the words coming out of my mouth."

Christina and Suzy reemerge with our drinks, totally oblivious. Jeremy reenacts the whole thing for them, and it takes on epic comic proportions, which helps me calm down. But I can still hear the girl talking to her girlfriend just a few feet away.

"I can't believe he was so mean to me," she's saying. "Why was he so mean to me?"

"She still thinks I'm a guy," I marvel to Jeremy. "I almost want to flash her my pussy, but that might just add to her confusion."

"Girl, you just gotta face it: you're a full-fledged androgyne. You're the child Bowie and Grace Jones would've had."

"Thanks, that's flattering," I say, laughing, "but what am I supposed to do if even lesbians think I'm a man? Even after feeling me up?"

Looking like this is making people think I'm something I'm not, but what are my options? Go back to girls' clothes, even though I'm enjoying wearing men's? Throw on some dangly earrings just so people will identify me as female? That would feel stupid; plus, I'm not really a regular woman anyway. The problem is there is no way to show people what I really am.

CHAPTER 5

Gendercide

SAN FRANCISCO, CALIFORNIA
MAY 1996

IN THE *SF WEEKLY* article I read about people who are intersex, a group for intersex people was mentioned, and it becomes clear to me that I need to get in touch with them.

I manage to dig up the article, which I had saved somewhere, and just as I remembered, the phone number for the group—the Intersex Society of North America, or ISNA—is listed after the piece. I sit for a moment, staring at it blankly.

I go to my room, find a ruler, pull down my pants, and measure my clit. Then I pull my pants up, pick up the phone, and call. I'm a little thrown off when an actual person answers. I had expected—had *wanted*—to just leave a message, because even though I've picked up the phone, I'm still nervous about actually having this conversation.

"Hi," I sputter out, "I'm calling because I think I may be intersex, and I want to find out for sure."

A woman whom I'll call Brittney responds.

"What makes you think you're intersex?" she asks.

"Well, I read the article in the *SF Weekly*, and I sound like the women in it—how they might have been before the surgeries," I reply. I proceed to briefly describe my body and the size of my clitoris.

"And you've never taken hormones to increase its size?" she asks.

"No. I've never taken anything."

"Well then, it sounds to me like you're definitely intersex," Brittney says.

As we're talking, she invites me to what she says is the first-ever intersex gathering in known history. As luck would have it, it's coming up in three months, and it's only a few hours' drive away.

LIKE SO MANY RELATIONSHIPS that start off quickly, mine and Christina's ends the same way, and for not a great reason. She wants me to tell her she's beautiful and brilliant more often. I believe that she is, but I start feeling put upon, and I eventually suggest that we see other people, for which she promptly breaks up with me.

After our breakup, I'm plagued with regret and I cry about it on and off for weeks. Not only do I miss our connection, but I miss how easy she had made my transition. I had a beautiful woman by my side almost immediately after feeling more like a "he," and now I feel a little like a fish out of water without that yin to my yang. Thankfully, the intersex conference is coming up, because I really need to talk about things like this with other people who are like me.

SONOMA COUNTY, CALIFORNIA
AUGUST 1996

The conference is held at a retreat center in Sonoma County. There's a multicolored, mosaic-covered Goddess Temple on the grounds, a teepee, and an animal sanctuary with rare and endangered species, in addition to the usual hot tub and sauna. It's very New Age Northern California.

I walk into the retreat's office and find Brittney there. She looks like a lot of professional lesbians: short haircut, high-end sporty clothing, and smart-looking glasses on a makeup-less face. You'd never suspect there was anything physically different about her.

She greets me warmly, gives me a schedule of the conference events, and walks me over to the lodge where we'll all be staying. There's a large living room, kitchen, and conference room on the lower level. The bedrooms are upstairs.

"I thought you and Alicia might like sharing a room," she says after introducing me to a woman unpacking her bag on one of the twin beds. "I think you're about the same age."

Alicia is a little younger than me, and she's also Latina. She has long, curly hair and a pretty, slightly made-up face. I feel comfortable around her and I'm glad that we're sharing the room. She doesn't seem to want to talk much though, so I decide to go for a walk.

I head over to the animal sanctuary and hang with the emus and other odd birds. It seems perfect that we're here together as rare varieties of our various species.

I'm also excited that I'm finally going to get to talk to other women about the fact that we can penetrate women, with our own genitals, and how weird and amazing it is.

A few hours later the conference attendees and I are seated around the living room. Its appearance reeks of the seventies: beige carpets, wood-paneled walls, and bulky furniture with floral upholstery.

There are only eleven of us, but we come from all over the country—Illinois, Boston, Wisconsin, and Atlanta, among other places. There's even someone who's flown here all the way from New Zealand. After basic introductions, we each share a brief history of our experience being intersex.

Brittney, the group leader, begins. She was born with ovotestes, or what doctors call "true hermaphroditism." She was labeled male on her birth certificate because she had what appeared to be a penis, and was raised as "Ben" for the first years of her life. But then her parents decided that something wasn't right, that Ben's penis wasn't big enough.

After myriad trips to different doctors, it was decided that Ben was actually female but needed to undergo surgery—a full clitoridectomy—in order to live as a woman. The doctors believed that Ben was young enough to adjust to his new sex as long as he was given a girl's name and clothing and raised with female social customs, like dolls. Apparently, the doctors had been taught that these practices would aid the transition by a psychologist at Johns Hopkins named John Money, who had built quite a career on promoting the theory of gender malleability and the presumed benefit of practicing it on intersex bodies.

So eighteen-month-old "Ben" got a clitoridectomy and left the hospital as "Brittney." Soon afterward, "her" parents received a new birth certificate confirming her new name—and life. But try as they did to raise Ben as Brittney, she retained memories of being a boy and continued to recall them throughout her childhood.

The doctors had warned Brittney's parents that if they ever told their daughter about her past life as their "son," she'd grow up confused, so they never did. Instead, they lied, and Brittney grew up so confused, alienated, and miserable that she even considered suicide. Fortunately, instead of going through with it, she decided to order her medical records and finally discovered the truth. She was stunned but ultimately decided she wanted the lies and secrecy surrounding being intersex to stop.

Helen, who looks like a linebacker, speaks next. She's six foot two and, despite her large breasts, seems incredibly "male." I discover it's because she was born an intersex boy with an undersized penis. Doctors made the decision that she would be better off female, but the genital "normalizing" surgeries and breast-inducing hormones hadn't eliminated her broad shoulders, husky voice, or rugged face.

Looking at her, I'm reminded of the women I've seen over the years who really seemed like men. Now I wonder how many of them might have actually been born that way.

Helen's father was at work when her nineteen-year-old mother had gone into labor. So her mother had given birth alone in the hospital and then was sedated for forty-eight hours while her doctors ran tests to decide what sex to label her baby. When Helen's mother awoke, dazed and confused, they told her that her baby "daughter" urgently needed several surgeries. They promptly castrated him, removed his testicles, and later began hormone therapy to cause breast development.

Despite everything that was done at an extremely early age to try to make her into a girl, Helen never really bought it. She always felt like a guy and says she wishes she could cut off her surgeons' penises with a dull, rusty knife and ask them what they thought of their technique after that. Hearing what she's gone through, I think it's perfectly natural that she's still pissed off.

Alicia, my roommate at the lodge, vividly remembers the removal of her clitoris because she was twelve years old when it happened. Her clitoris had gone through a growth spurt and shortly afterward her mother had accidentally seen it while Alicia was changing. After a trip to the doctor, her parents told her she was going to the hospital for a routine surgery, and when she awoke, her clitoris was gone. She was able to enjoy it for only a few months, but she can still remember the intense, pleasurable sensations it gave her.

Hearing her story makes me want to scream.

It seems crazy to me that this was done to her just because people had decided that this one, very private part of her looked too different. Especially because I grew up not even realizing just how different I was.

Robin is next to speak, and she also remembers growing up before her surgery. She was initially raised as a boy, but then her parents and doctors decided she wasn't developing enough as a male. So they performed a surgery on her in what she calls a "teaching theater," where hordes of doctors and med students shuffled through the OR to study her unusual genitals.

Oh my god, I think to myself.

I've heard about and experienced a lot of disturbing things in my own life, but I'm sickened by everything I'm hearing right now. Genitals that were removed can't be brought back. It's a wound that can't be healed.

I feel like I can't listen to any more, but I have to. I don't want to make it worse for my new friends by leaving the room, or even crying. I don't want them to think I pity them, because they're not the ones to be pitied. How could the medical community believe this is a good idea? The article I read had mentioned these surgeries, but I hadn't really understood that they were the *norm*, that these horror stories defined what being intersex was about for most of the people I had met.

It's almost my turn now, but I don't know what to say. Why was I spared the trauma that all of these people went through? It's obvious I can't talk about how amazing it is to use my clitoris to penetrate women. It would be rubbing salt in their wounds. Even the deeper gender-identity issues I was hoping to discuss feel minor compared to the fact that these people were robbed of the opportunity to explore who and what they were, from the very beginning. So when it's time for me to speak, I just blurt out something about always feeling different and finally realizing how different my body actually was when I started having sex with women, about being confused and wanting to meet others like me.

In a flash it's over, and we're on to the next tale of woe.

By the time we're through I'm exhausted and head to bed immediately. I have to let this all sink in. I have to reposition myself within
this new reality.

Alicia comes into the room shortly after I've slipped into bed.

"I'm so sorry about what happened to you, Alicia," I whisper.

"Thanks," she says, and adds, without a trace of self-pity, "so am I."

A heavy silence fills the room.

After several minutes I hear her ask, "You know what though?"

"What?"

"At least they didn't get to all of us."

Why didn't they get to me though? I wonder again, as I lie there
trying to fall asleep.

It must have been because of my father. As a physician, he cor-
rects anyone and everyone who calls him "Mr. Viloria" by saying,
"That's *Doctor* Viloria."

The doctors attending my birth wouldn't have been able to convince him that I should have surgery like they did all these other
parents. He would've known that the surgery wasn't medically necessary, but elective. Cosmetic.

Still, it's a little difficult to imagine why my dad would have opted
out of the surgery, since one of the reasons doctors do it is to ensure
that kids will grow up to be "men who act like men" or "women who
act like women." And my father wanted this for his children so badly.
But then I remember something Brittney said earlier, that these
procedures started being taught in the late 1950s at Johns Hopkins
University. My father went to medical school in the *mid*-1950s, in
Colombia. So he wouldn't have been taught that he should "fix" girls
with large clitorises or they might grow up to be overly masculine—
or worse, *lesbians*!

Because of the medical education he received, I'm inclined
to believe he thought that having his baby undergo surgery was

unnecessary. In fact, he probably would have assumed that, like all surgeries, it was dangerous, and he always thought he was right about everything. For instance, once when we were driving to visit some distant relatives in Maryland, he refused to admit that he was lost until we reached a sign that said "Welcome to Georgia."

So my dad's arrogance, which I've always resented, may have very well been one of the things that saved me. How ironic—and how oddly grateful I suddenly feel, for the first time in my life, that I had him as a father.

THE NEXT DAY WE have a workshop about intersex policy and goals, and I volunteer to take the minutes. We all agree we've been defined by outside forces for too long and want to create a definition of intersex for ourselves. After a few minutes of tweaking, we come up with this:

> Intersexuals are people born with reproductive organs, chro-
> mosomes, and/or external genitalia that are different enough
> to make them vulnerable or subject to stigmatization, dis-
> crimination and/or medical intervention.

As I'm taking these notes, I realize that I'm witnessing the birth of a movement. We're making history, right here, right now. Never before have this many hermaphrodites gathered together to shape their own lives.

At the end of the meeting, Brittney suggests we all do something very bold after dinner: show our genitals to one another. The last time I disrobed in public, in front of a group of people, was seven years ago, during the summer of 1989. I had been badly in need of a change of scenery after my ectopic pregnancy ordeal, so I found a sublet in San Francisco and lived there for a couple of months before I moved out to California permanently.

SAN FRANCISCO, CALIFORNIA
SUMMER 1989

The wind is blowing as I make my way up Grant Street for my "interview" at the Lusty Lady. It's one of San Francisco's best strip clubs and two girls who went to Wesleyan with me now work there.

I've never thought of being a stripper before. Being a self-proclaimed feminist since early high school, I've always thought stripping was somewhat demeaning to women. But I need spending money. Fast. Plus, a few of my Wesleyan friends made a great case for the job: I'll get good pay, short shifts with flexible hours, and can dress however I want since I'll be undressing anyway.

I walk up to the velvet-covered booth in the lobby and ask for Allison, the woman I talked to over the phone. I watch men walking in and out while I wait. Some of them glance at me. They're probably wondering what I'm doing here, so clothed. Am I waiting for someone? A customer, or a stripper?

Allison is a bleached-blond rocker type in her thirties, with the look of someone who started partying in high school and never stopped. She explains the job as she shows me around.

The tour ends at the stage—which is just a private room surrounded by mirrors, about twelve feet by sixteen feet. There, six women dance in various states and styles of undress. Around the stage are private booths where the customers sit, feeding dollars into a slot to watch the peep show.

"That's pretty much it," Allison says. "Wanna give it a try?"

My mother's voice echoes in my mind.

"Poor women," she'd said when we were in Times Square once and passed by some strip clubs, "lowering themselves that way. Thank god you never have to do that, Hida Patricia."

But when I look at the naked girls, I realize that—despite what

I previously thought about stripping—I'm perfectly ready to throw off my clothes and dance with them. In fact, given how much, as a lesbian, I like being naked around naked women, I'm somewhat thrilled that *this* is the job requirement. "Heart of Glass" by Blondie comes on the jukebox, egging me on.

Within seconds I'm nude, but right before I head out to join the other girls, I remember that gynecologist's words about my clit.

It just isn't normal.

I quickly tuck it down and walk out onto the stage.

The other girls are all wearing something—see-through panties, a mesh bodysuit, lace-and-pearl lingerie—that looks Victorian and super sexy.

I hadn't thought to come prepared with stripper gear, so I'm the only one baring all and I feel more naked than ever. What will happen if they notice my clit? You can see it a little even when I'm not aroused. When I *am* aroused, it gets erect and looks like a tiny dick. Until now, only my lovers, a few doctors, and people I've skinny-dipped with have ever seen it. So the prospect of revealing it so publicly is pretty nerve-racking.

The strippers are dancing in front of small windows, which are conveniently placed at crotch level. They're swaying, sometimes removing garments, sometimes touching themselves. When I glance at them in the mirror, they don't seem to be looking at me; they're mostly just looking at their own images in the mirrored walls. *Must be stripper etiquette,* I think to myself. Just like when you're walking down the street in Manhattan, you don't look other people in the eye.

I position myself in front of a window and realize, happily, that my back is to Allison. Most of the girls are angled out of view except the ones to my right and left. Sometimes they turn around and flash the guys a bent-over view, but mainly their privates are close to the glass for maximum viewing pleasure. I follow their lead, and my privates and I are just starting to relax when the window in front of me opens.

The face on the other side of the glass surprises me. I'm not sure what I expected, but it sure isn't the little, old Chinese man eagerly eyeing my cunt. He looks like he's about eighty-five years old, with a long, white beard and long hairs sticking out of his moles. But the weirdest thing about him isn't his age or looks. It's the efficiency with which he pursues his orgasm. His penis is already out by the time I see him, and he's jerking it methodically.

His eyes widen with surprise for a moment when he sees my clit. Then, a kind of hunger takes over him. He barely notices my face, his eyes glued to my swaying pelvis. His right arm moves in a rhythmic motion. When his peep show window starts to slide shut, he slides down with it to extend the viewing time as long as he can.

He's in the same position when the window reopens, crouched low in his seat so he can see me as soon as it opens up a crack. His hand is moving faster now, as fast as his eyes dart over me. He starts to grimace a bit and looks up at my face quickly as the window starts to close, an expression of determination in his eyes. I keep swaying, wondering if he's looking for more change, but the window doesn't reopen.

I guess he finished what he started or ran out of money. Or both.

I dance around to compensate for my lack of a window guy and accessories. I might not be in slutty garb, but at least I know how to move. The music, the mirrors, and the other women only make it more fun. I notice, though I'm trying not to stare, that most of them are pretty hot. Even the men on the other side of the windows, their eyes shining with that look of doing something forbidden, are a perfect part of the landscape. It is exactly as easy, in many ways, as part of me had imagined it would be.

"That was great," Allison says as I walk off the stage in a daze. "The job's yours if you want it."

I tell her that I'll start work as soon as possible.

My friend Charlotte from Wesleyan does not approve.

"Hida," she says to me over tea the next afternoon, "you know you're just perpetuating the idea that women are objects, something for men to buy whenever they feel like it."

I stare at the ornate moldings around the tall windows of her apartment, which is in an old Victorian home. The sun is streaming into the room and warming the hardwood floor we're sitting on. It's so much nicer than my apartment in New York—and cheaper too.

"I know what you're saying," I respond, "but you know, guys leer at me on the street all the time and undress me with their eyes. At least now I'm getting paid for it."

Charlotte smiles at me, pushing a strand of hair behind her ear.

"But being leered at on the street isn't really the same thing as dancing naked for them," she says. "Is it?"

"No. One is being done with my consent and the other isn't," I reply.

Charlotte laughs, then shakes her head. "I just couldn't do it."

"Honestly, I don't care what those guys think," I say.

Strippers have to have fake "stage names," so I choose Cruella de Vil, the evil dog killer in *101 Dalmatians*. My inspiration is the evil kick I get out of getting paid well just because these guys are so desperate for the sight of a naked woman, one who normally wouldn't have anything to do with them.

My fellow dancers are great—strong and progressive, with a very empowered sex worker, prowoman kind of vibe. In some ways, they're even more counterculture than I am. They don't give a shit *at all* about what society thinks of them, and it makes me realize that, in some ways, I still do.

I realize that if I were more confident, I'd show my anomaly off proudly, like a trophy of my uniqueness. Instead, I position my body right in front of the window so as to block it from everyone but the customers. I know from previous reactions by men to my clitoris that *they* won't mind.

In fact, these customers see my clit up close, and I swear they love it. It probably isn't often they see a woman get hard before their very eyes. And get hard I do—it is fairly impossible not to, with all the touching. There are only so many hip swirls and turns I can perform in one shift. It gets tiring after four hours. I find it more comfortable to just stand there and sway, touching myself here and there to kill time, like the other girls do.

But as I dance and watch these men masturbate, I notice something: in some ways, I understand men. As someone with a high sex drive and a small phallus of my own, I relate to the way their penises respond so quickly to the stimuli. And to my surprise, I feel a kindred spirit as I, too, touch myself and watch myself grow. In some strange way, I feel like I am out there with them.

I feel like I'm on both sides of the window at once.

I'm fascinated by the wide range of guys that come into the club. There is every type imaginable, all races, ages, and social classes. There are the horny young guys who seem thrilled to be at a strip club, maybe for the first time. There are the tired-looking middle-aged guys with a vibe that says, "This is the only pleasurable activity left in my life." There are immigrant types like the old Chinese man that first day, and the occasional homeless-looking guy looking to get the most bang for his buck. They usually start by talking to me through the glass, telling me what to do, which every customer is informed when they come in is strictly forbidden and grounds for getting thrown out. In fact, we're told to report them, but I usually just hold my finger up to my lips to warn them because I hate to see them blow what little money they have.

Then there is the slew of white businessmen in nice suits who come in during lunch hours. They're the types who probably have a wife and kids at home, and I wonder what their families would think if they could see them here. When they go home and are asked, "How was your day, honey?" their answer probably isn't "I had a great release at the strip club, which helped me relax before my board meeting."

The weirdest customers for me, though, are the straight couples. Some of the other girls like when these couples come in and add a woman to the mix of male clientele, but I always move to another window to avoid them. It feels sleazy being the thing used to "spice up" their sex life, and I can't help but feel kind of sorry for the women in the couples, because they usually seem uncomfortable.

For the entire three weeks that I work at the Lusty Lady, nobody says anything about my clitoris. Nobody, that is, until the divinity student. His black skin and navy shirt blend into the dark background of the booth, so I barely notice him when he opens my window.

He stares at me in awe as my hard-on grows more pronounced. I'm pretty used to this reaction by now, but I'm not used to customers waving twenties in the window and wanting to give them to me. Unfortunately, the club doesn't allow tipping, "in order to discourage familiarity with the girls." So I never see the money he tried to leave me.

I do, however, get the note they let him leave.

Dear Cruella: Very few females have a vagina as beautiful as you do. I have never written to a female of your quality and quantity in 33 years. You are the first and last. I should be in a monastery. I'm an activist and a journalist and I'm in the process of becoming a priest. Never sell your body to anyone. Your body does not even belong to you; your body belongs to our creator. Bless you Cruella.

On the bottom of the note he had scrawled a drawing of a church steeple with a cross on top. The irony of being told not to sell my body by a priest-in-training who just paid to see me naked is not lost on me; I find it funny, even. But his letter is the first description of my genitals and their uniqueness that I've ever seen in writing, and it has an impact on me.

In the five years since I've started having sex, almost no one has said anything about my body being different. In fact, other than my girlfriend Linda giving my genitals a nickname, there's been only one comment, in college. It happened when I slept with the friend of a girl I had briefly dated.

"So *that's* why Jackie called you a hermaphrodite," she'd said upon seeing me naked.

Somehow, oddly, I managed to brush the comment off and put it out of my mind. But now I'm more aware of just how much bigger my clitoris is than most women's, and it's been starting to feel like something that should warrant a mention, so it's nice to read this patron's comments.

The words clear through the strange fog of indifference toward my difference. He might as well have drawn a lighthouse instead of a steeple.

SONOMA COUNTY, CALIFORNIA
AUGUST 1996

At the retreat, we discuss how revealing our bodies will be a way for the people whose genitals have been mutilated and shamed to share them in an environment of love and respect, and counter all the awful, nonconsensual viewings they were forced to undergo as children. Everyone agrees to it, and even though I didn't have that experience, I do too, in support.

We gather in the living room and sit in a circle on the floor, everyone with a towel underneath them. One by one, each person reveals their most private parts with the rest of us gathered around to see. But these are not clinical, disapproving stares. Everyone is gentle and loving with the one who's exposed.

I've never seen anything like what I'm seeing, and it borders on unbearable. Almost everyone has scars—scars that aren't covering their elbows or knees like the ones I'd gotten as a kid. These scars cover the most sensitive of all human flesh, carved by hands seeking to correct things they saw as mistakes. One person doesn't have anything where a clitoris or penis should be. There's nothing but skin. It's like looking at a Barbie doll crotch, but it's human.

I have to look several times just to prove to myself that what I'm seeing is real.

My stomach suddenly drops, and I swallow hard to fight the tears struggling to stream out of me. I need air. I take a deep breath and look away, not wanting anyone to catch my reaction.

I'm worried I'll be seen as too normal to be here. My genitals aren't scarred like the others. I can't back out though, especially now that everyone else has had the guts to share theirs with me. So I go ahead and pull down my pants.

I don't end up feeling the judgment I was worried about from the survivors. In fact, Robin smiles as she looks at me and says, "It's beautiful."

I leave quickly once it's over, unable to speak and needing to escape. I see a sign for the animal sanctuary and head over that way.

Each footstep I take leads me farther away from the horror that I've just seen.

I find a bench when I get there and sit down. There was another person at the retreat who, like me, escaped surgery, and we had a lot in common. She wasn't exactly sure why her clitoris hadn't been removed. Still, this didn't come close to making up for, or outweighing, the impact of learning about the nonconsensual surgeries that most of the intersex folks I'd met had undergone. It was kind of traumatizing just *hearing* about them. I couldn't imagine having lived through one.

As my breath slows, I try to regain my composure and clear my mind. I sit there for quite a while before I spot a group of peacocks in the nearby aviary. Two of them are squawking as they spread their beautiful tail feathers. I know they're the males and that they're doing that to try to impress the female. In fact, the term *peacocking* is sometimes used to describe human males who do the same thing.

I am interrupted by the sound of one of the groundskeepers locking up the aviary for the night. The sun has almost fully set, and it'll be dark soon.

I decide to head back to the lodge, and I run into Robin on my way to the bathroom.

"Hey, can I ask you something?" I say.

"Go ahead," she says, smiling.

"Do you think it's okay that I'm here?" My voice starts to crack, on the brink of tears. "I didn't go through anything like what you all went through—"

"Hida," she says, cutting me off and staring me straight in the eyes, "I'm happy you didn't go through what we went through."

"But my clitoris isn't even that big," I continue. "I mean, maybe it's not big enough to make me intersex—"

"Who's to say mine would've been any bigger?" she interrupts again.

She makes a good point.

"So you don't think I'm out of place here?" I ask tentatively.

"Of course not. In fact, I'm glad you're here," she says, "because looking at you I get to see what I might have been."

CHAPTER 6

The Grass Is Not Always Greener

SAN FRANCISCO, CALIFORNIA
AUGUST 1996

FORTUNATELY, THERE IS SO much going on when I get back from the retreat that it's impossible to let my heartache about my breakup with Christina distract me. I have not only just met a bunch of intersex people, but I am working full-time and back in classes full-time at Berkeley after the summer break. And my classes are *good*.

After being confused for years about what to major in in college, I've just decided, finally, to go the interdisciplinary studies route, which will allow me to create my own major. It's funny because when I had seen that option, first at Wesleyan and then again here, I thought it seemed crazy to make more work for myself by doing that. Now here I am, doing it.

My major is gender and sexuality, which, unsurprisingly, I find fascinating. For example, I'd had no idea that, until 1973, homosexuality was listed in the *Diagnostic and Statistical Manual of Mental Disorders*. It suddenly made sense that my father had told me, after my brother, Hugh, outed me, that I needed to stay away from "those people with their 'psychosexual disorders'"—that was actually the label he had learned to describe us when he was in med school.

I also learn about the history of the lesbian and gay civil rights movement. One aspect of the movement that sticks out to me is that even though mostly "drag queens" and "bull dykes" of color participated in the Stonewall riots that played a big role in starting the movement, once the community got organized, white, older, and more conservative gender-normative gays and lesbians had tried to ban them from participating in gay pride marches. They thought drag queens and other gender-nonconforming gays and lesbians made the community look bad and would incite more prejudice.

"Man, isn't that just typical?" I say to my friend Todd.

He's taking the course with me, which makes it even better.

"Yeah, girl, they never want freaks like us representing—get used to it."

Todd's not even a person of color, but he gets it because he's always stuck out and been criticized as a visibly gay—meaning, not typically masculine—man.

In another class I read about how gays and lesbians were described as hermaphrodites from the 1500s through the 1700s, with speculation that lesbians, for example, had large sex organs that they could use to penetrate other women. *Wow!* I think. *I'm the prototypical lesbian!*

Also, since the nineteenth century and throughout much of the twentieth century until the seventies, the term *third sex* was a popular descriptor by and for gays, lesbians, and other gender-variant people. The stigma against nontraditional sexual orientation and gender expression was so strong that it was easier for community members to conceptualize their differences as being related to being born a different sex—like intersex people. It was also a way of countering all the religious opponents who accused them of "choosing" a sinful lifestyle.

It is amazing for me to realize—as someone just finding out I am intersex but having known I was a lesbian since I was a little girl—how old and deep the connections between intersex people and gays and lesbians are. It somehow makes me feel better about being both. More whole.

To my surprise, some of my courses also cover intersex people. I learn that in other cultures and at other points in history, intersex people were acknowledged and sometimes even revered. Many Native American tribes, for example, had a place for us in their culture, as born spiritual leaders and shamans. They believed that, unlike regular people, we had an elevated view of life's experiences and could "see down both sides of the mountain"—male and female—and provide this valuable vantage point for the community.

I see a picture of *Hermaphroditos Asleep*, a marble sculpture that sits in the Louvre, and learn that it's actually a replica of a bronze statue dating from 155 BC. Many like it were found in ancient Rome, which indicates to me that we were accepted, if not glorified, members of that society. Even Plato had said in his *Symposium* that "the original human nature was not like the present, but different. The sexes were not two as they are now, but originally three in number; there was man, woman, and the union of the two—a third gender known as 'androgynous.'"[1]

Somewhere along the line though, society stopped accepting intersex people, and we went into hiding. According to my professors, the only documented reason for the shift comes from records of North America's colonization. According to historic accounts by European settlers who encountered intersex and "two spirit" (transgender) Native Americans, they found them strange and ungodly, and highly discouraged their social acceptance. Native American accounts, in turn, document how these negative attitudes, fortified by the strong impact of colonization, slowly infiltrated tribal consciousness and drove sex- and gender-variant communities into hiding.

Only a few preserved accounts exist from earlier times to give us hints as to how sex- and gender-variant people lived. My favorite is that of Catalina de Erauso, a fifteenth-century Spaniard from the Basque Country.[2] Catalina had been raised in a convent but was constantly in trouble due to her "explosive" temperament, so at fifteen, she escaped from the convent, disguised herself as a man, and became a fugitive. The similarities of some of our lives' details impress me.

Catalina first found refuge in the town of Vitoria, then "he" (I use *he* because Catalina was now living as a man and using male names) returned to his hometown, living and working, unrecognized, among his former convent colleagues and family members. In 1603, Catalina traveled to the Americas, landing in Venezuela (my mom's homeland), where he battled a Dutch pirate fleet—and won. Best of all, when it was finally discovered that Catalina was not a man, he was not punished.

I'm relieved to read about someone who, unlike Herculine, *voluntarily* chose their new gender and adapted well to their new life. In fact, Catalina describes very much enjoying being a soldier and the freedom of living like a man—much like I'm also doing now.

"I WOULDN'T EVEN BE here right now if 209 had existed when I applied," my friend Marcos from Berkeley is saying.

He's talking about Proposition 209. It's on the ballot for tomorrow's November 5 election, and if it passes, it will get rid of affirmative action in California.

"What do you mean?" I ask him.

"I got in here because of affirmative action."

"How do you know that?"

"It said so right on my acceptance letter," he says.

When I get home, I head straight to the metal box where I keep my important papers and dig out my acceptance letter. I skim it and see nothing about affirmative action. I'm relieved.

Unlike me, Marcos had to help raise his younger siblings because his single-parent mom had to work long hours. Not surprisingly, his grades had suffered. I, on the other hand, had parents who paid for anything I needed, including a tutor when I once received below an A on a chemistry test.

Granted, as an immigrant kid I had more challenges than my peers—a lot more. English wasn't my first language and my parents didn't speak enough English to ever help me study or do homework. But other than those things, I had received the same financial breaks that well-off white kids get, like access to a good private school education, so it wouldn't really seem fair to me if I had gotten in because I'm Latina.

The potential unfairness had me a little confused about affirmative action at first, until the signs around campus reminded me that white people, specifically white men, have had affirmative action from the start. They pulled the strings, and they had always given preference to one another when admitting and hiring. Plus, unlike me, *most* Latinos and blacks did not have it financially easy. I was actually the minority within a minority that way.

Even the conservative General Colin Powell makes a public statement in response to the proposition, about how he wouldn't be where he is without affirmative action. It seems the little diversity that *does* currently exist is due, mainly, to affirmative action, and it will likely go out the window without it. I find myself going to rallies and anxiously awaiting the election results on Tuesday night after going to the polls myself. It's close, but when all is said and done, 209 passes by 54 percent. Affirmative action is over in California. The next day all of my friends at Berkeley are in an uproar, and a big protest march is staged for later that week.

After classes let out on the day we decide to protest, we gather on campus and hundreds of Berkeley students and residents begin to march across the city. The march ends back on campus, and the students go over to the Campanile, which is this tower that has a great view of the city. Five students have chained themselves up at the top, and our plan is to block off access to the tower so no one will force them down until the chancellor agrees to talk to us.

It's pretty tame compared to what I did at Wesleyan during the antiapartheid protests in 1988. Here at Berkeley we'll just be stopping a few tourists from getting a nice view.

Television crews come by while we sing and chant and wait for the university to send in cops or negotiate with us. But they don't, and the news crews and most of the students end up leaving. When night falls, the group decides that those of us who are left should stay overnight.

I wasn't planning on doing that, but it feels like one of those do-or-die moments, like at Wesleyan. There, a group of students, including me, demanded that the university divest its funds from South Africa to pressure them to end apartheid, and eventually the university did because enough of us made a stink. We blocked the admin building for fifteen days, and I'm proud to say that I was one of the 110 who finally got carted away in an arrest that made the pages of the *New York Times*.[3]

I find a spot to lie down with some of my friends and manage to doze off using my backpack as a pillow.

But I eventually wake up to the sound of someone screaming, "Get up! Get up! They're coming!"

In the dim light of sunrise I see a bunch of cops running toward us in full riot gear.

"Everybody, quick—get in place and lock arms!" one of the organizers yells.

I stand up, jam my feet into my boots, and link arms with the others in a circle around the Campanile. Then I watch as the cops start randomly grabbing and hitting students to my right. One of them puts a neck hold on this big Latino guy, trying to get him to leave the circle. I watch in shock as he screams out in pain.

Then suddenly, without warning, I'm on top of this porky white cop. He's screaming, "Let go of me! Let go of me!" and when I look down, I notice that I've got his arms pinned to his sides.

When I first moved to San Francisco, I began studying martial arts. It's been three years since I stopped training, but somehow, without even trying, I've got this cop trapped and in a tizzy.

I hadn't even seen him coming, because I was so busy watching the Latino guy getting fucked with. I'm guessing he must have grabbed me and tried to throw me out of the circle, and I must have instinctively grabbed on to him when he did, because here I am on top of him.

"Let go of me!" he screams again.

He is in a panic and I'm kind of surprised, considering he's the big cop with the riot gear. Then it hits me: *Oh my god, you're pinning down a cop—stop it!*

I release my grip, and when I do, he pushes me forcefully. I go flying off him and land on my ass. His baton lands on the ground right next to me. He must have knocked it off his belt when he pushed me.

I look around and see a frenzy of students crying and screaming while cops grab them and hit them. If I leave the baton here, one of these cops is just going to use it to hit another student. It seems like a good idea to get it away from the mayhem.

I pick it up and start walking away from the scene, toward a group of cops far away on the periphery. I'm thinking that I'll give it to them, since they're not attacking people. What I'm *not* thinking about is what everyone but me seems to know about picking up a cop's baton.

I make it about a step and a half before I hear someone scream, "Get him! He's got the baton!"

Get *him*.

Next thing I know I'm on the ground, tackled from behind. We roll around. Again I hear a cop yelling, "Let go of me!"

Apparently, my body likes to go into autopilot self-defense mode without bothering to ask my brain's permission. I have to consciously tell it to keep still. When it finally does, I end up on my stomach with the cop who tackled me sitting on my back.

I turn my head to get a look at what is happening, and all I can see is a circle of cops surrounding me. Then the cop who's sitting on me starts pushing hard on the skin under my eye with his thumb. It hurts a lot and he doesn't stop until I start screaming and begin to go limp.

A bunch of the cops proceed to grab me by the arms and jerk me up off the ground. One of them does something painful to my arm, some kind of armlock, but within a second I'm out of it. Another one tries but again my body instinctively twists out of it.

"Stop resisting arrest!" I hear one of them screaming.

You're resisting arrest, my brain tells my body. *Not a good idea. Stop moving.*

I do, and the cuffs are immediately slammed on my wrists.

Geez, I wouldn't have resisted if you had just told me you needed to cuff me instead of putting me into such a painful hold, I think to myself as the two cops walk me over to the booking area they have set up. I'm having a bit of a hard time walking and I notice I never got my boots on all the way when they stormed us at sunrise. One of them falls off.

"Can you let me put my boots on?" I ask the cops.

I notice a look of surprise on their faces upon hearing my voice.

"Oh," one of them says, looking at the other, "you're not a guy."

"Nope," I say.

"Uh, yeah, sure—you can put on your boots. Go ahead," the other one says, suddenly sounding a lot nicer.

When I'm done, they walk me over to the table, book me, and let me go. I'm tired and on edge from hunger and manhandling, but I remember that my backpack is still somewhere over by the Campanile. The students still gathered around stare at me with wide eyes as I walk up.

"Oh my god, Hida!" one of my friends screams. "You're bleeding!"

I touch a finger to my cheek and it comes back bloody. It must have happened when that cop was pushing his thumb under my eye.

"Wow, I didn't even realize," I say.

"Holy shit," another friend says, running up to me. "We saw what happened. Are you all right?"

"Yeah, I guess," I say.

They grin ever so slightly in badass admiration.

"Hey!" a girl with blond dreads yells, running up to us. "I'm with Copwatch. I got a bunch of pictures of the cops attacking you. Here's my info in case you wanna get them."

A FEW WEEKS LATER I'm looking for her number because I've just opened a letter telling me I'm suspended as of the end of the semester and can't register for next semester unless the "charges against me" are cleared up.

"Do you fucking believe this?" I ask Jade, who is living with me again. "They're saying I stole university property—which I guess is the baton—and attacked a bunch of police officers!"

"Well, girl, like I told you after it happened, you picked up their baton. What did you expect?"

Jade is that friend who always tells you the things you don't really want to hear. It's one of the many things I love about her, but right now I'm kind of looking for some sympathy.

"Yeah, but I obviously wasn't going to do anything with it. I was walking it away from everyone."

"Doesn't matter," she says. "That's their weapon. It's like taking their gun."

"I guess, but they're also saying I attacked them. That is *total* bullshit!"

"But didn't you say you went into some kind of martial arts reflex mode?"

"Yeah…"

"You're basically a deadly weapon because you know that stuff," she says.

"Yeah right!" I proclaim in disagreement. "There were, like, eight of them and they were all six foot two and two hundred and fifty pounds!"

"Oh, so now you're saying being small makes you less fierce? Puh-leeze! Look at Bruce Lee—he was only, like, five foot six. Anyway, I know you, girl. You're an animal when you get triggered. You probably could've taken all of them down!"

"I doubt that, but okay, I get your point," I say, cracking a sheepish smile. "But still, what the fuck? I can't register now unless I pass this court hearing?"

"I'm sure you'll be able to find some lawyer to help you, girl."

I do, and the lawyer says she'll do it pro bono since I'm a working student. I put on one of the remaining girly outfits in my closet and some makeup to go see her. I figure it'll be good for her to see how nonintimidating I can look in court.

"I don't think you have anything to worry about," she says, looking over her desk at me with ice-blue eyes. "I mean, look at you. You're so petite and pretty. I think the judge will take one look at you and these charges and laugh."

"Well, that's good news," I say, relieved.

"For now your homework is to look over these police reports to see if there are any inconsistencies with what you experienced," she says, standing up and handing me a manila envelope. "I think you'll get quite a kick out of them."

"Okay," I say, taking the envelope. "Thank you so much."

"You're very welcome," she says, shaking my hand.

"By the way," she says as I turn to leave, "did you realize that the police officers thought you were a man?"

"Yeah, because I heard them scream, 'Get him! He's got the baton!'"

"I just find that amazing," she says, laughing a little.

"I know I don't look it now," I explain, "but I can actually look like a guy if I'm dressed like one."

"I'll have to take your word for it," she says, "because I just don't see it."

I start reading the police reports on the BART train home.

"Thin, black-haired male approached Police Officer A and stole baton from his hip..."

"Short male, approximately 5′5″, disarmed Police Officer A and..."

"Small Asian male, thin, disarmed Police Officer A of his baton and proceeded to attack group of eight officers at periphery of student protest scene..."

"Aren't these hysterical?" I squeal with laughter as I read the reports to Jade.

"Yeah," she agrees, laughing. "You really don't look Asian."

"And what kind of maniac student attacks a group of eight cops? They're making me out to be some kind of martial arts ninja or something!"

"I told you," Jade says. "You *are* a little Bruce Lee ninja!"

I see my lawyer again the following week.

"I can't believe they lied so much," I say to her. "They totally made up all that stuff about me taking the baton off his body and attacking eight police officers."

"Well, the officer probably thought it would look incompetent to say he had dropped his own baton. Plus, this is the UC Berkeley police force. They're private, so they're not overseen by the city and have historically been more abusive."

"Huh, I didn't realize..."

"There is no question that you'll have these charges dropped, but you should think about whether you want to sue them for police brutality. I would be willing to take the case."

"Wow—okay, I will," I say.

"Do," she says. "Somebody ought to show them that what they are doing is wrong."

That somebody, though, will not be me. This whole situation has already resulted in two incomplete courses that I'll have to finish over winter break, and I really just want to graduate and get on with my life. A lawsuit would be too much to deal with.

Just as predicted, the charges are dropped, which makes me eligible to register for my final semester at Berkeley.

I know getting out of trouble wouldn't have been so easy if I hadn't been able to hide behind being a girl. I'm completely aware that I played that card. Utilizing sexism to my benefit bothered me a little, but since the Berkeley police had lied just to try to fuck me over, I had gladly used every card in my deck to defend myself.

I also find it interesting to consider whether any of this would have happened if the police hadn't thought I was a guy. They weren't attacking women like they did me, and I could tell by the way they became kinder after discovering I was a girl that they were uncomfortable with what had just happened.

I had entered the world of male violence, and for the most part, it sucked. It wasn't fun being thrown around and tackled, or having sensitive parts of my body jabbed at until they bled, even if I did know how to fight the officers off.

Still, I would never have known that I could pin a man twice my weight and nearly a foot taller than me if it hadn't happened. Most male initiation rites feature some form of violence, and it seems like I've gone through mine and passed. This had been my initiation. A little scar even begins to form under my left eye to commemorate it.

The problem is, now that I'm here, I don't know that I want to be. Until now, living as a guy had been all about novel experiences and cocky, sexy shenanigans, as well as getting taken more seriously. However, my encounter with the campus police had shown me the darker side of being a man.

JANUARY 1997

"Hey, good to see you," I say to Howard, one of the intersex people I've met through ISNA.

He wasn't at the retreat, but he works in San Francisco, right near me in the Castro. He's also gay and looks like a lot of the other professional gay men I see here in the Castro: muscular and handsome. One would never know, looking at him now, that his doctors hadn't known if he was a boy or a girl when he was born. But I guess a lot of people would say the same thing about me when I'm wearing feminine clothing and makeup.

"Nice to see you too. How's Berkeley going?" he asks.

I fill him in a bit and then we get to talking about being intersex. It's so hard to meet other folks who are out as intersex people that I want to connect with them as much as I can.

Howard tells me his story, which, like so many others, is shockingly traumatic and terribly sad. His penis was different—he has something called hypospadias, where the urethral opening is not at the center of the tip, but off to the side, or underneath—and he underwent sixteen surgeries by the time he was twelve because each time doctors tried to "fix it," the surgical sites would later reopen as his body grew. His urine is also now a spray rather than a stream. Like the other altered intersex people that I've met, none of what he went through was medically necessary. I begin to suspect that doctors often misinterpret what they see as a *social* necessity to be a *medical* necessity, as well as conflating the two.

MOTIVATED BY ALL THAT I've seen and learned about being intersex, both in person and in my classes, I decide to write my thesis on the "medical management" of intersex people, comparing those of us who had surgery to those of us who didn't. For my research, I read the medical articles and books upon which the practice of "normalization" was based. Sure enough, the early medical pioneers and proponents of these practices focused on the fact that children with ambiguous sexual traits might grow up to have an ambiguous *social* identity—or "gender identity," as one scholar calls it. This was in turn coupled with the unsubstantiated belief that such children would grow up to be social recluses or misfits—or worse, sexual deviants, which, decades ago, meant gay or lesbian. The stigma against such an outcome was so strong that doctors concluded that something must be done, and the solution of surgically "correcting" our bodies, to make them typically male or female, was born.

I decide to interview intersex adults who have not undergone surgical or hormonal treatment of their intersex variations. I can find only three, but it's still much better than nothing. Conducting the interviews, and then transcribing them all, is going to take a lot of time, but I think it's worth it.

CHAPTER 7

Finding the Vocabulary to Talk about Being Intersex

So do you ever think about just becoming a guy—I mean *legally*?" Beth asks me over dinner one night.

After over a year of constantly looking like a guy, it's almost like I am one. Oddly, in the lesbian world, it's like being a star. I get such a warm welcome everywhere I go that I don't even bother going places with anyone most of the time. I just show up alone, knowing I'll meet my friends, or make new friends, there—something I'd been way too insecure to do when I looked like a girl.

"It would be so much easier, in some ways," Beth continues, "since everybody thinks you're a guy anyway."

"Yeah, it would make using public restrooms a lot easier," I begin, "but I'd also be buying into a lot of things I don't agree with. Like, why do I have to be a man just because I look like this? I'm still the same old me. Plus, as much as it *would* make things easier, I don't really want to make an effort to become a man officially in this sexist culture—you know what I mean? It's already bad enough that I get taken more seriously now that people think I'm a man."

"That must be really annoying," Beth says.

"Yeah, it's like discovering firsthand that the worst of everything you ever believed about sexism is true: that, basically, most people out there still believe that men's views are smarter, *sounder,* and just generally more important. It's insanely depressing, in a way, and yet it's so nice being treated with that level of respect that I can see why people would want it and look like men, or be men, if they could. But then that's so fucked up because it's just buying into it..."

"Fuck. I totally get it," Beth says.

We're sitting out on the small back deck off the laundry room in Beth's flat. It overlooks the yard below, and I watch a cat chase some squirrels as I smoke a cigarette, which I occasionally do, especially when I'm having deep or heated conversations.

"But if you tell people to use 'she' when they say 'he,'" Beth continues, "that's not really accurate either..."

"I know—that's the whole thing," I reply. "I'm kind of in the middle, right? I'm kind of both. I know most people don't even know intersex exists, but that's what I am, and I want to try to be it anyway. Be who I really am."

"Yeah, I get it," she says, "but it's hard because everyone always wants to make you one or the other."

"Tell me about it. I've had so many women in the lesbian world say, 'Oh, you're really femme,' or, 'Oh, you're really butch.'"

"That must be really annoying."

"Yeah, it makes me feel like I have to choose a side, but I've tried and I can't. No matter how masculine I am sometimes, this other side is still there, and vice versa."

"What you really need is a new pronoun," Beth says excitedly. "You need an intersex pronoun!"

Beth is straight, but she completely understands my predicament. *How lucky am I that we've been friends for so long?* I think to myself.

"Yeah!" I answer. "But what would it be?"

"Maybe something similar to *he* or *she*..."

"I kind of like *v*," I say.

"Yeah, me too, but wasn't there some alien show named V?"

She's right. It was a television series that ran from '84 to '85.

"Oh yeah—I remember that," I say, laughing. "Maybe not the best choice."

"How about *z*?" she asks.

"Huh...I like it! How would you spell it?"

"Um, I don't know—maybe z-e?"

"Yeah!" I shout. "That's awesome."

After our conversation, I continue to think about new pronouns, though I later discover we weren't the first ones who had come up with *ze*. It was first used in the eighties by Dungeons & Dragons players for some of their nongendered game characters. Then the fabulous trans performer and writer Kate Bornstein had used *ze* in her novel *Nearly Roadkill*, which came out last year, in 1996. Even though *ze* hasn't caught on, the thought of establishing a third pronoun for intersex people intrigues me. It seems necessary in order to accurately refer to ourselves.

I volunteer for ISNA the following week. While mindlessly stuffing envelopes for a mass mailing, I remember my conversation with Beth and decide to run the idea of *ze* by Brittney.

"So my friend and I were brainstorming about a third-gender pronoun the other day," I say, "and we think *ze* would be a good choice. What do you think?"

She pauses for a moment then says, "I think it's stupid. I think all third-gender pronouns are stupid."

When she says this, tons of thoughts race through my head. Thoughts like, *But ISNA's newsletter is called* Hermaphrodites with Attitude. *Doesn't that imply we're not solely male or female, he or she?*

And if we're saying we need doctors to acknowledge us instead of trying to make us "normal" men and women, don't we need language that supports that?

I don't bother saying any of this though, because I think Brittney's smart enough to understand this. So instead I just tell her what I'm feeling.

"Okay, but it kind of insults my sense of gender identity for you to say that, because I basically feel like I'm both. Or something else altogether."

"I'm sorry if it does," she says coldly, "but I just don't see third-gender or gender-neutral pronouns as a good idea."

I feel tears starting to well up and it takes all the energy I have to keep them contained. I don't want to cry in front of her, because she's so unemotional I feel like she'll just judge me for it.

Why do you care so much what she thinks anyway? I scold myself silently.

I *do* care though. She's a leader in this fledgling movement and I've had so much respect for her, *and* this wasn't just a theoretical idea I'd run by her; this was me trying to embrace my identity as intersex.

She thinks it's stupid, and it feels bad that the first openly intersex person I've met thinks that using words to accurately reflect my gender identity is not "a good idea."

It reminds me of the early gay and lesbian activists of the sixties whom I read about at Berkeley—the ones who had tried to ban bull dykes and drag queens (most of whom were black, Latino, and/or working class) from the first gay pride parade because they thought they made the movement look bad. They thought gender nonconforming identities weren't a good idea, just like Brittney does, almost thirty years later.

I finish stuffing the envelopes as quickly as possible. Then I say good-bye to Brittney and dart out to the elevator. As soon as the door closes I start crying, surprised by how much worse judgment feels when it's coming from someone in my own community.

APRIL 1997

A few weeks later, I'm flipping through the San Francisco International LGBTQ Film Festival catalog and see a documentary called *Hermaphrodites Speak* listed among the entries.

On the last day of the intersex retreat I attended, Brittney had asked a group of us if we would mind having a conversation about being intersex videotaped for the purpose of potentially creating a documentary out of it, and everyone agreed except another participant named Karen, who volunteered to film it. Based on the description of *Hermaphrodites Speak*, this appears to be that documentary. I also notice that the catalog says there will be a Q & A session after the film.

However, Brittney hadn't told me that the documentary had actually been created and submitted to a festival. On top of that, she didn't invite me to speak on the panel for the Q & A session either— even though I'm the only person featured in the documentary who actually lives in San Francisco.

When I realize these things, I get a sinking feeling in my stomach. The feeling is pretty terrible. I immediately call Beth.

"I can't believe she would do that!" she says. "I mean, given how few of you there are, it almost seems like she *purposely* dissed you."

"I know. I'm kind of reeling."

"I can imagine! Do you think it's because of the thing with *ze*?"

"I don't know..."

"What are you going to do?"

"I guess I'll just talk to her and see what she has to say."

ISNA is still very small in its membership, and I'm one of just a few people who volunteer in person at ISNA's office, so Brittney sees and speaks with me frequently. I call her the next day, but she tells me to take it up with Karen.

"You were at the retreat too," I tell Karen after I get her on the phone, "and you were too shy to even be videotaped. But *I'm* supposed to be okay being outed to hundreds in my own town without even being notified?"

"I'm sorry, Hida; I didn't realize," she says. "I guess I thought Brittney had told you."

This doesn't make me feel better. I do want people to see this film, because I want them to learn more about intersex people and our experiences, but that doesn't mean I shouldn't have been warned about the screening, especially considering how the theater is just blocks from my apartment.

At least Karen is apologetic, and she tells me she'll see if there's something that can be done so I can be involved. A few days later, she offers to let me speak on the discussion panel after the film, and I agree.

JUNE 1997

I haven't been able to find the time to conduct the interviews I need for my thesis paper, so I have to graduate "upon completion," which means I get to walk in the graduation ceremony but don't officially get my diploma until I complete the thesis. Still, I'm elated. I received high honors, having never gotten lower than an A minus in a course. I decide I deserve to take myself on a vacation to celebrate, which I've never done as an adult.

The next week I get a message from a man who says he works for the television show *Inside Edition*. He's producing a piece on intersex and had found my name when, while researching the topic, he came across an interview that Brittney had asked me to do for a Sacramento news station shortly after the intersex retreat last summer.

I'm not that familiar with *Inside Edition*, but it strikes me as being potentially sensationalistic, so I decide to proceed with caution. I ask him questions and listen carefully to his answers to ascertain if he's cool. I decide that he is.

The following week, on June 22, *Hermaphrodites Speak* premieres at the Victoria Theatre in the Mission. I'm nervous to be coming out in the very same room with my San Francisco community, but the showing and the panel go great. I'm comfortable speaking to the crowd and answering questions. I even make them laugh a few times. Toward the end, a hip-looking lesbian with funky glasses directs a question to me.

"Hi, I'm here from New York, and I'm just wondering if you have any suggestions for a third-gender pronoun," she says.

"Yeah, actually, I do," I answer. "I like *ze*."

I'm happy Brittney is here to see that I'm not the only one who thinks third-gender pronouns are a valid idea.[1]

Some of the trans people at the film also love that I mentioned *ze*.

"Thanks for putting that out there," one of them says, shaking my hand.

I see my friend Christopher running up to me.

"Hey, that was great!" he chimes in. "Listen, the transmen are gonna be right behind Dykes on Bikes in the parade this year. You should join us."

Christopher and I met each other about six months ago through a mutual friend. I like him; he's smart, funny, flamboyant, cute, and obviously creative, at least in his attire.[2]

"I was actually planning on riding with the Dykes on Bikes again," I tell him.

"Oh c'mon—transmen will be much more fun!"

"Yeah, probably," I say, laughing, "but I'm not trans."

"Oh, I'm not so sure about that…" he says with the sexy glint he's always got in his eye. "I think you're a perfect tranny!"

"Oh, I am, huh?" I smile.

"Okay, well, if you won't ride with us, will you at least help me with the marketing for the film festival I'm putting on this fall? It's called Tranny Fest and it's going to be the first trans film festival ever."

"Wow, that is so awesome!" I tell him. "But I'm still not sure I'm such a good person for it since I'm not trans."

"Okay, well, will you at least think about it?" he asks.

"Sure," I say with a smile.

I'm flattered that he asks me and happy that, unlike the reaction I've received from Brittney, the trans people I've met have had a positive reaction to my gender expression. It almost makes me wish I were part of *that* community, because its members have been more accepting.

But from what I can tell, being a transman means feeling that you're a man even though your body was originally female. I guess it *looks like* I've been moving away from being female to being male, but it's not how I feel inside.

I've been through too many experiences that are uniquely female—like getting pregnant after being raped—to disconnect completely from that part of myself. Plus, the rebel activist in me has always preferred to side with the underdog anyway. So for now, I'm holding on to my *f*, even though what I *feel* inside is different—something I still haven't found the perfect name for.

I feel like I'm not a regular "girl," but I'm not a "boy" either—in my body or my mind—so I come back to that question: What am I? I know I'm "intersex," but that doesn't exist as a gender category. It's just a label for certain biological sex characteristics, like the words *male* and *female*. In terms of *gender*—social gender—biological males and females use the term *man* or *woman*, and so do trans people, identifying as men or women, or "transmen" or "transwomen," regardless of their biological sex characteristics.[3]

There actually *is* a word that could similarly be used for us, as a social gender category for intersex people: *hermaphrodite*. It works in the same way that the labels *man* and *woman* do, as it's a nonscientific term that's associated with certain biological sex characteristics and gender expression. And it's also a noun, which is useful when talking about people. In fact, 99 percent of the time, when I come out to someone as "intersex," they've never heard of it, so I'll say something like, "I'm basically a hermaphrodite, on the female side," because they're always familiar with *that* word, and it accurately conveys that I'm referring to having different physical sex characteristics. Then I'll elaborate and explain that we have a blend of sex characteristics, not both sets of fully functioning sex organs.

The fact that *hermaphrodite* is our older, better known label is probably why ISNA's newsletter is called *Hermaphrodites with Attitude* and their documentary is called *Hermaphrodites Speak*. Given how much they use it, I'm a bit surprised that Brittney had the reaction she did to third-gender pronouns. After all, one would almost *expect* a self-acknowledged hermaphrodite to use a different pronoun.

Three days after the *Hermaphrodites Speak* premiere, I film my interview for *Inside Edition*. It's a long one, and it's even kind of fun, especially filming the footage of me riding my motorcycle up Market Street. We finish the shoot with me standing next to it, gazing out at the San Francisco skyline from Twin Peaks, as if I'm pondering the nature of human existence, which is exactly what I've been doing.

CHAPTER 8

Invisibility

SAN FRANCISCO, CALIFORNIA
JULY 1997

I GUESS BRITTNEY MUST think I did well on the post–*Hermaphrodites Speak* Q & A panel, because she invites me to be on a Seattle talk show with her to discuss being intersex, and I agree to be a part of it.

The show's being filmed the day after I get back from my post-graduation vacation, which I've decided will be in Costa Rica, but the producers tell me that I can be a call-in guest if I send them pictures of myself to show on-screen while I'm speaking. While browsing through my limited selection, I realize that I look noticeably female in the older photos I have of myself and male in the recent ones.

Since looking and feeling like both a man and a woman are a central part of being intersex for me, I send them a variety of pictures that reflect this.

SAN JOSÉ, COSTA RICA
AUGUST 1997

"Stop right there!" I hear someone yell in Spanish: *"Parense allí!"*

The voice is coming from a jeep full of cops. They're dressed in fatigues and they don't look too friendly.

Oh god, really? On day two of my vacation? I think.

Eduardo, the sweet gay boy I met earlier tonight at the club, looks alarmed. He's only eighteen, and this city has a curfew: midnight if you're under twenty-one, unless you're with your parents. I think it seems extreme until we've started walking back to my hotel along the city's deserted, late-night streets.

My Lonely Planet guidebook describes parts of San José as seedy—the parts we happen to be walking through—but despite that and the fact that the cab fare would've been only about three bucks, I've decided we should walk back so I could get a real sense of the city. It feels different than the sketchy neighborhoods I know in New York and San Francisco, where crime often involves theft, drugs, and prostitution. Here, there's a quiet, spooky quality hanging in the air, like murder or rape is being plotted by the figures lurking in shadowy staircases and dilapidated doorways.

"Shit, the cops," Eduardo whispers.

I turned twenty-nine recently, so I have nothing to worry about in terms of the curfew, but I do have a bag of weed in my pocket, and marijuana possession is a serious crime in Costa Rica. I got it from one of the friendly guests at the gay hotel I checked in to last night, and I'd hidden it under the air-cushion soles at the bottom of my boots earlier this evening. I was careless, though, after smoking with my new friends at the club I'd gone to.

I consider dropping both my pipe and my stash on the ground, but the cops are eyeing us so closely there's no way they'd miss the movement.

"*Pongan sus manos en la pared!*" the tallest cop in the group yells at us. "Put your hands on the wall!"

I understand what he's saying, but I don't understand *why* he's ordering us to put our hands up against the wall.

"What are they doing?" I ask Eduardo.

"They wanna frisk us," he answers.

"I have marijuana in my pocket," I whisper.

"Hurry up!" the tall cop yells angrily.

As we walk over to the wall, Eduardo says, "Not her—she's a woman."

"What did he say?" they ask each other.

"She's a *woman*," he repeats, "an American."

I look over at Eduardo. He mumbles, "Men aren't allowed to frisk women," under his breath.

The cops just stand there, staring at me.

"Yeah, I'm a woman," I say. "I'm here on vacation."

"You have to be kidding!" the head cop says.

He and his cohorts begin to laugh as they look me up and down.

"I'm not. I'm serious," I continue. "Look, here's my guidebook."

Fortunately, I brought it out with me and am able to hold it up.

The cops look confused.

"Where are you from?" one of them asks.

"From the United States."

"Let's see your passport!" the leader demands.

I hand it over to him, and the other cops gather around for a closer look. Finally, the head cop glances at me and says, "Now this is *really* getting weird."

I knew my passport wouldn't help. I had recently renewed it and had to have a new photo taken, and I happen to have a buzz cut that makes my neck look unusually thick in the picture, like a bodybuilder's.

"I just can't believe that's a woman," I hear the head cop say to his partner.

"Look," I finally say, putting on my best air of privileged-American-tourist impatience, "in America some women look like this, okay? It's the *style*."

"Well, what are you doing out at this hour?" the leader asks, still displeased.

"I was checking out the city. I'm a tourist, remember?"

"Okay...fine," he says after some thought. He then orders the others to frisk Eduardo.

Luckily, Eduardo passes inspection, but the cops turn their attention back to me when they're finished with him.

"What were you doing out with him?" the head cop asks.

"He was walking me back to my hotel because I couldn't find a cab."

"Okay..." the head cop says to Eduardo. "We're going to let you go this time, but don't be out at this hour again."

"Thank you! I won't!" Eduardo says.

"Get back to your hotel!" he orders as he and the rest of the cops pile back into their jeep.

We watch them slowly turn a corner and drive off.

"Oh my god, that was scary," Eduardo says once they're out of view.

"I know! For a moment I thought I was going to jail."

"You might have if they had been able to frisk you," he says.

"I don't think I've ever been so happy to be a woman!" I blurt out, realizing that it's true.

THE NEXT MORNING, I grab breakfast with Sebastian, a gay poet who's here on a writer's grant and whom I met on my first day in San José. I tell him about last night's events.

"Well, shit, girl, of course they thought you were a young little fag!" he says. "I told you we all thought you were somebody's hot trick when you walked up to the breakfast buffet."

Most of the guests here at San José's one gay hotel (according to Lonely Planet anyway) seem to be enjoying the barely legal local boys a lot more than the culture. Sebastian is no exception. He's been enjoying the locals in San José for a week. He tells me he's been meaning to check out the beaches on the coast but keeps getting distracted. The young guys are cute, and apparently they're easy to hook up with if you're willing to throw some cash around. I imagine that's pretty tempting for a guy like Sebastian. His face has a youthful look to it, like Andrew McCarthy's in *Pretty in Pink*, but he's at least one hundred pounds heavier, meaning he probably doesn't get this kind of action back home, where there's not the same incentive.

"Well, I'm definitely ready for some mellow beach time," I tell him. "You wanna come?"

He says yes, and we decide to check out Punta Uva, a small town on the Caribbean side of the country that a friend of mine told me about. We catch the first bus after breakfast and watch the city disappear behind us.

The town turns out to be just as deserted and idyllic as I was told. There's the bus stop, a restaurant, the beachfront cabanas we're staying at for the next few days, and a scattering of small houses and farms. That night, we get dinner and go to sleep serenaded by the sounds of the tropics.

The next day we swim in the warm, tranquil Caribbean Sea and eat great food. A tropical rainstorm later in the day forces us to head back to the cabanas and take shelter under a large outdoor palapa. When we get there, Sebastian busts out his notebooks, saying it'll be good for his writing, but I can tell he's going stir-crazy. The next morning he announces that he's heading back to San José.

I, on the other hand, feel like my vacation is just getting started, so I decide to stay in Punta Uva. The cabana we were sharing is so cheap that I keep it all to myself. It's got a balcony with a view of the water and all kinds of tropical animals, like howler monkeys and toucans, which I fondly associate with Froot Loops cereal. One toucan is so tame it starts coming into my cabana and trying to make off with things, like my toothbrush.

After a few days I decide to check out the larger beach town of Puerto Viejo. There's another cabana my friend recommended that's right on the black-sand beach, and it's lesbian owned. But the lesbian owner, it turns out, isn't as friendly to me as she had been to my friend. For example, she doesn't invite me to hang out with her and her family. I'm guessing it's because I look more like a local boy—especially with the dark tan I've already acquired—than a fellow American lesbian.

The next day I head into the town to explore. When I get there, I'm hungry, so I grab some food, sit down at an outdoor table, and check out the scene. Unlike Punta Uva, there actually is one.

The scene consists of the Ticos, as the Spanish-speaking Costa Ricans call themselves, and the black, English-speaking Rastafarians. Then there are the tourists, made up mainly of backpackers, surfers, and rowdy, red-faced Australians. The latter stare at me very openly and rudely when I walk into the beachside bar to get a beer.

The bartender gives me an oddly amused look as he hands me the beer and says, "Here you go, sir."

I'm so used to being called sir that I don't bat an eyelash at his remark—until I remember that I'm wearing a two-piece bathing suit. Suddenly, I understand all the dirty looks I've been getting. The tourists think I'm a boy walking around in a girls' swimsuit, and they're clearly not the types who appreciate that kind of thing. I chug my beer and decide to stick to the beach by my cabana.

After several days of bliss on the black sand, I buy a bus ticket back to San José. I find a place to grab some lunch by the station and order plátanos, which my mom used to make, from a woman with caramel-colored skin. She calls me *mijo*, an affectionate abbreviation of *mi hijo*, which means "my son" in Spanish. I haven't heard that in a long time—and never directed at me—and it takes me back.

When the plátanos come, they're even better than my mom's. The waitress watches approvingly as I gulp them down.

"What are you doing here all alone?" she asks me.

"Just visiting," I answer.

"From where?"

"San Francisco."

"San Francisco de Las Cruces?" she asks, referring to a similarly named town in Costa Rica.

"No, San Francisco, California. In the United States."

"The United States!" she practically shouts. "And you came alone?"

"Yeah."

"Wow, you're a brave one!" she says, pinching my arm affectionately and winking at me as she walks away.

There's something oddly appealing about the way she treats me. I make my way onto the bus, and as it drives off it hits me: she was flirting with me! Flirting in that not exactly sexual way that older women sometimes do with boys. She was stroking what she perceived as my budding male sexuality, and it felt awesome.

I'm jealous of all the guys who got to feel this way growing up. I'd never understood why so many guys, even average-looking ones, had such a high level of confidence that girls would like them—*should* like them—but for the first time I do. The older women in their lives had probably been stroking their egos for years, making them feel like god's gifts to women, just like that waitress had done to me. No wonder so many men seemed to have a deep, subconscious belief that women would love them.

I'd always been told I was beautiful by my dad and other older men. It had annoyed me, though, because I didn't need or particularly *want* to be attractive to men. Plus, because their praise was always about my looks, it sometimes came off as shallow and even kind of sleazy—certainly worlds away from the sweet, flirty warmth that I'd felt from the waitress. *That's* what I'd wanted to feel.

I settle in for the ride and after a few stops the bus is packed. A guy sits down next to me and strikes up a conversation. I can tell he thinks I'm a guy, and when he asks me my name, I decide not to correct him because I think it'll be easier for him to accept my being a guy.

"Juan," I answer.

I'm surprised that it pops out of my mouth, since I think it's one of the least sexy of all Spanish names, but it's common and simple, and I'm trying to keep it simple. I tell him I'm seventeen and that I'm visiting my uncle. He seems satisfied and we talk about what subjects I like in school and what California's like. There's no drama; it's perfect.

Except for the fact that it's now easier for me to live in the world as a boy than a girl. And I'm not sure I want to be a boy. I'm getting tired of the limitations around expressing my emotions and the tough veneer that I have to put on to protect myself every time I get around a group of young men. Or any time I want to be respected as a man by the mainstream world.

But how can I *live* as anything other than a man or a woman in this world, when those are the only categories that exist?

SAN FRANCISCO, CALIFORNIA
AUGUST 1997

The day after I get back from Costa Rica, I call in to my television interview for the Seattle talk show. I can't see what's happening in the studio, but I can tell that they've put the pictures I sent them side by side because one of the hosts of the show asks if it's me in both pictures. They respond with positive fascination when I tell them it is, saying something about how cool it is that I can look so handsome *and* so pretty.

When it's over, I get off the phone feeling happy. I realize that even though it felt impossible to be anything other than a man or a woman in Costa Rica, it doesn't feel totally impossible here. In fact, I had kind of done it just now. I had presented myself as both a man *and* a woman on television, and the hosts reacted positively and were accepting.

I'm relieved to be back in the US and grateful to live in a place where people are more open about gender expression.

A few weeks later, the *Inside Edition* producer contacts me. The episode on intersex I was interviewed for is going to air on September 15 on CBS. I'm kind of nervous, so I invite some friends over to watch it with me.

Once the show airs, I'm pleasantly relieved.

The segment features only one line from my entire interview, but it's a good one, where I speak about intersex people being denied the right, because of nonconsensual surgeries, to grow up with their own unobstructed experience of their gender. Professor Anne Fausto-Sterling, whose gender studies work I admire and studied while at Berkeley, is also interviewed in the segment, and I feel honored to be a part of this conversation with her.

Overall, seeing my face on national television, talking about such an important subject, is a remarkable experience. My friends agree, and when they see the footage of me riding my motorcycle while my unzipped jacket is blowing in the wind behind me, they say I look like a hermaphrodite superhero.

MARCH 1998

I get a message from Howard, one of the local intersex people I know, asking me if I'd like to be on the *Montel Williams Show* with him.

"I told them that you're really cool because you can look like both a pretty woman and a handsome boy."

"Oh, thanks," I say.

"So do you want to talk to the producer, see if you like him? I think they want to do a very educational, respectful segment."

I call the *Montel* producer, and sure enough, he seems cool. He says we can do a phone interview, and if Montel likes it, they'll fly me out on Tuesday night's red-eye to film on Wednesday. By late Monday I get the call that it's a go.

This is a bigger show than the others I've done and the first where I'll be sitting on a stage while I'm interviewed, so there's definitely potential for high anxiety. Fortunately, I have to leave the next day so there's not a lot of time to dwell on it.

While prepping for the trip, I start thinking about what to wear on the show, and it becomes a somewhat difficult decision to make. On the one hand there's the *just be yourself* philosophy. But "myself" is pretty radical these days, and the reason I'm doing this is to make people—and especially parents—realize that it's okay not to operate on infants who are born intersex. So I decide that since I can look both masculine and feminine—and have—I'll look more feminine on the show but still true to myself. I pick the same outfit that I sometimes wear to work: black women's slacks and a dark-purple short-sleeved top with a feminine neckline.

When I arrive at the television studio, I'm immediately whisked off to hair-and-makeup. I tell the makeup stylist to go ahead and do whatever she regularly would. It's pretty fun, actually, not having to deal with it myself but just sitting back and letting someone else do a great job.

When she's finished, I'm taken to another room where I will wait until I head out onstage. The producer comes in and introduces himself. He tells me that Montel likes to meet his guests prior to the shows and may come by if there's time. Ten minutes later I hear a knock on the door.

"Come in," I say, and stand up to greet him.

"Hi," he says, shaking my hand. "I'm Montel. Nice to meet you."

"Nice to meet you too," I say.

"*Hida*, right?" he asks, looking me over. "You're actually not what I expected."

I can tell by the twinkle in his eye that he means that I'm *prettier* than he expected. He's polite about it though.

He goes over some logistics with me about who else is on the show, besides Howard. He also tells me that if anyone in the audience, or any of the other guests, is disrespectful, I should just lean over and give him a "help me" look.

"Thanks," I say. "Hopefully I won't need to do that, but it's nice to know I can."

The next thing I know I'm onstage, getting interviewed by him, and he's just as cool onstage as he was backstage. One of the other guests though, a doctor, is not so nice. He's on the show to advocate for "corrective" surgery, and he reeks of being an arrogant asshole.

During the commercial break he walks over to me and asks me if I've ever had to take cortisol. I know he's asking because people with "salt-wasting CAH," one of the conditions that can cause the clitoris to become enlarged, have to take cortisol for their health. Salt-wasting CAH is a severe form of congenital adrenal hyperplasia (CAH), in which the adrenal glands make too little aldosterone, causing the body to be unable to retain enough sodium. For infants born with CAH, sodium, or salt, is lost in their urine (thus the name "salt-wasting"), and if they go undiagnosed and don't get cortisol, they can dehydrate and die.

I tell him I haven't taken it, and I'm glad that's my answer, because if it weren't, he could make a big deal about how I've needed medical treatment to survive, in order to make the audience think that being intersex is some kind of sickness that needs medical attention. I've noticed that doctors often do this, even though the truth is that only some of us require medical attention for our immediate health, and this is true of "regular" males and females as well.

Later, when describing intersex bodies like mine, the doctor says, "If the clitoris is enlarged, and it can be *grossly* enlarged and look like a bent-over big boy's penis and kind of frighten parents in a way...then they need *something* done to allow them to be their full potential."

He sticks his finger out when saying "big boy's penis" to indicate how big the clitoris could be, and he does so with an attitude like, *Of course you'd wanna chop that off.* It's difficult not to interrupt him. He's trying to make the whole audience think that my body's gross. *Fuck him,* I think.

Finally, he stops talking, and I'm able to go in on him.

"You said if there's *gross* enlargement; you used the word *gross*. I think that's a problem right there. It's used in all the medical text-books and that right there displays the medical establishment's judg-ments that even when there's no salt-wasting syndrome, even when there's no threat to life, there *must* be something done. You said 'must.' Now, that is *your* opinion, but it is not necessarily the *child's* opinion, or the parents'."

The audience bursts into applause. The doctor had tried to inter-rupt me as I spoke, but I didn't let him.

When it's his turn to speak, he says, "You saw the pictures, Mon-tel," as if to prove how "gross" intersex genitals are. Montel jumps in and says that yes, he saw the pictures, but that if he had a child and they were born that way, he wouldn't touch a thing.

The show cuts to a commercial break.

I feel victorious. I've just challenged our oppressors. I've disputed the bullshit theories that they've used to mutilate us, right on national television. And from the reaction, the audience was clearly on my side.

MAY 1998

I've heard about a health clinic with great sliding-scale rates from my trans friends, and I decide to go there to try to find out what type of intersex variation I have. Some intersex people look male, some look female, and some look in between, and I've learned that there are different medical conditions associated with intersex people's appearance. For example, according to my intersex friend Craig, who has Klinefelter's syndrome, most folks with Klinefelter's are registered as male and look and identify as men as adults. Craig shows me old pictures in which he looked different, but still male, even before he was pressured into taking testosterone (as often happens to Klinefelter's men because they have low levels of testosterone). The T made him grow a beard and a lot of body hair for the first time, which he's angry about, as he preferred his previously boyish good looks.

I've never cared to have a "diagnosis," and I don't have any health issues, but now I'm kind of curious. I figure since I'm talking about being intersex more publicly and frequently now, I may as well know. The clinic sees mainly transgender patients, but I imagine that training will help them understand, or at least be sensitive to, my needs.

After telling the physician that I'm intersex and explaining why I'm there, to my surprise she looks me up and down and asks me which gender I *feel* more like, man or woman. I explain that I don't have an issue with my gender, or with being intersex. I'm simply there to get some medical information.

The doctor ignores my statements, asking me once more whether I feel male or female. I can tell she's not trying to be rude though, so I just answer truthfully that I feel both. I repeat that my visit isn't about my gender identity, though, but about finding out which medical condition is responsible for my large clitoris, with which I have no issues.

"Okay, you feel both, but which one do you feel *more*?"

"I don't know," I reply. "It's really hard to say..."

"You must feel like one a little more than the other though, right?"

I'm surprised, and a little annoyed, that she seems unwilling to continue without a binary answer. But I want to get on with this, so I finally give her the answer she's looking for.

"Well, if I *have* to choose, I guess I'll say female."

"Okay, great."

She does a blood test and sends me on my way.

The next week my test results are ready. While I'm sitting in the waiting room, I notice some people staring at me. Finally, one of them—a woman—walks over.

"Excuse me," she says in a German accent. "I am working on a documentary about gender benders in San Francisco, and the filmmaker wants to know if you'd be interested in being in it."

"Oh," I say, surprised. "I'd have to hear more about it, but maybe. Who's the filmmaker?"

"Her name is Monika Treut."

"Oh, I've heard of her!" I say excitedly. "I've seen *Virgin Machine*, and I used to have the ad for it hanging up in my room in New York!"

It's true. The picture for the movie poster was a gorgeous shot of two women in a sexual embrace. I'd had it hanging by my bed for months before I'd even seen the film.

"Oh, wonderful; let me go tell her."

A few minutes later, another woman approaches me, and she

looks exactly like what I'd imagine an artsy German filmmaker would look like: a woman with angular glasses, black patent leather boots, leopard-print coat, and dyed dark-red hair.

"Hello, I'm Monika," she says. "I'm so happy you're interested in being in my film. I have to run but here's my card. Please call me to discuss it."

She scurries off with her entourage and soon afterward, I'm called in to see my doctor. She seems rushed.

"So the tests came back negative," she says. "You have nothing to worry about."

"What does that mean?"

"It means you are a perfectly normal woman."

"But, I'm intersex, and there are different types, so which type am I?" I ask her.

She looks at me with a puzzled expression.

"If you want to come back, we can do more tests, but you're a normal woman, okay? Don't worry!" she says, as if I were seeking reassurance.

The incident leaves me feeling invalidated and makes me aware of a pattern in the medical response to my being intersex: denial. I hadn't been subjected to medical procedures to eradicate my intersex status, as others have been, but it is in a way being *verbally* eradicated.

"SO THE DOCTOR SAID the test came out negative," I say to Brittney on the phone the next day.

"Which test did they use? Check the paperwork."

"It says 17OHCort…"

"Oh, the seventeen is the worst one out there!" she says. "It's been shown to have false negatives. The twenty-one is much better. You should go back and have her do that one."

I doubt I will though. The whole experience just confirmed my suspicion that doctors don't get where I'm coming from. I'm healthy and I know what my body's like, regardless of what caused it to be this way. Although the scientific part of my brain is curious about what the diagnosis would be, I can't shake the feeling that I would be buying into the idea that I'm something strange that needs to be studied.

I decide to call Monika Treut instead.

"So the film is a documentary about transsexuals in the San Francisco Bay Area. I see them as being pioneers in the exploration of gender, so I've titled it *Gendernauts*, as a variation on *astronauts*," she tells me.

"Oh, wow. I like that, but I'm not transsexual," I say, a little disappointed.

"You're not?" she asks, surprised.

"No, I'm intersex."

"Oh, intersex! I didn't even try to get intersex people for the film because I thought they'd be too hard to find, so it's actually fantastic if you would be in it!" she says.

JUNE 1998

Brittney calls to tell me she finally got a tape of the Seattle talk show we filmed after I came back from Costa Rica. Recently, I've been volunteering at ISNA more often since I have extra time and decided to let go of the grievances I had with Brittney. Even though it hurt to know she was against gender-neutral pronouns, I'm okay with people having different opinions. Plus, she eventually apologized for being inconsiderate after I discovered on my own that our intersex retreat had officially been turned into a documentary. At the end of the day, I'm so grateful to her for her role in the intersex movement that I figure I can forgive her mistakes.

Brittney says maybe we can watch the Seattle show this Friday evening and then finish stuffing envelopes for the mailing we started last week.

Friday rolls around, and after we're done watching the show, Brittney asks me what I thought of it.

"It was great," I say.

"You didn't feel exploited?"

"No...Why would I?"

"Because of how they put those photos up side by side of you looking like a girl and a boy."

"Well, *I* sent them those photos, so no, I don't feel exploited. Besides, being both masculine and feminine is part of my intersex experience."

"Hmm," she says. "I don't think we'll use this piece for outreach, then. I don't want parents thinking their children are going to want to be little girls one day and little boys the next."

I don't really know what to say, because I actually think I came across well on the show. Sure, I'm a little different, but I seemed healthy and happy. Isn't that the whole point? Don't we want parents to see that intersex people can be happy without the surgery?

On the show, Brittney had talked about how horrible her life had been after surgery, and then it cut to me being bubbly and lively. One of the hosts had even said to Brittney, "I bet you wish you could be more like Hida though."

I know he meant, "I bet you wish you hadn't been *operated on*, like Hida wasn't," but Brittney probably felt bad being compared to me that way. Maybe that's why now she's being so critical instead of congratulatory.

Still, her comment makes me feel like she doesn't approve of me, and it's the final straw. I had expected this level of criticism and lack of support from straight outsiders who might think my gender duality was weird, but from *her*, another intersex person? She's surprisingly managed to be more negatively judgmental about my being intersex than anyone else has ever been. Most nonintersex *strangers* have been more supportive, in fact.

When I finally walk out of the office, I think, *With friends like you, I don't need enemies.*

THE FOLLOWING WEEK, I film my interview for *Gendernauts*. Monika is cool and easy to talk to, so the interview's fast and fun. Also, she's received international acclaim for her other films, so this one has a good chance of being shown internationally as well, which is *awesome* for intersex visibility.

Perhaps best of all, though, is that I lined this film up on my own—without any help from Brittney. She doesn't think I'm a good spokesperson for the cause, but I'm not going to let her stop me, because I know she's wrong.

CHAPTER 9

Girl/Boy, Lesbian/Gay?

SAN FRANCISCO, CALIFORNIA
JULY 1998

I FINALLY FINISH THE INTERVIEWS for my thesis and they reveal that, as children, the intersex people that had not received "corrective medical treatment" did not experience the trauma and confusion that doctors and others often presume they would, despite having ambiguous genitalia and unusual social circumstances to navigate. As adults, they had found long-term, committed, seemingly happy, healthy relationships. They appeared mentally healthy, were gainfully employed, and had friends and a social life. Unlike the common predictions, they seemed just as happy and successful as any other group of people I've encountered.

I conclude that, given the evidence that we *do* have of harm resulting from cosmetic, "corrective" medical protocols, the *lack* of any evidence that these procedures do indeed help us, and the healthy outcomes in those of us left as we were, doctors should help parents determine which sex traits are more dominant in their child, male or female, and assign them that sex *without* removing or altering their vital sex organs. They should do this with the awareness that their child, like any, might grow up to feel like a different sex than the one they were assigned and that they should be supported if that does indeed happen.

My advisor gives my thesis an A, which makes me officially a college graduate. It's been eight years since the friends I started college with graduated from Wesleyan, but I know that a lot of poor, disowned queer kids never end up graduating at all, so I'm happy I did and that I did it well. My advisor even tells me that with a little tweaking, my thesis could be a doctoral dissertation, which is exciting to hear.

"HEY, YOU WANNA GO to the beach with me and some friends?" my friend Tom asks me one Saturday morning.

I'm always up for the beach on hot days like today, which don't happen too often in San Francisco. Even if it's hot in the rest of the city, the sky is often fogged over by the time you get near the ocean, and I'm not one of those people who like the beach in all kinds of weather.

Twenty minutes later, Tom shows up in a friend's convertible BMW. In addition to owning expensive toys like luxury cars, most of Tom's friends often dress in trendy, well-made clothes and have the attitude of people who don't have to worry about money.

"We're going to Black Sands Beach," Tom says merrily. "Do you know it?"

"I've heard of it but I haven't been there yet."

"Well, honey, you're in for a treat!"

He's right. The ride alone is amazing. We cross the Golden Gate Bridge and then take the first exit, which loops under the highway and off into the Marin Headlands, a state park that borders the ocean, across the Bay from San Francisco. The road into it is steep and winding, but the view is spectacular. After driving a bit farther, we park in a lot and embark on a brief, but rugged, hike down to the beach.

When we reach the sand, which is indeed black, Tom spots his friends, and we head over to join them. They're all cute and gay, and it turns out so is Black Sands Beach, which I learn is a nude, gay beach. Luckily, I find it much easier to be totally nude these days than having to figure out what kind of bathing suit to wear.

The issue is that I like wearing men's swim clothes, like comfy surfer shorts, but men's bathing suits don't include tops. Of course, no one's *stopping me* from wearing a top though, and sometimes I do. However, even in California, doing so sometimes spurs a less than positive reaction from onlookers because it causes them to think that I'm not actually a man but a lesbian dressed like one.

The other option is to not wear a top, which I've also done. I did it in L.A., for example, when I visited my Wesleyan friend Angie, and it wasn't easy. A group of young guys started mocking me when they saw my tiny tits, and I had to get macho and confrontational to ward them off.

Ultimately, these things made me realize that no matter what kind of bathing suit I wear, I'll likely have to contend with some people's negative reactions to it.

I happily strip off my clothes the minute we finish putting down our beach towels at Black Sands Beach, and Tom's friend Jonathan joins us shortly after. Jonathan has a slight accent that I imagine is either Italian or French. After briefly chatting with him I find that he's very witty; I like him.

I note that he's also quite handsome, in a distinguished kind of way. His hair is closely cut and slightly silver with neat sideburns, and his green eyes are quite arresting against his nicely bronzed skin. He must be a jet-setter, I muse, because it doesn't look like the work of a tanning bed.

"So, what did you study at Berkeley?" he asks me.

"Oh, I majored in interdisciplinary studies, where you make your own major. Mine was gender and sexuality."

"Ah, that's great," he says. "What did you write your thesis on?"

I take a deep breath and mentally prepare myself to come out to him. He's cool, but I'm naked—we both are—and that definitely makes it a little more awkward than the other times I've come out about this.

"Um, intersex," I answer, exhaling. "Do you know what that is?"

"No," he admits. "Is that like transsexuals or something?"

"No. Actually, it's the modern word for hermaphroditism."

"Oh," he says, his interest piqued. "What made you interested in that topic?"

"I'm intersex, actually, on the female side."

There, I said it.

"*Really?*" he says, his voice unable to contain his fascination. "I thought you seemed different."

"You didn't think I was a butch lesbian?" I ask.

"No, that's the thing. I don't see you that way, in your looks or your personality. So many lesbians have this tough-guy attitude, like they're trying to prove something, which personally I find distasteful. But you—you're just as sweet as can be," he says, smiling.

"Oh, thanks—I guess!" I say, laughing.

"No, trust me—it's a compliment. And your *body*," he continues, "well, it's not very womanly as far as I can see. You certainly don't have to go to any effort to hide your breasts, do you?"

We both laugh.

"No, not really," I answer.

"You're actually quite lean and muscular," he says, studying my physicality in typical gay-male fashion. "And your hips are small and your stomach is tight. You seem like a boy to me. A *cute* boy."

He peers over his sunglasses and into my eyes as he says this. I think I feel a flutter in my chest. Is that possible? He's a man, and they don't make me feel that way. But I realize he's a handsome *gay* man, flirting with me as a cute queer *boy*; it feels different.

"Thanks," I say, a little embarrassed. I quickly change the topic.

He's a good conversationalist, and he tells me he owns several businesses, which seem of little importance to him, but they do seem to give him the means to travel quite extensively. He speaks intelligently, engagingly, and sensitively to the others around him, a skill I seldom see in straight men.

We spend the afternoon alternately sunning, jumping into the water, and drinking the bottles of expensive white wine that Jonathan has supplied. At one point I'm lying on my back, warming up after my last dip of the day, and I notice Jonathan discreetly looking down at my crotch. I guess he wants to see why I'm a hermaphrodite, and I can't help but wonder what he thinks.

Is he disappointed? Have I experienced shrinkage?

I'm always significantly smaller anyway when I'm not aroused; but I guess he knows all about this, being a man and all.

"I've really enjoyed meeting you," he says as we're packing up to go. "You know, I have a guest cottage in the back of my property on the beach in Cape Cod. You're welcome to visit me any time you like. It's really quite lovely."

"Thanks so much," I say genuinely. "That's very nice of you to offer. I enjoyed meeting you too."

"Here's my card," he continues, "in case you're ever in the area."

"*GUURRL...*" TOM SAYS LATER that evening when I pick up the phone, "my friend Jonathan really liked you."

"I liked him too," I reply.

"Yeah, but he *liked you* liked you. We went to dinner after dropping you off at home, and he kept talking about how smart and cute you are—and he even said he noticed that you have a little somethin' somethin' going on down below!" he says with a giggle.

"I thought I caught him sneaking a peek!" I say, laughing.

"And he said he was curious about it..."

"Oh, honey, isn't everyone?" I jokingly ask.

We both laugh.

"He told me he invited you to visit him in Cape Cod," Tom says.

"Oh god, do you think he's serious?" I ask. "I mean, he's *gay* and I'm not a man."

"Yeah, but you're not exactly a woman either, and he's always been into younger guys since I've known him. Cute ones—like you!"

I laugh.

"Okay, but seriously," I say, "don't you think the fact that I don't have a penis would be a problem?"

"Well, he *did* see you naked..."

"I *guess*," I say slowly.

"And he said you felt very boy-like to him *after* seeing that little thing of yours," Tom says, giggling.

"That's true," I say.

"So what do you think?" Tom asks.

"As in, would I actually stay with him in Cape Cod as his *lover*?"

"Um, *yeah*. That's what we were talking about!"

"Okay, Miss Thing," I joke back, "give me a second. No need to get all bitchy."

"Can't help it. And another thing," he adds. "I don't know if I mentioned it, but in case you didn't notice, he's *loaded*."

"You know I don't care about that," I say.

"I know, I know, but it doesn't *hurt*. He'd probably spoil you silly."

"God, it's weird," I say. "I've never thought about something like this before. I've always been so into girls!"

"I know, but you seemed to really like him. You talked to him the whole day."

"Yeah, I know. I did like him, and I found him kind of attractive, actually."

"I thought so!" Tom shouts.

"Wow, what a trip..." I muse.

"*Soooo?*" he asks, tentatively this time.

"Honestly," I reply, "I'm kind of shocked that I'm even considering this. I mean, I've had all sorts of escapades, but I'm just not sure..."

"Well, the offer's there for you, if you ever wanna find out how we fags live," Tom says.

It's the first time since high school that I've contemplated having a relationship, even a very casual one, with a man. And this man is gay. I guess I shouldn't be surprised by this situation, since I often do things differently than most folks, whether I mean to or not. But still, I am.

I'm aware enough to have noticed how gay men respond to me since I started looking this way. I know I look like a cute boy. But I guess I had assumed that all gay men are size queens and that one look at my genitals would nip their interest in the bud. It's nice to see there are exceptions to every rule, but what I find even more surprising than the proposition itself is that I'm considering it.

Even though I've always preferred women, I've also always been intrigued by new experiences. And I *have* enjoyed sex with men in the past, if I find them attractive.

So what's stopping me with Jonathan? Because *something* is.

"HEY," TOM SAYS WHEN he calls the next weekend, "have you given any more thought to whether you want to visit Jonathan? He asked me about you."

"You know," I say, sinking into my feeling of resistance, "I have been thinking about it, and it's appealing, but I think the problem, more than him being gay and me not being male, is the age dynamic."

"Huh," Tom says. "So he's too old for you?"

"No, it's not that, really. He's in great shape and everything, so he doesn't feel too old. It's more like I feel too young."

Tom sighs. "I don't get it."

I attempt to explain. "It feels like because I *look* similar to a teenage boy, and he's obviously this wealthy, older gay man, I'll just become his cute little boy toy if we got together."

"Oh, yes you would!" Tom says, laughing.

"Yeah, very funny, but I'm serious," I say. "Even though I look young, I'm thirty years old now, and even when I *was* younger, I was often the more dominant person in the relationship. I'm not used to it being the other way around, and it feels kind of weird."

"But you're not always 'the top' with every girl you date, right?" he asks.

"No, but they're girls, and they're my age—or close to it—so the power thing is totally different if I'm not."

"Okay, I kind of get it, but geez, girl, really? Do you know how many queens would be dying to be fawned over by a rich, handsome, intelligent, genuinely *nice* guy like him? If I wasn't with someone, I think I'd wish he were into *me*."

"Yeah, it's tragic," I say, making Tom laugh.

CHAPTER 10

Nonbinary Blues

I KNOW YOU'VE TOLD ME you think I'm both masculine and feminine," I say to Jade over lunch one day, "but which do you think I *look* better as, boy or girl?"

"Oh my god, girl, *I don't know*!" she proclaims. "I think you look cute as a boy, but I've always thought you were a beautiful woman too. It should be about what feels right for you."

"They *both* feel right," I say. "That's the problem. If someone is masculine, it means, by definition, that they're not feminine, or vice versa. People aren't supposed to be both."

"Says who?" Jade asks. "Plenty of people like androgyny."

"Yeah, you *hear* that," I say, "but I haven't met any of these people. All the girls I meet seem to want one or the other, butch or femme..."

"Well, I don't know what to tell you. I think you've just got to be yourself."

"Fine," I say, dejected.

Jade knows me better than anyone, and I trust her taste and sense of style, so I was kind of hoping she'd have a preference about which version of me she preferred, masculine or feminine. And that she'd just tell me, so I could express myself that way, because I'm so tired of fluctuating between the two and feeling judged by other people when I do.

"I'm sorry, girl," Jade says sympathetically. "I forgot how much this stuff tortures you. I guess I just don't get it, because I think you're so attractive and I know other people do too. I mean, I can't think of anyone that so many girls, gay *or* straight, have been into."

"But girls always like me more one way or the other, pretty or handsome, you know? And then when I switch, it bugs them, but no matter how hard I've tried to pick one, it just doesn't work. After a while I want to look like the other again. It's like I'm both, but I don't know how to *be* that, or if anyone's ever going to be into it…"

Nobody seems to understand why it's so upsetting and difficult for me to feel like a gender that doesn't exist. It makes me feel totally alone. I let myself break down in tears. Jade knows me, so fuck it. I don't have to pretend I'm less upset or confused about this than I actually am.

"Girl, look, I know it must be hard. This whole world is built on male/female archetypes—I'm sure that's why not many people are out as intersex. You're one of the few people on the fucking planet who *is*, right? You, Brittney, and that guy Howard from Mill Valley—like on TV and stuff? And that's just because you're such a crazy fucking badass!"

She gets me to crack a tiny smile.

"But you know what?" she asks.

"What?"

"Every spiritual philosophy talks about how important it is to unite the feminine and masculine polarities. Even Jung talks about the hermaphrodite representing the union that's necessary for psychological transformation."

"Really?"

"Yeah. That's why all those yogis and spiritual masters look androgynous when you see their pictures. You're supposed to become more androgynous the more enlightened you are."

"Wow, I didn't know that."

"And you were *born* that way, girl! That's why I love you so much!" Jade exclaims with a big smile.

"Now you're just being nice!" I say, laughing. "But you know, maybe that explains this thing I heard about the psychologist who started all the intersex surgeries."

"What? You didn't tell me about this."

"Yeah, his name is John Money, and for his doctoral dissertation at Harvard[1] he studied a group of about two hundred and fifty intersex people to see how psychologically healthy they were. This is before the surgeries existed, so the subjects hadn't been traumatized by that, and his results actually found that they were psychologically *healthier* than the *non*intersex people."

"*See*, that's what I'm talking about."

"But the weird thing is he still promoted doing the surgeries even though he knew that," I say.

"Maybe he just saw it as a way of making a name for himself, you know? Or maybe he was still so closed-minded that he couldn't accept the results of his own study and still thought he could 'help' intersex people by making them 'normal' males or females. You know, that whole bullshit philosophy," Jade hypothesizes.

"Yeah, maybe..."

"In any case, thank god you escaped that, right? *That's* something to be happy about!"

"Yeah, totally," I say, nodding my head in agreement.

"And look, your androgyny is *hot* and you know it. That's why all these girls, *and* guys, are always after you," Jade assures me. "The right person's gonna come into your life one day, Hida—I know it. And she's gonna be lucky to have you!"

This is why I've been friends with this girl since high school. I'm lucky to have *her*.

JUNE 1999

Gendernauts is premiering at the San Francisco International LGBTQ Film Festival, at the infamous Castro Theatre, just a few blocks from me. This time, the filmmaker, Monika Treut, informs me and invites me on the panel in advance. There's a huge line down the block for the screening, and it's a smash. I'm elated.

SEPTEMBER 1999

A few months after the film's premiere, I begin school again as a law student. The decision to pursue a law degree came as a surprise even to me, because until last year, the thought of being a lawyer had never crossed my mind, save for the time when I took a career aptitude test in high school that said "lawyer" would be a good choice. But I'm thirty-one at this point, and I feel like it's time to commit to a career.

Although both of my academic advisors at Berkeley had encouraged me to pursue a doctoral degree, which would lead to an academic career, I wasn't interested. Instead, I realized I want to do something where I can help people in a more direct, hands-on way. In fact, I'd wanted to become a firefighter after graduating, but a serious injury prevented me from pursuing it.

So I'd turned my attention to going to law school to pursue public interest work. I didn't study for the LSATs as much as I was supposed to, but I managed to do well enough to get into my safety schools, Georgetown and Hastings, the latter of which won out because it's in San Francisco.

I'm here with the hopes of using my degree to advocate for intersex people, but it's not exactly a picnic having to watch my professors' mouths drop whenever I come out to them as female. I figure I need to because some of my classmates have seen me use the restroom and know that I'm legally female, so it'll look strange if I don't correct the professors when they call me "he." It happens so much that after a couple of weeks I wax my upper lip and tweeze my eyebrows a little, just so it will seem *possible* that I'm a woman.

Then, as luck would have it, I meet a girl.

Her name is Audrey and the first time we meet is at a social gathering for law students and lawyers. Our eyes lock the minute she walks into the room, and we soon become inseparable the rest of the evening. She is beautiful—kind of like a brainy Elizabeth Hurley—funny, and apparently very interested in talking to me.

I learn that she's an Ivy League grad who had also gone to law school and graduated at the top of her class. Now she's fighting the good fight at a public interest law firm. She is basically everything I could ask for and more.

Audrey e-mails me a week after the gathering, and by the following Friday night we're making out on her couch.

"You're beautiful," she says.

I'm surprised to hear that after looking like a boy for almost four years, but as the weeks roll by and I continue to see Audrey, I realize how much she sees me as a beautiful woman. And how much that turns her on.

She doesn't ask me to change my style; I just sort of fall into it given the effect that my looking feminine has on her. I start wearing some of my less boyish outfits and wearing makeup, because I love seeing Audrey's eyes light up when I do. I'm crazy about her, and I want to turn her on as much as possible. However, I'm also discovering that I don't want to live out the rest of my days as solely a man or solely a woman.

I am someone that society has been trying to hide or get rid of for centuries, and the rebel in me feels like I should put my duality out there as much as possible, rather than trying to fit into one of society's acceptable gender boxes.

One evening, while Audrey and I are hanging out, I decide to show her the tape of my appearance on *Montel*.

"Oh my god, that was brilliant!" Audrey shouts when it's over. "I love the way you just nailed that doctor for being such a bigot. I'm so proud of you!"

Audrey likes to brag to her friends about my activism for intersex people.

"So I told Jane you're intersex, and she asked me how big your clit is," she tells me one day.

Jane is Audrey's ex, with whom she is still friendly, and even though I like her, I'm not thrilled about her knowing the exact size of my clit.

"What'd you say?" I ask nervously.

"I said, 'It's big enough to fuck me with,'" she says bluntly.

I smile. She's perfect.

Law school, however, is not. For the first time since Costa Rica, I'm struggling a lot with the day-to-day reality of having a sense of gender expression that confuses people. It's a bit ironic given that just months ago, at the *Gendernauts* premiere, I was speaking comfortably and openly about being neither male nor female, man nor woman, and making the whole theater laugh. It's not funny in law school, though, when professors refer to me as "he" in front of dozens of my classmates and I have to correct them.

I've been using *ze* as much as possible in my private life, but I don't even think about doing it at Hastings. It's been hard enough getting my friends and allies to use it, and my professors are more traditional. They're dedicated to the letter of the law, which excludes intersex people and gender-neutral pronouns. That doesn't leave much room for me to express who I am.

In my classes, we're also taught that, regardless of how awful the situation is, at the end of the day all that matters is whether or not something is "legal." It's a strain for me to think this way, to check my ethics at the door in order to win a case, and now I don't know if that's something I want to do.

It's useful, though, to think about how much intersex people are impacted by this phenomenon. Other than what happened during the eugenics movement in Nazi Germany, I've never heard of another community being altered in the ways that we are. Many of the adults who were subjected to nonconsensual medical procedures would sue in a minute if they could—but they can't, because these procedures are completely legal.

Parents have the legal right to make decisions like those about their children, and the only way to prevent these horrible things from happening is to prove that the genital corrective surgeries doctors perform on intersex children cause great harm. The problem is whenever intersex adults step forward to say they were harmed by these surgeries, doctors often respond that intersex people would be worse off if they had been left as they were, and sadly, because the social stigma against us is so strong, most people believe the physicians. There needs to be evidence to disprove these doctors' claims, but it's difficult to get a sufficient amount of it.

Knowing this is the prevailing social attitude sometimes makes me want to hide—to go back to living like I did before I became vocal about being intersex, when only my closest friends and lovers knew who and what I really am. But I feel an obligation to live honestly and openly. My parents couldn't hide being different—their looks and their accents immediately gave away the fact that they were from a different country—and throughout my childhood I always stuck up for them, so now I feel compelled to stick up for this.

NOVEMBER 1999

My mother is so happy I'm in law school that she comes out to visit.

"I'm proud of you, Hida Patricia," she says, hugging me.

It feels good to be doing something that makes her feel this way—if for nothing else than to see her this happy.

She takes me and Beth out to dinner after she arrives. Beth is married now, and my mother asks her question upon question relating to her recent wedding and new husband.

After about twenty minutes I venture to say, "So, Mom, I'm dating someone now—"

"Oh, that's nice, Hida Patricia," she says, cutting me off. She turns to Beth. "So, do you think you two will have children?"

When we get back to my place, I confront my mother about her reluctance to ask about Audrey, and she confesses that she's always thought that my liking girls might be a phase I'd eventually grow out of.

"Mom, I've been this way my whole life, and you've known about it for a good twelve years now. Does this really seem like a phase to you?"

"I guess not, Hida Patricia," she says sadly. "I guess I was just hoping that it was."

I realize in that moment that she still doesn't see me for who I am, and at this point in my life, she may never.

MARCH 2000

"I'm falling in love with you, Hida," Audrey says to me, looking deep into my eyes.

She had warned me in the very beginning of our relationship that she didn't say the *L* word quickly, or use it lightly, but that when she did, she meant it. Now, she just has, and I'm so happy I almost feel high. She's gorgeous, so fucking gorgeous, and so fucking smart and established . . . and she loves me.

But I also get the sinking sensation that this might be too good to be true. How can *she*—this incredible woman—be in love with *me*, a law school dropout?

I made the decision last week over spring break. The lack of possibilities for me to be who I am became too much to bear. Lawyers are supposed to be strong, professional, convincing advocates for their clients, and it seemed impossible for me to do that when a core part of my identity—my gender—was constantly in question. I considered the possibility of having to falsely present myself as strictly a man or strictly a woman for the rest of my professional career, and it filled me with dread.

So now here I am, a directionless law school dropout.

I take some comfort in the fact that Audrey is proud of my activism, which makes me happy because I am too, and I've heard from numerous intersex people that my story has had a positive impact on their lives. However, I want to be someone she can be proud of career-wise and achievement-wise.

As much as I want to believe that my brains and beauty are enough for Audrey to love me, the pressure to succeed in all aspects of my life makes me feel like they're not.

OUR LOVE STORY DOESN'T have a happy ending.

The beginning of the end is when I ask Audrey to participate in a threesome, with me and another guy. She reluctantly accepts, but then I end up getting mad at her for doing it—so mad I make her break down in tears.

To her credit, Audrey tries to put the incident behind us, but I can't pull myself out of the horrible headspace I had created. I had been so worried about trying to please her, to live up to her love for me, that I inadvertently manifested a situation where I had to see her having sex with someone else, in front of my very eyes. It only causes me to sink into a pit of my own insecurity.

Things are never quite the same after this, and Audrey breaks up with me a few weeks later.

JUNE 2000

Although we're no longer officially together, Audrey and I still hang out. With the exception of not having sex, things gradually become more like they were when we were really happy together. I can't tell if that means there's potential to reignite our relationship, but I'm hoping it does, because I still want to be with her.

I've been dealing with the confusing are-we-friends-or-are-we-more situation since I was little. Starting in first grade, I was always in love with my best friends. In fact, the reason we'd become friends in the first place was because I had a crush on them. They didn't know this, of course, and I never told them.

Audrey's seen me sob about losing her, and all the emotional honesty has made our friendship stronger. The problem is I don't know if it means we might get back together, or if I'm just being delusional.

Luckily, Jade and I have started hanging out more again, and she's always good for advice. She recommends I take a meditation course for women that she just finished. It's all about finding your inner power and purpose, which sounds like just what I need right now.

In the second class I attend, I learn that we'll be practicing meditations involving our feminine and masculine energies. I didn't know this would be a part of the course, but I'm psyched, being who I am and all.

When the teacher, Lisa, begins to guide us through the meditations, she tells us to imagine an elevator and us stepping into it. Then she tells us to imagine what it looks like as it begins to go down. She's going to count down from ten, and when she reaches zero, the elevator will open. When we step out, we'll be stepping into our yin (or feminine) energy.

I step out into a feeling, not a visual. I feel engulfed by a soothing sensation that's warm and cozy, a lot like sinking into a water bed... or a woman. It's delicious.

Then Lisa guides us into our yang (or masculine) energy. This time I see a figure on a horse, holding a long staff. It's a warrior and somehow I know that it's me. Then it's replaced by a young man, kind of Asian-looking, doing martial art moves and acrobatics.

When I tell my meditation group afterward that I think I felt connected to my yang energy, Lisa responds, "They're both you."

The next meditation class focuses on the yin and yang in relation to each other. After I'm guided into meditation, I see a man and a woman, then two women. One's very jubilant and outgoing and one's serene and silently powerful. Then I get another image of waves pounding at the beach. The breaking is the yang and the receding is the yin, but it's all one motion. My lesson, as Lisa helps me understand, is that the two energies complement each other and work together.

Lisa explains that yin and yang are always relating within one person. She says it's usually the yang that acts first and the yin that responds. She says if the yang isn't listening to the yin's response, then it will accidentally hurt it.

I think maybe all the ideas about masculinity and femininity that I got from my childhood have left my yin and yang out of balance. I thought I had rejected all the bullshit messages I received when I was younger about how I was supposed to present myself as a woman, and about how femininity was somehow inferior to masculinity, but now I'm starting to realize how much had lodged into my subconscious.

Lisa helps me see—and helps all of the women in the class see—that our feminine, yin side isn't weak at all. It's actually wise and powerful.

"How could I have been so blind?" I ask. "I've been doing exactly what I hate about mainstream society: I've been valuing masculinity over femininity because I thought masculinity was stronger. I'm so embarrassed."

During this time, I realize I long to be with Audrey sexually, but she doesn't want that and it hurts. I miss her so much as a lover I take to crying about it almost every day.

I start seeing Lisa, the meditation course teacher, for private sessions. I share everything that happened with Audrey, down to the latest phone call, and Lisa says I should stop hanging out with her. She says a three-month separation is necessary to break the sexual connection. Even though continuing to see Audrey is only making me sadder, because she doesn't reciprocate my feelings, I don't want to let her go. But I decide I have to.

Audrey keeps trying to hang out after I pull away, but I won't give in, even though I start having vivid sex dreams about her. In them, she tells me she desires me again, and we start making love.

"So how's the separation been going?" Lisa asks during our next private session.

"It's hard," I confess. "I've been having these sex dreams about her almost every night, and in them she still wants me. They're making me feel like we're meant to be together, but I feel like I ruined everything."

"Hida, if you're meant to be together, you'll be together. You can't ruin what's meant to be," Lisa says.

"But I feel so stupid for starting that threesome. I'm such an idiot!"

"You need to stop putting yourself down, Hida. You're having a lot of feelings and that's fine—they're your access to wisdom and they're meant to guide you. You need to ask yourself why you sabotaged things with Audrey, what you were so afraid of."

I take Lisa's words to heart.

I think about the most formative relationship I witnessed in my life: my parents'. But thinking about their relationship only makes me recall terrible memories.

One of these memories is of a particularly bad fight between my parents. It was worse than usual, and it started sounding so bad that I instinctively ran out of my room to try to stop it.

I remember seeing that my parents were in the hallway by the top of the stairs, and my dad was furious.

"You think you can get away with calling me that?" he screamed in Spanish before hurrying back into their bedroom.

When he came back a moment later, he had a gun in his hand, and he was pointing it at my mom.

I remember time suddenly took on a different quality. It wasn't faster or slower, but it felt as if I were in a different dimension.

"Dad, what are you doing?" I yelled.

"This is between me and your mom. She knows why," he said, still looking at her, still pointing.

"Your child is *right* here," my mother snarled under her breath, her eyes locked on his. "Don't be crazy. Put that away."

"Yeah, put the gun away, Dad," I said, a little hesitantly.

I knew how angry he could get when anyone defied him.

"Not until this bitch apologizes!" my father yelled.

"Apologize for telling the truth?" my mother asked him, her voice shaking with fear and hatred.

"Do you want me to shoot you right now?" he yelled.

"Dad, no," I said, starting to cry.

My mother glanced at me quickly, her gaze softening just a little as she did.

"Okay. I apologize," she said to my father, "for *the children*."

My dad lowered the gun down to his side.

"See," he said, looking at me as if nothing crazy just happened. "That's all she had to say. We could have avoided all this."

I have so many bad memories about my dad from my childhood; my siblings and I all do. Hugh and Eden don't share this particular one, but they have their own. Hugh, for example, says he remembers our dad chasing Mom with a baseball bat.

Usually, I don't like to think about these memories and rarely feel strong enough to do it, but when I force myself to seriously consider the long-term effect they've had on me, my fears about relationships become clear. I'm afraid that if I love someone and they say they love me, and we commit to each other, I'll end up trapped and controlled—or even worse, abused, just like my mom was.

When I think about how I pushed Audrey away because of this, I can only cry.

She was in love with me and it was so sweet and I just killed it, I killed her love, I think to myself. It's like it was too much or something. Like letting myself love so openly and purely wasn't safe.

I spend hours sobbing about the end of my relationship with Audrey, but when my sobs subside, I feel lighter, purged—like you feel after you've been nauseously drunk and you finally throw up.

I also see, clear as day, how I've been trying to push my more emotional and sensitive feminine side away for years, not just because I'd been taught by my dad that masculinity—and masculine behavior— was superior, but because it *felt* vulnerable and scary to be soft and feminine. I'd also absorbed these ideas that feminine women are into masculine men—or masculine women if they're lesbians. So I had tried to be more masculine, for both reasons.

I thought that because Audrey is feminine she would want a more masculine partner—someone who was powerful and successful—but it was my dad who cared so much about success and accomplishments, not Audrey! She loved me for who I really was, even when I felt like I was failing. She really loved me, and I couldn't even recognize it as such. In fact, it scared me. So I pushed her, and her love, away.

I feel totally broken.

Then I hear Lisa's voice in my head, telling me that if Audrey and I are meant to be, then she'll come back, and if not, our relationship wasn't meant to be long-term. It was just meant to help me learn an important lesson about love—one that I apparently needed to learn before I could be with my soul mate.

CHAPTER 11

Burning My Man

My friend diana's been trying to get me to go to Burning Man since '95. We met a few years earlier, at an art opening in the Haight where she was showing her work. I loved her work and her loud, crazy laugh, so we hit it off immediately.

Diana's the most driven, dedicated artist I know, and she lives up to all the stereotypes: dramatic, emotional, and always on a financial or romantic roller coaster—usually both. Despite all that, she's still managed to make it to Burning Man for the past five years, so it *must* be pretty damn good.

"Will you at least *think* about going this year?" she asks.

My life is in transition since leaving law school and I'm in the process of doing some heavy healing, but I feel like I could use an exciting new experience.

"I'm in," I tell her.

"Awesome!" she shouts. "You better start packing, then, because it's next week."

I manage to talk Devon, my current roommate, into going as well. Devon is the gay younger brother of my Wesleyan friend Angie.

Angie was my first "girlfriend" ever (as opposed to the love interest of my closeted high school self), and we had remained good friends after the breakup. I don't see her often though, because we've always lived in different cities since leaving school.

I first met Devon while Angie and I were at Wesleyan, and I've hung out with them and their family dozens of times over the years—more often than with my own, actually. Then Devon had decided to move to San Francisco, where he's now living with me in my rent-controlled apartment in the Castro.

We decide to take his car to the festival, where we'll be meeting Diana, Eric, Beth, and some other good friends.

BLACK ROCK CITY, NEVADA
AUGUST 30–SEPTEMBER 3, 2000

We arrive after nightfall, but luckily there's a map in the guidebook that festival volunteers gave us at the entrance to help us find the campsite.

Burning Man, aka Black Rock City, has become so big that two years ago they created a street grid so festivalgoers could navigate it better. Last year the festival became even more official by creating the map. On the map, the streets were named by the hour, from two o'clock to ten o'clock, to fit in with the theme that year, "The Wheel of Time." The streets running perpendicular to those had been named after the planets of the solar system. That meant people ended up saying things like, "Meet me at Three and Uranus" all week.

This year's theme is "The Body." I read about it aloud to Devon, who's driving, from the guidebook:

Nothing is so immediate as your experience of your body. Indeed, to even claim your body as your own is a kind of misrepresentation, for you are possessed by your body as surely as you possess it . . . Being and belonging to a body, feeling we are members of some greater body—this is primal to our sense of who and what we are.[1]

It's pretty amazingly apropos that this is the theme, considering my intersex issues, I think to myself.

I read the streets on the map aloud. There's Head Way, Brain Boulevard, and my favorite: Sex Drive.

"Hey, you guys!" Diana squeals happily when we pull into our camp. "Good news: I got the vial!"

She's talking about liquid acid.

Beth and I found a great connection in the East Village after we did it for the first time as juniors in high school. We used to say it was the best drug in the world because it gave you the most bang for your buck with the least side effects. Eight hours of fun for five dollars, plus no hard crash or hangover.

After unloading the car and having a snack, I'm ready to drop. We grab some sugar cubes that the acid's on, get on our bicycles, and go.

We see cool stuff everywhere: a big metal rib cage with a swing hanging down from the center that you can actually swing on; a mausoleum the size of a four-bedroom, three-story house, made out of thousands of bone-shaped pieces of wood; two giant cupcakes being driven by people wearing red hats that look like the cherries on top. It's a visual wonderland.

"How the hell did you neglect to tell me that this is the best place *on earth* to do acid?!" I yell at Diana.

We stay up all night exploring and then catch the sunrise over the desert. By the time I wake up later that day, lunch is served. Beth is an awesome organizer and she came up with a plan where everyone at our camp pairs off and makes one meal. That way there's always food but you only have to cook once.

After lunch a group of us go for a ride on our bicycles. The city's even cooler in the daytime, in some ways. I see things that I couldn't at night, because they weren't lit up, like a life-sized Pegasus that's half-buried, its wings sticking out like it's struggling to fly out of the sand.

I see a large open dome with people climbing up the rungs to see what's happening inside. As we get closer I realize that it's Thunderdome, just like in the eighties movie *Mad Max* with Tina Turner. The people inside look as postapocalyptic as the actors in the movie. I see an abundance of piercings, tattoos, Mohawks, and dreads.

"Fight! Fight! Fight!" people are screaming.

We look over and see two gladiator-type men swinging from ropes that are hanging from the top of the open dome, trying to hit each other with various weapons. *Probably welders,* I think to myself. The Burner guys who do that often look badass, in a kind of apocalyptic or medieval way.

"Let's check out the other side of town!" Eric yells.

Art cars pass us by as we go. My favorites are two giant matching heads made of metal. There's also a shark—or sand shark, to be exact—built out of an old Caddy convertible. I think it's amazing. I see the cute cupcakes whirl by again and wave to the cheerful drivers, who wave back.

When we get to the other end, we scope out the camps, like one called Hookahdome, which is, unsurprisingly, filled with hookahs. But then the vibe suddenly changes. Everyone seems to be rushing away somewhere.

"Looks like a sandstorm's coming," Eric says, looking out at the horizon. "We better head back to camp. Fast. Cover your nose and mouth with something."

I tie my black bandanna around my face, bandit style. Then we follow Eric in a line through the open expanse of sand, called the playa, pedaling as fast as we can.

Sure enough, the sand starts blowing, and unfortunately, we're pedaling against it. The wind gets stronger and the sand gets thicker until we can just barely make out the person in front of us. In a matter of seconds, we can't even see one another.

All I can see is sand blowing around me. It's like riding through a cloud. And it's exhilarating.

"Is everybody still here?" I hear Eric shout from up ahead.

"Yeah!" we scream in unison.

"Beth?"

"Yeah!" she says.

"Hida?"

"Yeah!" I yell.

"Devon?"

"Present!"

"I'm gonna keep calling out names in intervals, and you keep responding, okay?" Eric shouts.

It takes about twenty minutes to make it back to camp, and when we do, I find out why Eric pulled the Boy Scout leader routine. Apparently people have actually been killed during sandstorms because the big art cars rolling around can't see people in the fog, just like we couldn't see one another.

The next morning I finally see Diana at breakfast.

"Where the hell've you been?" she shouts across camp through a mouthful of eggs.

"Where the hell have *you* been is more like it!" I shout back.

"Oh, just catching up with my man," she says with a naughty smirk.

A tall, cute guy with dreads—white dreads, but nice ones

nonetheless—walks up and puts his arm around her. I learn he's Diana's boyfriend, Jared, and after we introduce ourselves, he disappears while Diana and I catch up.

"So we got caught in a sandstorm yesterday. It was pretty wild."

"Yeah, they don't call this the playa for nothing," she says. "That sand is crazy."

Jared comes back with three mugs of coffee.

"So do you take sugar with your coffee?" he asks, pulling the vial and some sugar cubes out of his pocket.

"Oh, definitely," I answer with a wry smile, and we all drop together.

An hour later we're whizzing around the playa on our bikes. It's fun having Diana as my tour guide since she's been here so many times. She knows a lot of the artists who built the big pieces and art cars. It's kind of like having a backstage pass.

At some point I hear a loud, strange sound, and when I look toward where it's coming from, I can't believe my eyes. It's hard to tell because of how far away it is, but I'm pretty sure the sound is being produced by a dragon shooting fire out of its mouth.

"Oh my god!" I shout out. "Is that a giant dragon?"

"Oh, yeah," Diana says, looking over. "That's Draka, Lisa's piece."

I guess she knows that artist too, Lisa Nigro, which is really cool. And what's even cooler is that this amazing, gigantic thing was built by a woman.

We ride toward it, and as we get closer I notice that it's made entirely of metal. It looks like a large version of the gothic dragon figurines I'd seen in toy stores as a kid. Then suddenly it starts moving away.

"Oh my god, it moves?" I gasp.

"Of course it moves," Diana shouts. "It's an art car. *Hell-o!*"

"I couldn't tell from here!" I say, hitting her arm. "It's so big I thought it was just a stationary piece."

"No, its body's made from a semitruck, actually, and then there's the separate head and tail on top of that."

"Wow," I say. "Can you ride in it? Do they let people on?"

"Yeah, but it's kind of hard because it's always moving. You just have to get lucky," she answers.

After riding around for a bit longer, I learn that Jared is a DJ, and he knows a lot of other DJs at the festival. He takes us to where one of them is spinning. The guy's name is Lorin, but he's known by his stage name, Bassnectar, and it turns out he's amazing. His music is some of the coolest dance music I've ever heard, and I was into the early nineties SF underground outdoor dance-party scene—before they were called raves—so I've heard a lot of good DJs in my day.

While listening to him, I dance my ass off. And my thighs off. And my feet off. I dance my way into another dimension—a dimension where I'm not dancing along to the music, I am *predicting* the music. I'm one step ahead of it, pouncing on every beat like I know exactly when it's gonna drop. Like the DJ and I are telepathically connected.

Through the glorious haze of my dancing, I notice that people are staring at me—a lot of girls in particular, and I like the expressions on their faces. I feel like I'm a magnet for both curious and beautiful girls and boys.

I'm wearing these low-rise velvet pants with a psychedelic pattern that I got with Beth ages ago at Patricia Field, our favorite clothing store in the Village. My top is a child-sized Teenage Mutant Ninja Turtles tee shirt that I pulled and stretched till it was big enough for me to squeeze into. The bottom makes it just past my breasts, so you can see my whole stomach, which is looking more cut than usual with the water loss I've experienced over the past twenty-four hours.

I look very *Is that a boy or a girl?* Some things about me are sexy in a womanly way, like my smooth skin and the way my body moves. But then I'm also flat chested and more muscular than most women, with small hips and an aggressive masculinity to some of my dance moves.

My energy moves back and forth from masculine to feminine and everywhere in between. It seems to mesmerize the crowd. Most people can't stop staring and gravitating toward me, although the boys can tell I'm a dyke, so they keep a respectful distance, god bless 'em. However, I throw some love at both the girls and the boys because I can tell they see me for who I really am.

I'm an andro freak (and that's "freak" in a good way), and they obviously love it.

I remember Jade saying my androgyny is the very thing that makes me attractive. As usual, I think she was right.

SEPTEMBER 2, 2000

Tonight's "the Burn"—what folks call the yearly burning of a giant wooden statue of a man (called "the Man"), which is the art festival's visual focal point—and it's supposed to be crazy. I'm having such a blast already that I can't even imagine it getting any wilder. Yesterday, for example, after the dance party, Beth's husband ended up running for mayor of Black Rock City in his gorilla costume—and he won! The story makes it onto page 2 of today's *Black Rock Gazette*.

This afternoon, Critical Tits will be happening before the Burn. The name's a spoof on Critical Mass, the big urban bicycling event that started in San Francisco. Critical Tits is basically just what it sounds like: a lot of women bicycling, topless. I'm in.

Diana rallies all the women in our camp to do body painting in preparation. I check it out but it's not for me. They're covering their breasts with things like butterflies and glitter and it seems like an attempt to feel less topless. One girl practically looks like she's got a bra on by the time she's done. I decide to wear just my red-orange pants, boots, and a hat—no top, no body paint.

Some of the girls I ride by smile right at me flirtatiously. It's nice that way here: people are friendlier than usual. It's a city but it's not New York or anything, where the first thing I'd learned was to never look strangers in the eye.

Critical Tits was designed to give women a chance to feel safe being topless, just like men get to feel. It's meant to empower us, and in this moment I think it's achieved its goal. I've never seen so many smiling, powerful, *happy* women all in one place.

Afterward, at camp, we all put on warmer layers as the postsunset desert cold kicks in. I choose the Teenage Mutant Ninja Turtles tee shirt that I love and a jacket that happens to be the exact color of the pants I'm wearing. They're both a dark, bright orange, which seems perfect for the night of the Burn.

Diana invites me to go with her and Jared, but I decide to hang out with the rest of our camp for the big event. I know I'll outlast them, but fortunately Diana knows exactly when and where some awesome psychedelic dance band is playing later, so we can meet up there.

Diana takes off with Jared and the rest of us ride our bikes out to the Man. This is the main event that everybody gathers in one place for, and it's totally crowded. I hear people saying there are twenty-six thousand people here this year, and I believe it. We park our bikes a fair distance away and ceremoniously drop acid as a group.

People are hooting and hollering but I'm kind of bored. After what feels like forever, the first flames light up, but the Man burns slowly. The acid's starting to kick in and I have to wait and wait for this thing to go up in flames. I don't even know why we're burning it, actually. After asking around, I find out that Larry Harvey, who founded Burning Man in 1986, says there's no real meaning behind it.

After about twenty minutes, the Man finally falls to the ground in an impressively sparkly display.

"Let's go over to where it fell!" I yell. "I wanna see what's going on!"

"You think we can make it through this crowd?" Beth asks.

"Yeah! C'mon, I'll lead!"

I grab her hand, and the next thing you know, I'm snaking us through. The crowd gets tighter and tighter and people start getting pissed as we squeeze by. If I weren't such a pushy Latina lesbian hermaphrodite from Queens, I never would've gotten us up there. But I am, and I do.

People are running around the remains of the Man in a circle, to the sound of drummers playing in the crowd. It's really hot, so I take off my jacket and the shirt underneath it and stick them both in my child-sized Dr. Seuss backpack. Then I put the backpack back on and join the throng of people.

I get so close to the fire that I almost get torched and one of the security guys pushes me back. It's kind of like being in a mosh pit, and I start dancing along, old-skool punk style, instead of just running around the fire. The heat feels good on my bare chest, and my red-orange pants make me feel like part of the flames.

There's something primal about this, with the drums and the fire and the frenzied crowd, and I finally see why people are into it. I'm fully here, fully me, not some put-on personality that people around me have encouraged me to be—like the boy I became because it's what all the pretty lesbians wanted and it got me more respect.

Fuck that! I think as I circle dangerously close to the flames. *I'm burning that fake man at Burning Man!*

"Hida!" I hear Beth yell.

I jump out of the ring to talk to her.

"It's too hot; we're gonna go. Do you wanna come?"

I look back at all the hooting maniacs.

"No, I'm gonna stay awhile."

"Okay, we'll bring your bike back to camp."

I'm dripping with sweat and flying high on acid and adrenaline when I finally work my way out of the crowd. It extends so far back I can barely believe I pulled us all the way through it. When I get to the outer edge, I stop to get my water bottle. As I chug I see two familiar profiles walking through the crowd.

"Diana? Jared?"

"Hida!" Diana screams out, running over and hugging me. "How's it going?"

"Awesome! I was just dancing around the fire ring."

"Where's everybody else?"

"Oh, it was too hot for them up there so they left."

"Ha-ha! You're all wet, you little nut!" she screams, looking at my gleaming torso. "C'mon, let's go find an art car to jump on."

We get on a big boat on wheels and the wind feels awesome on my sweaty chest.

Jared knows where the best dance party is, so we head there. When we're ready for a change of scenery, we head back outside and walk a bit. After checking out hundreds of beautiful, fascinating, glittery things, I hear something familiar. Where have I heard that sound before?

Then I see it: Draka the Dragon. She's blowing fire far across the playa. Every time a flame shoots out of her mouth her body lights up in the darkness.

"It's the dragon!" I shout.

Diana and I look at each other, sharing the same thought.

"Run!" we scream.

We run toward it as fast as we can. We're super high so it feels good to be suddenly sprinting. We manage to make some headway, but after a few minutes, to our dismay, it starts moving.

We eventually notice that it's not moving away from us though.

It's taking off to the left, toward us, and it seems like if we cut across the playa diagonally, we might intercept it.

"Oh my god," I scream after a few more minutes, "we made it!"

"Not yet!" Jared yells. "It's not gonna stop for us. We have to jump on. See that door with the step?" he continues between breaths. "It has a handle next to it, see? We can use that to pull ourselves up, but we have to hurry 'cuz she's picking up speed."

Jared goes first. He grabs the handle and pulls himself up easily. Then he turns around to help Diana, who jumps up grabbing his hand. I'm right behind her.

I jump up, grabbing the handle at the same time, and pull myself onto the step without a hitch. It's fucking awesome, like a stunt out of a movie.

And Draka's as impressive inside as she is out. We're in a room with velvet-covered benches stretching down the length of each side. People are lounging comfortably, enjoying the view. There are also velvet-covered poles with little drink ledges around them, every few feet or so, to make it easy for the people standing.

"Those of you who just came aboard," a gruff voice yells in some kind of working-class white foreign accent, "prepare yerself to face the paddle!"

I turn and see a sexy redhead dressed like a pirate wench standing next to a guy who looks like an escaped convict from the Australian outback. He's wearing a leather vest without a shirt underneath and has dozens of faded tattoos and a patch over one eye. The redhead's wearing a naughty grin and holding a big wooden paddle.

"Line up, lads, and get ready to drop yer drawers!" the guy with the patch yells.

Someone who must've jumped on before us is standing in front of them. He pulls down his pants, bends over, and gets a hard whack on the ass from the wicked wench. She laughs when he rubs his red butt cheeks, and the patch guy shouts, "Next!"

Jared does the same thing and the redhead winks at him afterward. I can understand why: he's handsome. Plus, I see he's hung like a horse.

I'm next, so I pull my pants down and bend over. Just as I'm expecting the whack, I hear the girl say, "Wait, um, you're not a guy!"

"No. I'm not," I answer, looking at her from between my legs.

"Girls don't have to get whacked," she says, "but since you're already down there..."

She gives me a light tap before patch guy yanks me up. He looks me over with an amused, curious stare.

"All right, on your way," he says, sending me off with a brotherly slap on the back.

I walk over to Diana with a spring in my step.

"You fucking nut!" she shouts, cracking up. "Didn't you hear him say, 'Line up, lads'?"

"No, I guess I missed it."

"I mean, I know you think you're such a man and all," she says, "running around with no shirt on..."

"Oh, shut up!" I laugh, hitting her arm. "She spanked me, didn't she?"

"Hida..." She's laughing so hard her eyes are tearing up. "You kill me!"

"Wanna go check out the next room?" I ask once she's caught her breath.

"You read my mind, sister."

The next room is a dance floor with a bar at the back. The music is weird—industrial. It's not my favorite, but it goes with the whole dragon theme. We hoot with glee and dance our way through the freaks to the bar.

After what feels like several glorious hours, we notice that Draka has stopped right near where a band is playing.

"Oh my god, Foxgluv's on next!" she yells. "Let's go!"

Foxgluv does not disappoint. The lead singer is this girl who's hot and seems possibly queer. I fantasize all through their set that she likes me. She certainly notices me, at least, since I'm freaking out for hours in front of the stage. When they finish playing and step out into the crowd, I run over to tell her how much I enjoyed the show, and she thanks me and kisses me right on the mouth.

Sa-weet!

When we finally get back to camp, I remember it's my and Devon's turn to make breakfast. We'll be eating in just a couple of hours, so I decide to stay up with Diana and Jared, laughing and smoking weed. By the time they're ready to crawl into bed, it's time for me to meet Devon.

"Well, look what the cat dragged in," he says when he sees me. "We made bets over whether I'd be making breakfast for everyone alone. Looks like I lost."

"How could you think I'd ever do that to you?" I tease back.

"Oh my god," Beth says when she walks out of her tent. "I guess I underestimated you. I was sure you weren't gonna be awake for this."

"Of course I'm awake," I answer cheerfully. "I never went to bed."

"Really? You've been out all night?"

"Yeah, it was awesome! We even got to ride on Draka the Dragon."

I make breakfast with Devon and entertain everyone with stories of my adventures since we had parted ways at the Man. Then I pass out.

When I wake up, Diana and Jared convince me to go to another dance party before tonight's Temple burn.

It's hot, so I wear a black velvet vest with no shirt underneath. It feels awesome walking around like this, so natural. As usual the girls stare, and Jared notices.

"You get a lot of attention out here," he says when we're sitting down for a water break.

"I know. It's been kind of surprising."

"It shouldn't be," he says matter-of-factly. "You're hot."

"You think? Even with my short hair and all?"

"Yeah, short hair looks good on you—really good," he says.

I can tell by the way he says it that he's letting me know he thinks I'm fuckable. Not in a gross way or in a way that's disrespectful to Diana, just kind of as one comrade to another.

Jared is cute and I've seen the kinds of gorgeous girls that like him and vice versa. So I find it fascinating that he finds me attractive, as boyish as I am. But it finally dawns on me that maybe I've been getting too hung up on the stereotypes.

All this time I've been trying to define my gender, define how I'm attractive: butch or femme, masculine or feminine.

It's suddenly ridiculously obvious that I need to stop defining myself by what's already out there. The truth is I'm something else altogether. Someone who likes to look like a boy *and* a girl, or something in between.

I'm someone who can do Critical Tits *and* get paddled by the pirate wench, who'll cry *or* throw down at a moment's notice. And to top it all off, I have a clitoris that's so supersized it looks like a miniature penis.

Basically, I'm a woman who's well hung. I know that that term usually refers to men—that such a person isn't even supposed to exist—but it's the perfect way to describe me. I am a well-hung woman, a walking paradox.

The next morning everyone starts packing up after breakfast. All around the playa, things are coming down. The remains look like bones in the desert. Devon and I finish by lunch and say our good-byes.

There's a long line of cars leaving, and it's dusk by the time we hit the long stretch of highway that'll bring us back to civilization. The sky is flooded with bright-orange streaks of color as the sun makes its way down under the horizon, the untouched, ancient sand glowing in the last light of day.

The desert spreads out as far as the eye can see, and it's almost hard to believe that such an amazingly unique city sprang up in this barren wilderness. That it arose, like nothing before it, solely from the vision of all its creators.

That's exactly what I'm doing, I realize. I am creating my identity with no rules and with nothing to guide me. And the process is as unpredictable as the playa.

CHAPTER 12

Going Public

Hi, HIDA," A VOICE on my answering machine says. "My name is Alice, and I'm a producer for the ABC News program *20/20*. We're doing a segment on intersex and I'm wondering if I could talk to you about possibly being in it."

I'd grown up watching *20/20* almost every Friday once I was old enough to stay up till eleven. Although I stopped watching TV almost entirely once I left home, it's still a popular and respected show. Also, my mom watches it.

"Geez, *20/20*—that's the big-time!" Beth says when I tell her.

I'm hanging at her place, as I often do on the weekends.

"How'd they find you?" she asks.

"From some article in a New Orleans newspaper, apparently, which is interesting because I haven't done any interviews in New Orleans, but I forgot to ask them for details . . ."

"Did I hear you say *20/20*?" Marina asks, walking into the room.

"Yeah," I answer. "Kind of crazy, right?"

"Yeah, a lot of people watch that show. Are you sure you're ready for that kind of exposure?" she asks.

"Yeah, I bet your mom still watches that," Beth adds.

"She does. Not religiously or anything, but often."

This means I'll have to tell her about it. It wouldn't be fair to her for it to be a surprise, or for a coworker who recognizes my name to see it and ask her about it. Telling her that I'm an intersex activist and that I'm going to out myself on a major television show is not something I have any desire to do, given what a hard time she has dealing with the fact that I'm openly gay. But I guess I'll have to because being on *20/20* is too important for intersex visibility to pass up.

Fortunately, the *20/20* production team is meticulous in their preparation, and filming won't take place for months, which gives me time to mentally prepare myself. Also, I learn that Barbara Walters will not be the one interviewing me, which is a relief. As much as I respect her, she's known for asking those blunt, difficult, and somewhat invasive questions that can sometimes make people cry. Just speaking about being intersex so publicly is revealing and stressful enough for me. Also, the fact that I do respect her and have been watching her for years would only make me more nervous.

"EVERYONE SAYS NAVY BLUE is a good choice for these kinds of things," Diana says.

We've been hanging out a lot since Burning Man, which is fantastic. I've also decided to go shopping way in advance of the interview so I don't freak out at the last minute about what I'm going to wear on camera.

"Good to know," I say. "I want to be myself, but not my superfreaky self, because I'm trying to appeal to conservative parents who might be thinking about operating on their babies."

"Yeah, navy blue is respectable and conservative, and it's not as boring on-screen as black. I think it'll be good."

"Okay, navy blue it is," I say. "I'll go get a bunch of tops, but do you think you can help me pick out the best-looking one?"

"Sure—what are friends for?"

I go to the mall where I used to work as a security guard, and I purchase six navy blue tops with a range of feminine to masculine cuts. I'm not sure how I'll feel about my gender expression when the day of the interview arrives, and my experience has been that my level of femininity or masculinity can change at a moment's notice, so I figure I might as well be prepared with some options.

When I get home, I call Diana and invite her over to check them out.

"Okay, let's see 'em!" Diana says when she arrives.

I lay them out across my bed.

"That's it?" Diana asks.

"Yeah—why?" I ask.

"Well, they're all the same," Diana says.

She's sitting in the big, comfy armchair that faces my bed and the ornate, nonfunctional fireplace in my room.

"No they're not!" I reply.

"Hida, they look almost identical," she says.

"No, look—this one's got a V-neck, and this one's got a round neck, and this one's got a maroon stripe..."

"Where?" Diana asks, bending over to take a closer look at the shirt.

"Right here!" I say, pointing to the small stripe on the side of the collar.

"Oh my god—that's so tiny I can barely see it!"

"Well, it's there. And this one's kind of girly, with the boatneck..."

It's a close-fitting, long-sleeved shirt with a neckline that reveals my prominent collarbones, which I've always been told are sexy in a feminine way.

"*That's* girly?" Diana asks, suppressing a giggle.

"Yeah, look at it. It's a girl's cut. It's from the women's department."

"Yeah, maybe the *masculine lesbian* women's department..." she says, laughing openly now.

"Okay, look—do you wanna help me or not?" I ask, starting to get frustrated.

I fling myself down on the bed, across the tops, and look up. The high ceilings make the room feel palatial; it comforts me.

"I do, I *do*," she says, starting to full-on crack up. "It's just that all these tops look almost identical to me..."

She's laughing so hard she has to stop, and even though I'm frustrated, as I look at the tops more closely I start laughing, too, because I can see her point. It feels great to laugh, actually, after being so stressed out about this.

"I kind of see what you mean," I finally say once I've regained my composure, "but you know, it's not like one of the options was ever going to be super frilly or anything! I said I want to feel like myself, remember?"

"Yeah," she says, reeling herself in. "Okay, try them on and I'll tell you which one I like best."

Twenty minutes later we've decided on the one with the small maroon stripe.

MANHATTAN, NEW YORK
APRIL 2001

I had wanted to hang out with Angie, whom I rarely get to see because she's practicing medicine in New York now. I thought it would be a good way to relax before the interview, but my flight was delayed and it's already ten by the time I get dropped off at my hotel.

The hotel is nice, a small boutique place on the Upper West Side. It feels more like a very large home than a hotel, which I like.

There's no one in the small, sophisticated lobby when I check in, which I also like. I feel the need to go into deep meditative mode to prepare for this. The less stimulation the better.

The room is small too—narrow, but with tall windows at the end that make it seem bigger. Within it are expensive-looking modern furnishings and I spot gorgeous metallic-colored sheets on the bed. *Ah, I made it,* I think, throwing myself down on them. I'll be seeing my mom and telling her about this, but not until after it's over.

I need to call Angie from the room phone to tell her I can't make it, but I switch on the TV and go to the bathroom first. When I walk back in, I see a bunch of punk rock–looking folks on the screen.

"Crowds have started to gather to pay homage to the lead singer of the musical group that many consider the best punk band of all time," the reporter is saying.

Huh?

"Joey Ramone passed away early this morning at the age of..."

Oh my god, Joey Ramone? I'm surprised to feel tears welling up.

Like so many people I grew up with, I love the Ramones. They're from Queens, which gave all us Queens kids something to be proud of, and I loved them so much in high school that they actually became one of the few American bands that my mother could recognize. She liked them too and would bop her head to songs like "Sheena Is a Punk Rocker" and "Rock 'n' Roll High School" when I played them.

Around the time I left Wesleyan, Beth had talked me into seeing Iggy Pop, another punk rock idol of mine, with her. It was one of the only things I'd been able to drag my depressed ass to that whole winter. And not only was Iggy incredible, but on my way to the bar I stopped for a few seconds, and when I looked up, I saw Joey, leaning against a post, looking even cooler in person and even taller than I'd imagined.

I couldn't help but stare for a moment, and as I did, he looked down in my direction. He was wearing those round rose-colored sunglasses he often had on, so I couldn't tell if he was actually looking right at me, but it felt like he was, and I know it might sound a little silly, but it was a special moment for me. It felt like having his energy so close to mine was a gift to help me get through that hideous time. And I guess it's not such a strange idea when you think about how people will travel far and wide to see spiritual gurus whom they admire, and benefit from being in their presence.

I admired Joey. He was weird-looking and weird-sounding, but his creativity and his spirit were so strong that they burst onto the world stage, forever searing a mark of rebellion onto our cookie-cutter society. He showed everyone that you don't have to fit into the mainstream mold to shine and soar.

"People are gathering for a memorial service being held at the legendary punk club CBGB..."

I call Angie.

"Hey! What took you so long? I've been waiting," she says.

"I know, I'm sorry—my flight got delayed, and I would've called sooner but the car was there waiting the minute I got out of the gate. I just got to the hotel."

"Oh, okay."

"Hey, did you hear about Joey Ramone?" I ask.

"Yeah. It sucks, right? It's been on the news for a while."

"I guess I missed it because I was on the flight. I hear they're holding a memorial service down at CBGB's pretty soon."

"What—you wanna go?" she asks.

"Yeah, kind of. I mean, it's Joey Ramone."

"Well, I'll go down there with you if you want," she offers.

I pause for a moment.

"Let me think about it," I say. "I *really* want to, but I worry that we might get caught up down there, and I'm getting picked up early tomorrow morning."

"Hmm, yeah, it's a tough call. This interview's important," she says.

"Yeah, tell me about it. I'm so nervous."

"Well, just think about it and let me know. I'll be up for a bit, and I'd be down to go."

We hang up, and I am torn. On one hand, it feels a little like fate that I should happen to be here and *able* to go to the memorial, since I'd regularly be three thousand miles away. On the other, this interview means a great deal to me, and it's why I'm here. I want to do the best job possible, and that might require getting a very good rest.

I close my eyes and meditate. I went to my first meditation retreat in 1994 with my martial arts school, and I've been what you could call a "moderate meditator" ever since, doing it mainly when I need clarity. It's not long before the answer becomes clear. I should stay at the hotel and go to bed.

I give Angie another ring to let her know.

"Okay, I'm a little disappointed 'cuz I wanted to see you, but I get it, and I want you to do well," she says sympathetically.

"Thanks, girl. I love you," I say.

"I love you too. Go get 'em tomorrow. I know you'll do a great job!"

I feel so lucky and grateful for the friends this life has given me. And for having had the opportunity to experience Joey's music and presence.

I wake up the next morning before my alarm, with plenty of time to shower and be ready and checked out when the car comes at eight thirty. I'll be going to my mom's home in Queens later, so I need to stay at the hotel only one night.

She and my dad have been separated since 1996—about five years now—and she's managed to do so well in her career in real estate that she was able to buy her own house in Bayside, Queens, a nicer neighborhood than the one I grew up in.

I'm proud of her.

When I arrive at the studio, I meet Alice, the producer, who is as wonderful in person as she's been on the phone. She seems to understand how vulnerable I might be in an interview like this, and she does her best to prepare me and make every step along the way as comfortable as possible.

The interview is being shot in the rented-out suite of a different hotel. They have plenty of food and a private room that I can relax in when Alice and I are done. The film crew is setting everything up in the main room. They have to check the angle and the lighting on me from time to time, but after a while, they don't need me anymore and there's still about fifteen minutes left before Lynn Sherr, the woman who is interviewing me, shows up.

I go into the private room and check my hair in the mirror. I notice that my heart is racing, so I decide to meditate.

I close my eyes and breathe deeply, knowing it will help. It does. I think about what it is that I really want to say and convey. My thoughts start to race and jumble when I do, but the Universe, that force that I feel connected to, has never steered me wrong. So I decide to just ask it to help me.

Universe, I say quietly as I look in the mirror, *please help me give the best interview that I possibly can. Please use me to convey the message that will best help intersex people all over the world and best reach the thousands of people who will watch this show. I thank you in advance for doing so, knowing that everything is happening just as it should. Thank you.*

I feel calm, and in a minute I hear them asking for me. I go out and meet Lynn Sherr, who is very nice, and I do the interview. When it's over, Lynn and the film crew tell me I did a fantastic job. We have lunch and then go to Riverside Park to shoot the B-roll footage.

Afterward, Alice takes me out to dinner, which is when I learn she's a Buddhist. I tell her about the prayer I did before filming, knowing she'll understand.

"Well, they showed me a few clips of your interview," she says, smiling, "and I think the Universe heard you loud and clear."

"HI, HIDA PATRICIA!" MY mom says an hour later, pulling me into a hug.

Although we have our differences, my mom is a sweet woman. Despite her lack of acceptance around my being a lesbian and so many other things, I can't help but love her. Deeply.

She makes us some tea and we sit down to talk. I consider telling her about *20/20* right then, but it's a little late and she's tired. So I decide to wait until tomorrow.

The next day, I wake up happy about the day before, but with round two of nerves. I know it'll only get worse the longer I wait, so I make the decision to tell her right after breakfast.

"So, Mom, you might be wondering why I'm here, huh?" I ask her.

"You told me it's for work, right?"

"Yeah." I take a deep breath. "I'm nervous to tell you about this, but you may find out anyway if I don't, so here it goes. You know how I've mentioned a few times that I'm doing some activism?"

"Yes, about gay things, right?"

"Uh, not exactly. I've been saying that's what it is because I thought it would be easier for you to understand," I confess.

"Well, what is it then?" she asks.

"I've been doing activism about being intersex, and that's why I'm here. I did an interview for the show *20/20*."

"*20/20*? The one with Barbara Walters?" she asks, looking surprised.

"Yeah."

"Oh, she's very good. What did you talk about?"

"About being intersex."

I can tell that the word *intersex* must have slipped by her the first time I said it.

"Intersex? What is that?"

I give her the briefest, simplest explanation I can.

"Oh, okay, but why are you talking about that?"

"Because *I'm* intersex, Mom."

My mother pauses, looking confused.

"What?"

"I'm intersex," I repeat.

"Oh my god, what are you talking about, Hida Patricia?" she says, starting to laugh.

"I'm intersex, Mom. I have a big clit."

She looks at me quizzically.

"You know, the clitoris?"

I try to pronounce it the way I imagine it might sound in Spanish.

"Cleetorees," I say, gesturing toward mine. "The part that women have."

"Oh yes, okay. But what do you mean? *Women* have that, right?"

"Yeah, but mine is larger than normal," I say.

"What do you mean? I don't remember that…"

"I don't know how often you changed my diaper, Mom, because you were working, but you must know what I'm talking about?"

"No!" she exclaims. "You're normal, Hida Patricia. You're a beautiful girl!"

"Thanks, Mom," I say, smiling, "but beautiful or not, I have a really large clitoris. So large that I'm considered intersex."

"Hida Patricia, I know you have always liked being different, but do you think I would not know about this? I'm your mother."

I find it odd that she's having this reaction to my news, given who she is. But I have heard the weirdest stories of denial from this community.

"Look, Mom, I don't know how or why you missed this, but if you need me to show you," I say, a little surprised that I'm saying it, "I will."

My mother locks eyes with me intently. My proposition is kind of a challenge, and even though she has always been extremely shy about nudity—her own or mine—she hates being told, or feeling like, she can't do something.

"Okay, fine—let's go," she says. "Show me, because I know you are my daughter and you are a girl, so I don't know what you are talking about."

We go to the bathroom upstairs. It's large, and for whatever reason, it seems like the appropriate place to do this. I have to admit that even though she's my mother, this feels unnatural, especially because I was not raised to be nude around others, including her.

"Okay," I say, undoing the top button of my jeans, "here you go. Take a look."

I pull down my jeans and she crouches down to get a good look. Seconds pass in silence.

Man, is this awkward, I think to myself.

"Well, do you see?" I finally ask her.

More silence. She stands up straight and looks at me with an expression I've never seen before. On anyone. It's a little surprised, but kind, and . . . something else I can't place. It's almost amused, but not in the regular way, like with nostalgia or something. A memory perhaps? It's difficult to tell.

"I mean, I don't know how many clitorises you've seen," I say, "but I think you can tell that this is not what they usually look like, right?"

"Yes, Hida Patricia. You're right," is all that she says. Then, "I'll meet you downstairs, okay?"

I head down the stairs to join her a few minutes later.

"So, Hida Patricia, I believe you now, but that doesn't matter that you are like that. Why do you have to talk about it?"

I can tell she's a little mortified, and I am not the least bit surprised. Sometimes I am too. So I tell her all about intersex genital mutilation, or IGM, which is what I've recently begun calling the nonconsensual genital surgeries that are inflicted upon intersex people. I tell her all about what I've seen. She listens intently, taking it all in.

When I'm done, she says, "I see, Hida Patricia. Yes, that's terrible. But it didn't happen to you. We didn't do that to you, and you are beautiful and normal, so why do you have to talk about it on TV? It's so personal...so private."

"I know, Mom. But the problem is that nobody talks about it. Nobody knows that we're here, and that's what makes it easy for people to keep doing it."

"But Hida Patricia, you could get fired!"

"No, Mom, it's cool in San Francisco," I assure her.

"Yes, but Hida Patricia, you don't know—"

"Yes, Mom, I do. It's okay."

"But somebody could hurt you!"

I can tell she's starting to get a little upset.

"Mom, look, it's going to be okay. Nobody's going to hurt me—I promise."

"I just don't know why you have to talk about these things in public. You know people don't always like people who are different, Hida Patricia!"

I clasp her hands in mine.

"I know, Mom, I know. But I want to help make these terrible things stop."

"I know; you were always like that, since you were little. You were always fighting with your father when he bothered me," she says, smiling at me, her love shining bright in her eyes. "But Hida Patricia, who is going to help *you?* These people aren't paying you to help them, right?"

"No. It's not like that…"

"So you have to take care of yourself. I know that it's bad, what is happening, and that you want to help, but you can't help everybody."

"I know, Mom, but I *can* actually help with this. And there are not that many people who can, because a lot of intersex people have been affected by IGM, so there are very few people who can say that we're fine just how we are."

I pause.

"See, other people are not talking about it," my mother says. "You have to think about yourself first. You're not in law school anymore. You need to make money because money is more important than this stuff, Hida Patricia. This is not a career…"

"But it is more important to me than a career, Mom," I say.

"How can you say that? Are you dreaming? You have to live in the real world!"

I try to think of a context that I can possibly explain this in that will make sense to her.

"Okay, Mom, remember when we were growing up and we used to see things on TV sometimes about Martin Luther King, and you used to say what a good man he was?"

"Yes," she says.

"And remember how you used to say how much he helped his people, black people?"

"Yes."

"Well, he gave up his career to do that," I say.

"Yes, but that's different. Black people were getting hurt—killed sometimes even."

"Yeah, but my people are getting hurt too. Every day. Doctors are cutting up their bodies when they're babies and leaving them mutilated in a way that they can never enjoy sex. They often become depressed, and some of them have even killed themselves."

"Yes, but why do you have to be the one to do this? You're not rich, Hida Patricia. You need help too!"

"I know I'm not rich," I say, laughing, "but Martin Luther King didn't have to do it, and I don't think he was rich either. I mean, there was no reason why, of all the black people out there, *he* had to be the one to do it, right?"

Judging by the look on her face, I think she may finally be understanding me.

"So it's not really about that. It's not about *having* to do it; it's just about wanting to do it. It's just about it being important to you. And if it hadn't been important to him, he would have had his career, but the black community would have never had his help—the help that you used to tell us was so good. So which one was more important in the end?"

I pause for a moment to let my words sink in.

"I'm not saying I'm Martin Luther King, but this cause is very important to me too. My people are being hurt, badly, and to me it's more important to try to stop the hurt rather than focus on having a great career—even money. I know not everyone feels this way— I guess maybe most people don't feel this way—but I do. Do you understand, Mom?"

"Yes, Hida Patricia, I do," she says.

And I can tell she means it.

CHAPTER 13

The Lows of Being Out

SAN FRANCISCO, CALIFORNIA
MAY 2001

SHORTLY AFTER I GET back, Jade asks me if I want to get out of town for the weekend. A friend and coworker of hers, Hallie, has a friend who owns a gorgeous house up in Sonoma that Hallie can invite people to.

"It'll be great," Jade says. "A little free vacay in the sun."

"Sure!" I reply.

Hallie is a thirty-five-year-old, all-American, long-legged blond beauty. I meet her for the first time when Jade and I arrive at her friend's place in Sonoma.

She's straight, presumably, but by the way she looks at me, I'm not so sure. She also drops the "I've always wanted to be with a woman" line when we're alone in her hot tub that weekend, which, in my experience, has often been code for "I've never been with a woman before, but I want to be with *you*."

When we get back to SF, I decide to ask her out on a date, and it turns out I was right. We have a really comfortable, fun connection, and after dating for about a month, she tells me that being with me isn't that much different than being with a guy. I'm a little surprised, since I see myself as so much more emotional than most guys, but hell, what do I know? I've never dated them for more than five weeks—and that was in high school, almost twenty years ago.

She also shares that all her lesbian fantasies leading up to this moment of Sapphic consummation had consisted of two feminine, beautiful women together. I can totally relate, having had the same fantasies myself.

I tell Jade about it.

"Well, she's obviously very into you," Jade says.

"What makes you so sure?" I ask.

"I can tell by the way she looks at you, and I've known her for years."

"Wow, cool..."

Then Jade says, "If you start looking pretty...bam! That girl will fall madly in love with you."

"You think so?"

"Oh, I *know* so," she says.

Jade has had a pretty good track record with these things, and I *want* Hallie to fall in love with me, so I decide to make her fantasies come true by giving her the gift of femme. Jade suggests hair extensions as the easiest, fastest way of making myself look feminine. Three hundred dollars, eight hours, and one hundred and thirty extension braids later (apparently I have a *lot* of hair to weave into), poof: I'm a pretty girl again.

Yes, I changed my entire gender expression to get a girl. Most people have strong feelings about their gender's true, fixed nature. Me? I find the entire spectrum of gender identity and expression fascinating, and I've explored as many spaces along it as possible and enjoyed them all—at least a little. So it doesn't seem that strange to go back to an earlier one.

Besides, looking like a girl can be fun—especially when riding a motorcycle.

When I rode looking butch, everyone just assumed I was a guy, even in my half helmet. Another dude on a bike—not that interesting. But when I rode in tight women's clothes, with my long extensions and lipstick showing under my helmet—well, that was a different story. I couldn't go a few blocks without someone honking or hollering something.

Femme girls on bikes have that whole I'm-pretty-but-I'm-not-scared-of-shit-and-could-possibly-kick-your-ass appeal.

It's hard getting all those braids into my helmet though, and they're itchy as hell. I have to take them out after only four months, but that's long enough. My real hair is longer by then, and Hallie, as predicted, is in love. So am I.

Hallie moves in with me five months after our first date, a few weeks after we get back from having spent Burning Man 2001 together. Tons of couples break up when they go out there, especially new ones, so we figured we had passed the relationship litmus test since we survived it.

APRIL 2002

I get word that the piece I'd filmed for *20/20* is finally scheduled to air on the nineteenth, Hallie's birthday.

"I know you wanna watch it with all your friends, but I always have a party," Hallie says after I tell her.

"Okay, I get it," I say, "but it's kind of a big deal, and I've been waiting so long to see how it came out..."

"I know, and I get it that your activism is important to you, Hida, but my birthday only happens once a year," she says pleadingly.

"Yeah, I know, but *this* has almost never happened..."

"Okay, I know, but my birthday is important to me. I don't want it to end up being all about you."

I guess I can understand where Hallie's coming from.

"Well…maybe we could do both," I suggest.

"Like have a party and watch it at the party?" she asks.

"Yeah, why not?"

"Huh…Okay, I guess that'll work."

We schedule the party early so people will be there by the time *20/20* airs at ten. As the time nears I realize that most folks already have a buzz on, and it's going to be hard getting them to sit in front of a TV.

"Hey," I say to Hallie in the kitchen, "it's almost time."

"Oh, okay," she responds, barely breaking away from her conversation. "Why don't you make an announcement or something?"

I consider asking her to help me, which I want her to do, since half the folks here are her friends. But then I start to get annoyed that I would have to.

I'm pretty certain other girlfriends would be bragging about their partner being interviewed on national television and proudly organizing a viewing. In fact, I've seen people be more supportive of their significant others for much less significant events.

"Hey, Hida! You wanna get high?" someone screams over the noise.

It's my friend Diana. She lives here now, in the Castro apartment I now share with Hallie and another friend. It's a big three-plus bedroom, so it works.

As I make my way over to her through the rowdy crowd, I realize that I don't have it in me to make a big announcement that I'm about to be on TV. I'm proud that I did it, but I'm also sick to my stomach with nerves about how it will turn out.

Since the vast majority of intersex people are still closeted, as far as most people know they've never seen one of us. That means I'm kind of representing the whole community. If I sound stupid, or look stupid, we all do—on some level.

I can't deal. Not right now, at Hallie's birthday party, without her help.

I grab the glass pipe from Diana and inhale deeply, deciding to blow the whole thing off. I'm recording it anyway, so I can watch it later.

The next morning Diana and I wake up early and watch the segment together over coffee.

Barbara Walters is the one who introduces it. She refers to me as "a woman talking openly about the most private part of her body ... There are thousands of others like her, and it is for their sake that she comes forward tonight. Lynn Sherr with a woman determined to change the way people with ambiguous gender are treated." I feel touched and honored to have what I'm doing understood and publicly acknowledged by someone I greatly respect.

"Holy shit, that was amazing! You rocked it!" Diana says once the interview is over.

I'm thrilled and relieved that I agree with her. I feel like I delivered the best possible message I could have. I even chose my words well, given how nervous I was.

When Lynn asks in the interview if I'm trying to tell the world to make room for intersex people, I respond, "I'm saying accept that we're here; don't try to cut us up or change us or shame us or hide us."

The interview cuts to a picture of me that I love as I continue to speak.

"I love my life right now, and I really want to embrace who I am, which is an intersex woman."

It's a lovely ending to a very respectful, intelligent, and sympathetic piece. I'm grateful to the Universe. Not only did it hear my prayers to use me for a higher good, it answered them.

A doctor—who, oddly, works at Downstate, the hospital where the doctor had wanted to "run tests" on me—is also interviewed for the 20/20 piece, but what he says only illustrates why the practice of nonconsensual genital correction surgeries is so messed up. He's condescending, and in response to watching a clip of me saying how happy I am that I didn't have a clitoral reduction surgery, he says he still thinks he could have helped me.

Even better, when the interviewer asks him why he believes these surgeries are necessary despite what he's heard from people who have experienced it and from me, he answers, "Society can't accept people of different colors, and now we're supposed to accept somebody with genitalia that don't match what their gender is. I do not believe that society is ready for it."

"*Ready for it?*" a friend of mine says when she sees the interview. "It's not like this is some new invention, like cloning or something. It's been around forever! There's nothing to be ready for—just accept it!"

She makes a great point.

I'm also fascinated by how the doctor's racism analogy reveals that social prejudice—not medical necessity—is what is truly at the heart of these procedures. It's actually one of the most honest statements I've ever heard a doctor make about what we are subjected to. His analogy makes it easy to see why the practice is misguided; after all, would you ever say we should lighten the skin tone of people of color just so they'd be more acceptable to society?

When I first heard about the nonconsensual surgeries, it seemed obvious to me as a person who had experienced racism that just like some people discriminate against those who have dark skin, they also discriminate against people with intersex traits. But some of the people in the—mainly white—intersex community I've met seem to view nonconsensual surgeries as an issue of improper medical care, rather than discrimination. The reason for this seems to be that if we call the surgeries discrimination, we're claiming discrimination against us as a specific *type* of people, and not everyone is into that.

For example, I like the word *hermaphrodite* because it allows me to say, "I'm a hermaphrodite" in the same way I've also said, "I'm a woman," but other intersex people seem to hate it for that very reason. I hear them say that they don't want to be identified as this third-gender *thing*, a hermaphrodite. They prefer to be seen as normal men or women with certain medical conditions or physical differences.

While I totally get that they feel more male or female, their negative reaction to the alternative is kind of insulting, because I actually *do* feel like something other than male or female, or *both* male and female—a third gender, if you will—and my body looks like it too. My body looks like what a hermaphrodite is thought to look like, so when intersex people say, "I'm not a *hermaphrodite*; don't insult me by calling me *that*," it's almost like they're saying that what I consider myself to be is gross, is wrong. It takes me back to the same kind of pain I felt when some of my classmates in elementary school would bully me because I looked different than them.

Also, it's worth considering that although some of us don't want to be identified as a specific type of people based on our intersex traits, doctors see us that way anyway, and intersex babies are vulnerable to surgeries because of it. I almost want to thank the doctor on *20/20* for saying what he did, because it demonstrates what I've been thinking all along: there are many kinds of discrimination, and discrimination against intersex people is another one of them.

I'm so happy about how the segment came out that I move past thinking about how Hallie reacted when I first suggested we watch it. I tell myself that other people might have doting partners, but maybe that kind of girlfriend's just not right for me.

MAY 2002–2004

Hallie and I continue to date for another two years. We do things together like go to a Brazilian dance camp, travel through Southeast

Asia for four months, and go to Burning Man again—this time with our own version of an art car.

Eventually though, we can no longer ignore the unease that's pervading our lovefest. Our differences begin to show, and they seem to be of the irreconcilable—rather than the "opposites attract"—variety. We see things, important things, very differently.

In the spring of 2004, my intersex friend Craig, who has been developing a relationship with the San Francisco Human Rights Commission, tells me they have decided to hold a hearing to examine the nonconsensual medical practices we're subjected to—the first government hearing on human rights for intersex people in US history. Craig invites me to provide testimony at this hearing, which feels like an honor and a duty to my humanitarian soul. After all, I am one of the few people we know of who can speak to the fact that I feel blessed *not* to have been subjected to medical "normalization."

But as the May 27 hearing date draws closer, I start itching to blow it off. Although I've been on national television several times and in two documentaries, those interviews happened one-on-one, in a private or semiprivate setting. In contrast, this will be live, in front of an entire panel of people I've never seen or spoken with, in a room crowded with both strangers and peers, not all of whom have been supportive.

I know Brittney will be there, and it kind of scares me, because just the thought of her brings up bad feelings and memories, memories of being deemed too weird to be a spokesperson for the community and treated less kindly than I am by my friends, specifically *because* of how I express being intersex. I wish that I could say that I didn't care, but Brittney's past judgments and negative reactions to my gender make me want to avoid her. Hallie, though, agrees to accompany me to the hearing, and I'm grateful because I don't think I'd be able to do it on my own.

Craig tells me the hearing will run for hours but says we can arrive after it starts, so no hobnobbing is necessary. After we do arrive and listen to some of the hearing, the moment comes for me to testify.

I decide to just speak from the heart, and it seems to work beautifully. The panel members react to me positively and are very receptive.

At the end of my testimony, one of them says, "You seem so confident and well-adjusted despite being part of such a stigmatized community. It's just amazing..."

"Thank you," I say a bit sheepishly, trying to take in the compliment.

"I'm just wondering, and I think I speak for the whole panel," he continues, "how you developed such a healthy self-esteem."

No one has ever asked me that directly, although it has certainly been noted, so I have to think about it. Within moments, memories of my father come back to me.

"I think part of it could be because of my father," I respond. "He always told me that I could do or be anything I wanted and how smart I was. He said it so much it actually annoyed me sometimes."

I pause as people laugh, which I'd expected.

"Ultimately though, I think it sank in and boosted my self-esteem, so I'm grateful to him for that."

The panelists nod and thank me. I return to my seat feeling relieved and thankful to the Universe. Just like after watching my 20/20 interview.

"So what'd you think?" I ask Hallie once we're home.

"It was great," is her reply.

"Cool," I say. "What'd you think of my part? I was pretty nervous, so I think it went really well, considering."

"Yeah, it was good..." she says absentmindedly.

I wait for more, but that's all she'll say.

"Really? Because it seems like you're not telling me how you really feel."

"It was fine." Her answer is curt.

"Just *fine?*" I press. I can detect she has more to say.

"Okay," she finally says, "it's just that you didn't seem really honest."

"Honest? What do you mean?"

"Like with the stuff about your dad."

"What about it?" I ask.

"You made it come off like he was this great guy, but he's actually an asshole who abused you."

"But that wasn't the point. They were asking me about my self-esteem, and he came to mind as a reason why it's good."

"Yeah, but it didn't feel like you gave an accurate portrayal of him."

"But he really did say all those things…" I begin.

"But you don't even talk to him."

"I know, but what was I supposed to say?" I ask, my voice rising. "Should I have told them all how abusive he was? How would that have helped the issue?"

"I don't know—whatever," she says. "It just didn't feel sincere to me."

Hallie doesn't want to think about the fact that the same man who'd given me so many of my wounds had also helped me thrive in certain ways, and I don't think the people on the panel would want to think about that either. And I didn't think they should have to, since my father's abusiveness had never quite affected how I feel about being intersex, specifically.

I can accept that Hallie disagrees, but I'm not sure why she seems so disappointed in me. Even if her critique *is* valid, the bottom line is that I need *support* doing this activism, not criticism. Her stance on this issue makes me feel terrible.

If I had more guts, or less optimism, I would end things with

Hallie, but I want to believe that love can conquer all. Like an addict, I hold on to her, to the fix her love gives me, long past the point when I know it isn't working for me anymore.

NOVEMBER 2004

Hallie breaks up with me around Thanksgiving—after she meets someone new, a guy. It's probably the easiest way we could end things. She gets someone to ease the loss, and I get to feel justified and secure in why it's over. A win-win breakup.

In the process, she also admits to me that she'd grown to miss the masculine energy I had when we first met. It's annoying to hear, considering the reason I had become more feminine to begin with was because that's what she had said she wanted. What I hadn't realized was that if my *look* got less masculine, so would my personality.

I guess it serves me right. This is what I get for changing how I look to make someone fall for me. In hindsight, it was a terrible idea. But it was easy, natural even, for me to tailor my behavior to meet others' desires.

I realize it may have something to do with the fact that I was raised in a home where love was conditional—well, my father's love anyway. I was reminded of this when he called me last year before my birthday, after about thirteen years of no contact.

It turned out he heard I was in law school from my brother, but I told him I had dropped out and was thinking about becoming a writer.

"Wow," he said with a sigh, "I really wasted a lot of time and money on you."

When I heard this, I was initially taken aback, but then I thought of the kind of person my father really is. People say that as you get older you realize your parents weren't so bad, but that isn't true in my case. Despite the praise he had given me when I was growing up, at his core my father was just a cruel and unloving man.

I tried to take pleasure in the fact that I'd been right about him all along, but it was fleeting. Try as I might, I couldn't fool myself into believing that I wasn't upset by the fact that he ultimately saw me as nothing more than a failed investment. It had always been that way: He "loved" me only when I did things that made him look good as a father.

I became depressed because of it, and Hallie couldn't comfort me through my pain.

Now, here I am again, recently dumped and despondent. My dream of finally being settled down having been just that: a dream.

I think about how my friends have often accused me of not being ready for a real, committed relationship. They've been pointing out the pattern of my dating previously straight women for years, and suggesting that I seek out women who are unavailable because I'm afraid of true intimacy and commitment. I was always reluctant to consider that a possibility, because I've wanted nothing more than to fall in love with, and spend the rest of my life with, one woman. Now I finally have to admit that they may be right. I know that my fear stems from my childhood, and I'm furious that it's still impacting me.

Within days of our breakup, I cut my hair short again. It's typical for me, this gender boomerang reaction, and although it's somewhat superficial, it makes me feel I'm moving on. I'd done it after Audrey too. I became tough-looking again, since she'd liked me softly beautiful.

This time though, something different happens: I don't transition to a rigidly "opposite" gender. I cut my hair, but I don't start wearing men's clothing exclusively or *stop* wearing makeup. In other words, I don't suddenly start presenting myself as a guy.

Instead, I get more androgynous than ever. I think I owe it in part to Burning Man. Diana has recently started dragging my ass to local Burning Man events, and the Burner crowd doesn't give a fuck how I express my gender. On top of that, my students at my new job teaching ESL to the elderly seem to love me so much that they don't care what I wear there either.

For the first time outside of college, I feel like I can dress however I want, all the time.

After a few months I realize I feel a new kind of relaxed. Like something stressful that had once been there is now gone, and the absence of that anxiety is allowing me to be more comfortable in my own skin.

I've been dealing with polarized gender-role requirements for so long that I had no idea how liberating it would feel not to. To be able to look however I want—butch or femme, male or female, both, or something else—all the time. I'm still not sure what I'm doing career-wise, but I feel free. I feel my*self.* And I'm happy with it.

FEBRUARY 2007

"Hi. What do you think about this new DSD thing?"

That's all that the e-mail from my friend Craig says. I'm obviously supposed to know what DSD is, but I've never heard of it. So I do a quick search online.

I discover that it stands for "disorders of sex development" and that the global medical community has decided to replace the term *intersex,* or *intersex conditions,* with it.

Huh? I think to myself. *Why?*

I see a link and click on it. It leads me to a post published by ISNA that argues in favor of the new term's benefits.

Why the hell would they do that? I wonder.

I stopped volunteering for and being a member of ISNA about eight years ago and haven't followed what they've been up to since, but apparently they've been working almost exclusively with medical providers for some time now and have come to think that DSD will make it easier for doctors to hear their message—to meet them where they are.

Many doctors are the ones who want to "fix" us. We can't meet them where they are, I think.

My head begins to spin. I need more information.

I continue to research DSD online and learn that some people think the word *intersex* has become associated with certain political or *gender* identities and that parents don't want to associate their children with that kind of thing. So they believe that saying babies have a physical disorder is preferable to saying they are "intersex."

For weeks, I unearth new information—like the fact that some intersex adults dislike the term *intersex* because their gender identity is either man or woman, or they feel like the word labels their entire self rather than just a part of themselves. I remember that people who didn't want to be identified as gay often said they felt this way too—back in the day.

Then I notice the date of a post I'm reading: *2006?* I almost can't believe I missed this development, and I cannot fathom why in this day and age ISNA thinks it would be preferable to use *DSD* instead of *intersex.* I mean, is it really better to denigrate ourselves and say we have a medical *disorder* instead of just calling ourselves intersex?

In a subsequent e-mail I receive from Craig, I learn that ISNA added a disclaimer on the acknowledgments page for one of their resouces that said some of the contributors to the resource did not support the term *disorders of sex development.* The fact that they opposed DSD makes me immediately respect them.

But what about the other folks who'd contributed to this resource? I wonder. Were they okay with DSD, or just too nonconfrontational to oppose it?

There used to be so much stigma against queer people that homosexuality was originally classified as a disorder—but gays and lesbians fought against it. In our case, I can't help but think that we have gone backward. I console Craig as best I can and continue researching.

I find a paper from the 2005 International Consensus Conference on Intersex that was held in Chicago and convinced the medical authorities to adopt DSD.[1] To my surprise, the three main authors of the paper are all ISNA members. While I understand how *doctors* might be biased toward using a term like *DSD* rather than one that emphasizes our androgynous nature, like *intersex*, it is extremely disappointing to see how prominently ISNA is endorsing the term too.

The article stresses the importance of finding a newer, more modern umbrella term for us after deeming *hermaphrodite* outdated and stigmatizing, and another article I find says *intersex* is too politicized and associated with the LGBT community. Putting aside the innate homophobia and transphobia I saw in wanting to dissociate intersex from LGBT people—which is troubling but unsurprising, as I'd already witnessed it—if ISNA was so hell-bent on finding a new umbrella term, couldn't they have endorsed a better term, something that didn't further the impression that we have a problem that should be corrected?

This all feels like a bad dream.

When I think about ISNA's promotion of DSD, I am only filled with anger and frustration, because we don't need a "disorder" diagnosis in order to talk about ourselves in clinical settings. In fact, there are already medical names for our various physical variations: androgen insensitivity syndrome (AIS), congenital adrenal hyperplasia (CAH), Klinefelter's syndrome (XXY), hypospadias, etcetera. According to what I read though, *all* the different variations that give people atypical sex anatomy are now considered DSDs, and it doesn't feel right to me.

Granted, there has always been confusion and debate over which variations should be considered intersex. For example, there's a variation called Mayer-Rokitansky-Küster-Hauser syndrome, or MRKH, in which people are born with bodies that look typically female but have a small or absent uterus and a short or absent vagina. I had wondered whether these people should be considered intersex, or would want to be, and I learned that most of them didn't because they identified as women.

Conversely, I learned that there are people who *don't* have visibly androgynous sex anatomy and *do* consider themselves intersex. Craig, for instance, looks typically male and is seen and accepted as a man in mainstream society, but because he has Klinefelter's, he has chromosomes and hormone levels that are atypical for a male. Although Craig has shared with me that the majority of people with Klinefelter's identify strictly as male/men and do not like to be called intersex, he uses the term *intersex* to describe himself.

So yes, it's confusing trying to figure out who and what is intersex, but to me, that's okay. I have concluded that the best way to deal with it is to let the individual decide whether or not they're intersex—or male or female, for that matter. If someone identifies as intersex, great, but if not, they can simply continue identifying as men with Klinefelter's, or women with MRKH, and so on.

I determine that because DSD ultimately pathologizes intersex people, it contributes to doctors' efforts to medically "normalize" us: the very thing we've all been working against. Thinking about this makes me livid.

I start writing frantically about my feelings regarding DSD, but my essays are too furious. I know it won't do anybody any good to put such insanely angry rants out there. People are turned off by that, especially when they can't relate, so I start to think that there's nothing I can do about this. The medical establishment has already adopted DSD—per the recommendation of what is now the biggest intersex organization in the US. Why would they care about what one lone intersex person has to say? I begin to feel despondent.

What's far worse, though, is the fact that I'm sure the new label will facilitate nonconsensual medical treatments as well. For ten years I've been coming out as intersex in order to help spare others from going through that. I came out to spread visibility and pride— not so that we could be deemed disordered in the eyes of the general public or so that intersex children would now grow up hearing their bodies referred to in that way.

I feel slimed by the shame this new label imposes on us. It's insidious, seeping under my skin and into my bones, corrupting the part of me that feels good about myself—like maybe, somehow, I've been wrong this whole time; like being intersex must actually be something horrible if even well-meaning folks think we're an unspeakable, inferior class. Like I might as well not exist.

Then, something gives me a glimmer of hope. I find an intersex group I haven't heard of online: the Organization Intersex International, or OII, which has members all over the world. Unlike US organizations, which have tried to support ISNA by accepting DSD, OII is highly critical of the term and how ISNA seems to have convinced doctors to impose it on us—vehemently, *scathingly* critical.

OII believes in the same things I do—a lot of the things I never vocalized because they seemed too harsh—and I have to admit that knowing others feel deeply disappointed and betrayed makes me feel *infinitely* better. As far as I'd seen, most intersex folks in the US—other than the three denouncers of DSD in the ISNA resource—didn't seem to have a problem with the new term. This had not only added insult to injury, but it made me feel like I was taking crazy pills.

Now I see that I was wrong. There are others, many others, who are just as dismayed as I am—who think, just like I do, that *disorders of sex development* is a very dangerous diagnosis and label for inter-sex people.

Unfortunately, while this makes me feel a little better, it still doesn't remedy the situation.

CHAPTER 14

The Highs of Being Out

SAN FRANCISCO, CALIFORNIA
APRIL 2007

I DIVE INTO PARTYING more than ever, and this time, I let my androgynous tendencies rip. For example, I've been keeping my hairstyle subdued because I know conservative parents will hear my message better that way, and those are the kinds of parents I need to reach. But hell, if my own community is going to throw in the towel and pathologize us, then fuck it—I'm doing what I want to do.

"Hey, is there time to do mine next?" I ask my friend Julie.

We're at her place, and she's almost done giving her friend a Mohawk before we head over to a party.

"*Really? Shaved sides and everything?*" she says, squealing with glee.

"Yeah, fuck it!" I reply.

"Yes! Finally!" she screams.

I've always loved the way a Mohawk looks on me, and I'm sick of compromising. I'd been doing it not just for my activism, but for Hallie as well. The two complemented each other, actually, since it was preferred that I be gender normative for both of them.

I love my new haircut, but I don't stop there. For starters, I've wanted to wear vests with no shirt underneath as an everyday cloth-ing option since I was in high school, so I do it. I start going semi-topless. It's summer, so the vest is great for the heat. It's enough to cover up my tiny breasts, and I think the style looks hot.

My bare torso looks boyish, as does my hair, but I wear eyeliner too, so my face looks pretty. I'm not sure what folks make me out to be, and for once I don't care. At all.

I think it's the combination of being almost forty, the Burner scene being so open, and feeling like I've got nothing to lose that gives me the guts to let my freak flag fly full mast. To my surprise, the hottest girls seem to love it.

I develop a theory that women who have known they're good-looking for most of their lives are fascinated by people who don't care about getting approval because of their appearance. The kind of people whose persona says, "I don't give a shit." That definitely describes me right now.

I'm living the high life—literally.

I've recently begun managing a medicinal marijuana bakery, and I'm partying as much as I had in college, including sleeping with beautiful twentysomethings. One of my friends says I'm going through a midlife crisis. I deny it until I realize that, at thirty-nine, I *could* actually be halfway through my life.

It's a little hard to believe, because in many ways I feel like now that I'm finally comfortable with being a full-on hermaphro*dyke*, my life is just beginning, but I know it's true. And I have a lot I still want to do.

SEPTEMBER 2007

To my great surprise, I discover I was contacted by one of *The Oprah Winfrey Show*'s producers while I was at Burning Man 2007 (at which, incredibly, I got to fight in Thunderdome—and *win!*). There's no cell phone or Internet access at Burning Man, so I had missed the producer's messages for almost a week. In the voice mail she leaves, she says the show will be taping soon. I leave a message on her phone as soon as I can and even try e-mailing her, but I'm worried it might be too late.

Only a few minutes after I do these things though, an unknown number calls me.

"Hello?" I answer anxiously.

"Hi, I'm a producer from *The Oprah Winfrey Show.* Is this Hida?"

The producer is nice, funny, smart, and she's obviously done her research. The conversation that ensues is great. I have no doubt I want to be on the show, despite the rushed timing.

"Oh, I have a question for you," she says toward the end of our call. "When I first started researching this segment, I was using the word *hermaphrodite*, but then I heard it wasn't PC, so I started using *intersex*. But now I've started seeing this new term, *DSD*, for *disorders of sex development*. So my question is, should I use that?"

I smile silently to myself. I had actually written numerous essays in response to this subject, but I never did anything with them. I realize now that I had needed to process all my feelings first. I needed to get through them to formulate a clear, logical, and convincing opinion about the issue before I could be ready for this moment.

I launch into my answer. Like a lot of my analysis of discrimination and equal rights, it involves intersecting forms of oppression. In this case, after examining the harmful medical implications of officially labeling us a disorder, I share my views on similarities with race rhetoric. Specifically, I talk about how the situation with DSD reminds me of when and why the term *black* was replaced with *African American* in the late eighties.

The argument for African American was very much like the argument for DSD. It was said to be a more accurate term because people weren't really the color black. However, I'd always thought it was crappy reasoning because people aren't actually the color white either, but no one seemed to need or want that label replaced with a more accurate one.

To me, it seemed that the only reason the term *black* was problematic was because some people had problems with black people. In other words, racism was still so strong back then that just acknowledging that someone was black, rather than the preferred white, was seen as an insult.

Similarly, proponents of DSD argued that the terms *hermaphrodite* and *intersex* were inaccurate and insulting. However, just like the word *black*, there wasn't anything inherently insulting about *hermaphrodite* or *intersex*—unless you thought they were bad things to be. While some argued that *hermaphrodite* was inaccurate because it refers to having both male and female sex organs, in humans it has accurately referred, for centuries, to having both male and female sexual *characteristics*. Also, ISNA openly states on their website that being intersex is not a disorder. So *disorders of sex development* wasn't an "accurate" label anyway.

To me, it felt like in both cases people had come up with new labels in an attempt to create new, less discriminatory attitudes toward two very stigmatized communities. However, I felt like it was the stigma and discrimination that we needed to deal with, not our labels.

"Wow, I'm black," the producer says when I'm done, "and I totally agree with you about the African American thing. I never thought there was anything wrong with *black*."

I hadn't guessed or assumed she was black, so I'm happy to hear she agrees.

"Also, I thought *disorders of sex development* sounded stigmatizing from the moment I heard it," she adds.

In this moment, I feel like there's a higher power on my side, trying to help me. After months of feeling tormented and completely disempowered to do anything to address this horrifying occurrence, the Universe sent me this. It sent me the opportunity, out of the blue, to ensure that when forty million viewers heard about us—most of them for the first time—they would not be introduced to us as a disorder.

The show is filming in Chicago next week, and they need to shoot my B-roll before then, so if this is going to happen, I have to hustle. The timing feels a little weird, but when I think about it, it's perfect. Coming out as intersex on *Oprah* is *huge*, and it seems inextricably linked to the fact that I'd been living my life so hugely. It feels like it couldn't have happened prior to right now because my energy wouldn't have been big enough to take it on.

The production team decides to fly out to San Francisco to shoot my B-roll. When that's done, I then need to obtain a doctor's letter of verification that I am, indeed, intersex before they can fly me out to Chicago to be on the show. I know the producers believe me, or they wouldn't have sent their film crew out here, but it's a technicality their legal department insists on.

I go to my regular medical clinic in order to get the letter. It's a clinic originally founded for lesbians, with a high percentage of lesbian, bisexual, and transgender staff and clientele. I explain the reason for my visit to the nurse who checks me in and wait for one of the doctors to see me.

The nurse returns and tells me that the doctors are out for the day, and she's not qualified to verify that I'm intersex.

I tell her that she doesn't have to be an expert, or to even use the word *intersex* if it's problematic. I suggest that she can simply examine me and give me a letter stating the size of my clitoris. I'm sure this will be satisfactory, as they know clitoromegaly, the medical term for my large clit, is considered intersex.

However, the nurse says she's not comfortable doing that. I start to get worried because it's Friday and I need the verification to fly to Chicago on Monday for the filming. I explain my time frame and ask her if she can speak with the supervising physician on call.

It's taking awhile and it's approaching 5 p.m. I start panicking. Suddenly, I think of my friend and former girlfriend, Angie, who's a doctor and can potentially help me. I grab my cell and wait anxiously for her to answer.

"Hey, girl," she finally says when she picks up the phone, sounding out of breath.

"Hey, are you okay? You sound weird."

"Oh, I was just running down the ten flights of stairs to my car. What's up?"

I explain my predicament.

"Wow, well, you're really lucky you caught me now. I was about to drive home, and I'll tell ya, I wouldn't have been too crazy about having to turn around in Friday L.A. traffic!"

Angie had left New York a few years ago and was loving California life in L.A.

"Oh, thank god!" I say. "So can you do it?"

"Yeah, sure. I know it's important. I'll run back up and print it out on our letterhead. Just text me a number I can fax it to. I think I even remember exactly what size you are."

"Ah, what a relief. Thank you so much, girl!"

The nurse returns from speaking with a physician and tells me she's been advised that they can't help me. I'm surprised—shocked even—that although I've been a patient here for years, they're refusing to help me. It's additionally insulting that they're known for being so good with San Francisco's gender-variant community, but somehow *my* variance as an intersex person, and assisting me in my needs around that, is something they won't give the time of day.

Were it not for my own personal access to someone with medical authority, I wouldn't have secured the confirmation letter I needed. My own health care providers would have prevented me from advocating for intersex people on such a far-reaching, well-respected venue. And what luck that I caught Angie before she'd left for the day! It feels like the Universe definitely wants this to happen.

A few days later I'm at Harpo Studios, sitting in hair-and-makeup. I agree with the producer who says that my Mohawk is distracting, so I let the hairstylists cut and color my hair for the show and let the makeup artist do her thing.

When they're done, I'm escorted to my chair in the audience. There are two people sitting in the chairs next to Oprah, and I watch them speak with her first.

BEFORE OPRAH INTERVIEWS ME I am sitting with the other guests in the first row in front of the stage. The butterflies I initially felt have now fled my belly, bred a bit in my outer limbs, and are threatening to carry me off. It's nerve-racking in and of itself to be sitting down with such a cultural icon, but I'm about to talk about stuff so personal that it's not even considered appropriate to talk about in public. I've been doing it for eleven years at this point, but it still feels like I'm about to jump off a cliff each time.

The next thing I know, a production assistant motions for me to come up onstage, and I find myself floating over to the chair next to Oprah. Then sitting in it. Then smiling at her and saying hello.

Oprah smiles and says hello back. She pulsates with energy the size of a small planet contained in a *very* familiar-looking human body, a body that I have respected *deeply* since I saw her in *The Color Purple* in high school.

It's surreal, but I'm *not* dreaming: I'm actually on *Oprah*.

Someone I know did a radio interview once about being involved in a local PTA group. Afterward, she said she couldn't remember what she said. She worried for days that she might have come off sounding stupid.

Unlike her, I wasn't being interviewed about something as wholesome and uncontroversial as the PTA, and it wasn't on the radio. I was being interviewed on *Oprah*—a show seen by forty million people—about being intersex. Specifically, in my case, about the fact that my private parts don't look typically male *or* female.

By comparison, *my* anxiety, as you can probably imagine, has transcended worry. It is an entity, a being in itself.

I take a moment to remind myself, though, that I'm outing myself to millions of people because many still think intersex people are inherently flawed. And because of this, they frequently harm intersex babies by trying to "correct" their unique qualities.

I think we intersex folks are just one of nature's marvelous variations—like redheads in a world of blonds and brunettes—but each time I out myself publicly I remember that not everyone feels this way, and the fear sets in. I have to remind myself that ultimately it doesn't matter what they think, because our separation is only an illusion—by which I mean that as much as people may view those who are different from them in a divisive, us-versus-them way, in actuality we are all fellow human beings who feel and want the same basic things.

Oprah's voice brings me back to the moment. She introduces me and the clip they filmed before the show. I watch it for the first time with the audience and hear myself say, "My clitoris is large enough that it resembles a small penis." I promptly float off to la-la land, far from the present moment.

Up until this point, I have never spoken about my privates in *such* a public way, and it frightens me to hear myself do it. But most intersex babies are never even given the option of privacy—their private parts are openly evaluated and decided upon, often with painful consequences. Then, if they complain as adults, they're often told they'd be worse off if they had been left alone.

I feel compelled to state, to share, on their behalf, that I have an intersex body and I feel blessed that it was never altered. I want parents and doctors to know that I'm better off because I was left as is. But therein lies the rub: in doing so, I have to explain what "as is" is.

When the clip ends, there's a commercial break, and the woman to my right, another intersex guest who had spoken before me, starts talking to me.

"It's so nice to meet you. I saw you in *One in 2000,* and I have to confess, I feel a little starstruck," she says.

One in 2000 is an intersex documentary I was interviewed for that came out earlier this year.

She looks at Oprah over my shoulder and adds, "Oh, with you too, Oprah."

I look over at Oprah, who has a pleasantly amused expression on her face.

The other guest continues. "I think I've been mispronouncing your name this whole time though. I'm sorry."

"Oh, that's all right," I say. "I've heard it all: Hilda, Heidi, Pita, Fajita, Turn on the Hida . . ."

Suddenly I hear a voice on my left say, "Turn on the Hida—I *like* that."

It's Oprah, and she's squeezing my forearm as she says it. She is *touching* me, and I'm shocked to the bone that she's joking around with me too! I am stunned, nearly paralyzed. As I try to recuperate, she gives my forearm another squeeze and says the phrase again.

Then, it's interview time. Oprah is fantastically warm, smart, and kind, but talking with her flies by at lightning speed, and I can barely remember a word I've said once it's over.

WHEN I GET BACK to San Francisco after the taping, I get lost while driving to a friend's place. Twenty minutes after I should've arrived, I find myself way out by the beach. The road has dead-ended at the Great Highway, which follows the coast along the Pacific. I pull into the parking lot and stare out at the darkness.

As my eyes slowly adjust, I begin to make out the waves. They're harsh and relentless, like the thoughts spinning around in my head. I'm panic stricken that, in addition to being revealed to millions as one of the oddest-viewed, least-known minorities on the globe, I'll also appear, to put it simply, *subpar*.

If a drop of water represents this fear, I have found a whole ocean and thrown myself in. My spiritual practices are no match for the strength of its force. I'm being flung about, with no shore in sight, no anchor.

I don't sit in quiet meditation daily, but I practice meditative awareness and breathing when uncomfortable emotions come up, which is often. I'm used to stopping and breathing into the discomfort when it arises and asking it what it is trying to tell me. The process does wonders to calm me and reconnect me with a place of loving acceptance, but in the days following the filming I can't calm down enough to even *remember* it, let alone *do* it.

The show is airing in just two days, and I spend most of them alone at home, lost in a sea of dreaded scenarios. I imagine I've done a bad job. I looked bad. Humiliated myself. Ruined my future. I've let down the people I represent, all over the world.

Finally, I'm so exhausted I just stop. I'm sitting on the deck of my apartment, the one I moved into when I had to leave my rent-controlled flat in the Castro due to an owner move-in eviction. It's in Hunters Point, right on the water's edge. I'm looking out at the Bay Bridge, and I stop thrashing around in my mind. I spot a great blue heron in the park between my building and the Bay, and I marvel at how it makes its life here in the last tiny bit of marshland left in this urban place. I decide to walk down there and try to see it for myself. When I do, I get lost in all the little things I see along the way. I come back to the present.

Soon, everything changes.

I realize there's nothing left to lose. I've lost it all already. I can't get any more vulnerable than telling forty million people about the size of my clitoris. But shockingly, life has gone on. I'm still here, living, breathing, and feeling the sun on my face.

I can almost hear the Universe saying, *See, you've survived! It's not such a big deal in the grand scheme of things. It's not all about you.*

There's something incredibly comforting about this realization. It makes me *part* of the Universe, rather than alone within it. I'm no longer lost in a frightening ocean; I'm floating freely in an infinite, soothing sea.

I spot the shore: it's the place in my heart where everything is all right just as it is. The former waves of fear are now the waves of this awareness. I let them bring me back to solid ground, knowing that I've done my best and there's nothing to do, nothing to improve. Nothing left but to enjoy the loving calm that was always there, waiting, beneath my fear.

*   *   *

I FINALLY REACH THE shores of mental calmness, and I invite my close friends over for the airing of the show. Incredibly, when we watch it, no one can tell that I'd been in shock over Oprah's unexpected gesture. I made all the points I wanted to and even some new ones, like explaining how the pressure to pick either a boy or a girl identity is similar to how society used to pressure mixed-race people to identify as either black or white.

My friends tell me that I sound confident, happy, intelligent, and inspirational. One even says I look beautiful, which wasn't my goal but is still nice to hear.

Jade has a lot of deep things to say about my appearance on the show, like how making intersex visible by sharing my unique experience was stepping into my life's destiny. I guess I would say that I agree with her, although I wouldn't have ever put it that way myself.

What I *will* say is that I definitely had a pivotal experience, right there on the show, while talking to Oprah. It happened when she was talking about how society tries to force people to choose between boy and girl. Without stopping to think, I said something about how I refused to choose, because "I have both." I'd rather have said, "I *am* both," but I guess "have" slipped out because I wanted to be clear that being intersex is a physical thing.

It was a moment my whole life had been building up to. The first time I was asked if I was a boy or a girl, at the age of nineteen, it pissed me off so much that broke the beer bottle I was drinking on the street beneath my feet and chased the two guys who'd asked down the block.

It was a badass reaction, which the person deserved because he had said it disrespectfully, but getting pissed meant I considered having my sex questioned an insult. By my late twenties I no longer did. I understood that I looked androgynous and I played with it.

I'd talked about feeling like I was "in the middle" in one of the documentaries I was in, *Gendernauts*. However, I had still been confused about how to embody this, so I'd swung back and forth from boy to girl, trying to figure out which one was the "real" me, because I was still attached to those identities.

It had taken me until now, the fall of 2007, to finally become comfortable with who the "real me" is. If someone were to ask me, "Are you a girl or a boy?" I'd answer, "I'm both."

Or alternatively, "I'm neither."

Before the taping of my *Oprah* episode, I asked a friend of mine who does web design if he could help me get a website up and running. Knowing how few people are "out" as intersex, I suspected that there might be some intersex folks who'd want to get in touch with me after viewing the show, and I wanted there to be an easy way for them to do that. Sure enough, I was right.

After the *Oprah* episode airs, I begin getting e-mails from all around the world. Mainly, people thank me for helping them accept themselves. There's an intersex woman in Brazil, for example, who says she'd felt so isolated with regard to being intersex that she felt "like an alien." It was so bad that she'd considered the "normalizing" cosmetic genital surgeries that doctors recommended to her—until seeing me inspired her to follow her gut and love herself as she is.

I feel something move in my heart area, literally, when I read that—a softening, an opening. I can't help but cry.

I remember how upsetting it had been, eleven years ago, when I met intersex people at the retreat, heard about their suffering, and saw the damage that had been surgically carved into their bodies, and their souls. It was horrific, and the worst part, perhaps, was that as much as I knew that the abuse needed to end, and as much as I wanted it to, I didn't think there was anything I could do to make it stop. At twenty-eight, I hadn't even been able to graduate from college yet, and I hadn't yet figured out how to properly deal with my pain and depression from my past, and my economic challenges.

Somehow though, I actually *had* done something. Some of the people who send me e-mails tell me that they saw me on *20/20* too. Or *Inside Edition.* Or *Montel.* They tell me that I've been their "hero," inspiring them for years. I hadn't realized how many people I'd reached—probably because I was so freaked out by every interview that I quickly put it out of my mind. Now, I'm grateful to know that all the fear and nerves were worth it.

My favorite e-mail, perhaps, is one from a dad of four in Kansas. He tells me that he and his wife have four daughters. He says that after watching my interview on *Oprah,* he can only hope that they grow up to be as "beautiful, well adjusted, confident, and happy with themselves" as I am. It's crazy flattering.

I realize that, as I'd hoped, I'm helping parents view us as equal human beings who don't need to be "fixed," and the feeling is more fulfilling than getting into Wesleyan, or finally graduating with high honors from Berkeley, or, frankly, anything else I've ever done.

Someone from *SF Weekly* contacts me about an interview, and when it runs it includes a drawing of me and Oprah—caricature-style! I'm thrilled, until I see that one of my positions is misstated *and* I'm quoted out of context. Fortunately, they offer to let me write my own correction piece, so a week later, when it's published, I get to also say:

> While some doctors and parents are...more comfortable referring to us as having "disorders" than associating with a label supported by homosexuals and transsexuals, I do not believe adopting a pathologizing label to distance ourselves from these groups is a solution, to say the least. Many have been calling for an improvement to the term, such as "Differences of Sex Development."[1]

Now I'm thrilled.

CHAPTER 15

The Struggle at Home and Abroad

SAN FRANCISCO, CALIFORNIA
DECEMBER 2007

CHRISTMAS IS APPROACHING AND I'm deeply depressed, not just because I find myself, yet again, without a supportive partner as well as a supportive family, but also because, at the age of thirty-nine, I'm about to be homeless. My plans of being a full-time writer and speaker have not panned out as quickly as I needed them to, financially speaking, and I will need to give up my apartment. I know that I'm lucky to have friends who have offered to let me stay with them, but I feel terribly hopeless nonetheless.

This is the best you could do, despite your brains? You might as well just end it now, because being this poor is only going to be worse when you're older.

My cat meows loudly just as I entertain the thought.

She's jumped up on the bed next to me and is staring me right in the face, as if to say, *Don't even think it.*

She meows again, insistently.

Fuck, I can't do it, I think. *Who'll take care of her?*

Later, my phone rings and it's my friend Catherine, from Wesleyan.

"Hey, you wanna come over to my place for Christmas? Beth and Margaret and their families will be there too," she says. "I know how you get depressed around the holidays and don't make plans and then feel even worse."

"I don't know if I can." My voice starts to quaver before I can finish.

I tell Catherine everything—that I feel so terrible that I don't even want to be around anymore. She listens and comforts me and makes me promise her that I'll go to her place on Christmas. So I do.

"Hida!" her daughter, Joan, screams when she sees me.

"Hida! Hida!" I hear more screams. It's Meryl and Amelia, Beth's daughters, and Lucy and Elizabeth, who belong to our friend Margaret.

They jump on me and cover me with hugs, and their embraces make me feel better. With their joyful, untroubled energy, they melt away my weariness, my sadness, and my fear about my uncertain financial future.

I may not have money or a supportive family, but I have the love of my amazingly supportive *chosen* family. It's more than so many people have, and somehow their very existence makes me know that it's all going to be okay.

AUGUST 2009

I learn that a black South African runner named Caster Semenya has had the gold medal she earned in the world championships taken away due to suspicion that she may not be female. *Huh*. I think I remember hearing about athletes getting accused of this once.

I read a piece in the *New York Times* that says she'll be forced to undergo gender-verification testing in order to determine whether she can compete as a woman.[1]

"These kind of people should not run with us," an Italian who came in sixth against Semenya is quoted as saying. "For me, she's not a woman. She's a man."

Oh my god, what a sore loser, I think angrily.

Sore loser or not, complaints from her and other athletes are being taken seriously. Apparently, any female athlete who falls "under suspicion" can be subjected to gender-verification testing. Then, if a private panel determines that she's "failed," she can be banned from competing as a woman.

I discover that from 1969 to 1999, all female athletes were required to undergo mandatory "gender-verification testing" in order to compete in the Olympics. It was supposedly due to rumors that men were cross-dressing and competing as women to try to win more medals.

In all those years though, not one such case had been found, but rather, untold numbers of intersex women had been. They had been banned because their chromosomes tested "XY": typically male. This happens in an intersex variation named androgen insensitivity syndrome (AIS). Women who have certain grades of AIS have bodies that look female, due to their bodies' inability to utilize male hormones (aka "insensitivity"), but have XY chromosomes and internal testes.

I heard things got so bad for some athletes following the rulings that some had even committed suicide. Many were from small, conservative, and/or religious towns where people weren't accepting of their differences.

I thought the practice had long been abolished, but I was wrong; it was just *mandatory* gender-verification testing that had ended when a Spanish hurdler named Maria José Martínez-Patiño had fought the regulations and won. She demonstrated that although she had XY chromosomes, she had *no* functioning male hormones—or complete androgen insensitivity syndrome, also known as CAIS.

It was determined that, if anything, she had a competitive *disadvantage* compared to "regular" women, who all have some degree of functioning male hormones. She was once again free to compete as a woman, chromosome testing was declared an inaccurate measure of gender, and the practice of mandatory gender-verification testing came to an end.

However, Patiño's kick-ass work rendered only CAIS women safe, and there are many types of intersex women. Consequently, regulations held that women could still be tested on a *case-by-case* basis—upon suspicion. Semenya's competitors had found her suspicious enough to complain to sporting authorities, as well as the press.

"HEY, CAN YOU STAY a little late today?" my friend Margaret asks over the phone, forcing me away from the computer.

She and her husband, Luke, have been good friends of mine for thirteen years. Last fall, she told me that she was stressed out because their nanny had just quit, and she was worried about finding someone good on such short notice. I was bored stiff with my office job, and the hours were terrible for my writing, so I quit the very next day and filled the slot. I've been their nanny for close to a year now, and it's been great.

"Sure," I answer easily.

Margaret's daughters, Lucy and Elizabeth, are four and six—and a total pleasure to be around. Actually, that's an understatement. They are such fun, funny, smart, sweet loving beings that they're probably the best part of my life right now. That may sound cheesy, but it's true.

To my delight, the love is mutual. So much so that my friends have been calling me the "kid whisperer."

One day, while I'm watching the girls, one of them, Lucy, tells me to come into their living room.

That's where her dollhouse is, and she is *obsessed* with dolls, specifically playing "characters" with them. Nannying these girls marks the first time that I've ever played with dolls, and the funny thing is I think it's kind of cool.

When I join her, she tells me she'll be playing "Bella" before pointing out the biggest bedroom in the dollhouse—which is packed with furniture, clothes, and accessories—as "her room."

She looks at me and we both giggle. She loves giving her dolls *ridiculously* lavish setups in these games, and this room is no exception.

"Who are you going to be? *Him?*" she asks, holding up her Prince Charming doll.

"Okay, fine," I say, laughing. Somehow, it's been understood from the beginning that I would play the boy characters, like Charming, as they call this one.

"So we've got the girl and the boy," I say.

"Don't forget the girl/boy!" her sister, Elizabeth, shouts, running in from their bedroom.

"Of course!" I yell, ever impressed by her. She's only six and she's already been a vegetarian for two years, by choice, even though her parents are meat eaters (and it's created a lot of work for them!).

"How about the girl/boy be this one?" Lucy asks, holding up a girl doll that lost its hair and is bald. It actually looks a little like Sinéad O'Connor, I think, and not just because of its lack of hair.

"Sure, perfect!" I say.

The first week I took care of them, they were both confused about whether I was a girl or a boy. They asked me straight out, and I said girl because it was simpler. They didn't seem satisfied with that answer though.

"Hida, you're a boy!" Lucy would say, poking me in the chest with her little finger.

Their parents are both liberal folks, and as one might expect of my friends, they have always been supportive and cool about acknowledging intersex people. So after a few days of this confusion about whether I'm a boy or a girl, they had let me just explain what intersex is to their daughters. It was actually easier to do than I'd thought since they already knew about human anatomy.

"Wait, really?" Lucy asked, looking a little incredulous.

"Yeah, really," I answered.

"*Really?*" Elizabeth asked seriously. "There are really people like that? You're not making it up?"

"Yes, there are," I answered, looking her straight in the eyes so she'd see I meant it. "It's just that there are not as many of us as there are girls and boys, and people don't talk about us, so most people don't know we exist."

"Wow..." they both said, looking at me wide-eyed.

"So you're kind of both...?" Elizabeth asked.

"Yeah," I answered, smiling.

"That's so cool!" they both screamed.

"That means you're a boy/girl!" Lucy said.

"No, she's a girl/boy!" Elizabeth insisted.

I'm still not sure which one I prefer, but I was completely amused and impressed by how quickly they had recognized the fact that sex comes in more than two categories. In fact, they're better at it than I am, because unlike them I've lived most of my life in the binary system.

These girls give me hope. Especially because so much of the world is so messed up.

"CASTER SEMENYA: GENDER ROW Runner Is 'Half Man and Half Woman,'" the headline reads.

It's been a few weeks since the story broke, and some of Semenya's test results have now come in. Details were supposed to be kept private, as they involve confidential medical information. However, it looks like somebody leaked something to the press, and they're running with it.

"Caster Semenya Is a Hermaphrodite," another headline reads.

It's a little stunning to see the word *hermaphrodite* sitting right there on the page. I'm not reading a gender studies or biology text, after all. I notice that the word itself doesn't bother me. In fact, it's a little thrilling to see our existence being openly acknowledged in the news for the first time in my life, given how much the world has tried to hide us.

However, the fact that the label *hermaphrodite* is being so freely imposed on Semenya, despite her right to confidentiality, *does* bother me. Even though I don't have negative associations with the label, I think it's safe to say most people do. This makes attributing it to Semenya quite problematic.

Yet there it is, over and over. "Runner Is a Hermaphrodite!"

Her private sex characteristics also make headlines. "Caster Semenya Has Male Sex Organs and No Womb or Ovaries." "Caster Semenya Has No Womb and Internal Testes." "Caster Semenya Has One of the 46 Types of 'Intersex' Conditions." "Testicles! Vaginas! Caster Semenya's Got 'Em All!"[2]

The tone of the sensationalist articles ranges from inappropriately invasive to downright disrespectful. What begins to bother me even more, though, is the way in which some of the people coming to Semenya's aid, or who are in her life, "defend" her—namely, by insisting that she couldn't possibly be something as horrible as intersex.

It reminds me of how fathers would sometimes "defend" their gay sons when I was a kid. They'd yell something like, "No one calls my son gay!" and possibly punch out the father of whichever kid had called his son that.

The one that bothers me the most comes, unfortunately, from the African National Congress Youth League (ANC YL). In response to the media's claims, they issue the following statement:

> Even if a test is done, the ANC YL will never accept the cat-egorisation of Caster Semenya as a hermaphrodite, because in South Africa and the entire world of sanity, such does not exist.[3]

The world of *sanity*? So they find the very concept of intersex people so "out there" that just saying we exist is insane? Ouch.

I'm thrilled and relieved to notice, however, that Semenya herself doesn't deny the claims. Instead, she tells *You* magazine, "God made me the way I am and I accept myself. I am who I am and I'm proud of myself."[4]

I'm proud of her too and very impressed by her strength. Sure, she did a girly photo spread in the same magazine to accompany the interview, and a lot of folks are saying it's terrible that she resorted to that, but I totally get it. To me, it seems like her way of saying, "These tests are bullshit because if I'd looked like *this*, I wouldn't have been questioned."

Nevertheless, I'm inspired to write something about the rampant denial by others of Semenya's possible intersex status. My essay ends up being published on CNN.com. It starts with the sentence, "A lot of people have been outraged by the gender verification testing that South African athlete Caster Semenya has been put through, and have been trying to be supportive of her; but in doing so, they often further prejudice against the very thing which she appears to be: intersex."[5]

Afterward, the editor tells me it was one of their top-performing essays of the week. It's thrilling not just as a budding writer, but because thousands of people got to read positive, perhaps never previously expressed things about being intersex. Things like, "While many doctors would refer to my clitoris as 'grossly enlarged,' I have to tell you, having an overabundance of the only organ in the human body whose sole purpose is pleasure is far from a negative thing!"

The whole situation makes me think back to when I first read Herculine Barbin's memoirs. Semenya isn't being tried in a court of law, but what she's being put through is nonetheless quite similar to what Herculine went through—except that it's nearly *one hundred and fifty* years later. Whereas other issues have advanced in spades, intersex people are still on trial, even in a first-world setting. We've been working so hard to bring attention to nonconsensual infant surgeries, but even if you're lucky enough to have escaped intersex genital mutilation (IGM), you can still be made to suffer later.

Seeing an intersex adult treated this way somehow outrages me even more than IGM. I can understand parents wanting to make their kids' lives as easy as possible, even though I dislike that this upholds heteronormative, and gender-normative, ideals. They're misguided—because surgeries don't produce heterosexual, gender-normative kids, and they really should be loving and accepting their kids anyway, even if they're *not* heterosexual or gender normative—but at least their intentions are essentially kind, unlike the ones behind Semenya's treatment.

Around this time, I'm contacted by *Inside Edition* about being on a segment about Semenya and being intersex. I'm nervous, as I always am about being captured forever on film talking about my privates. My nerves are outweighed, though, by the opportunity to educate about intersex issues and show my support for Semenya in another highly viewed venue.

The film crew comes over to my place and sets up. When the interviewer asks me what I would say to Semenya if I could, I answer, "You're a champion." I don't know if she ever saw it, but I like to think she did.

Meanwhile, American intersex advocacy organizations haven't stepped forward in Semenya's defense.

So far the American intersex movement has been focused almost entirely on ending nonconsensual medical practices. Thus, it's possible they don't consider Semenya's situation to be their issue, because she wasn't subjected to the practice. Also, her situation is a reminder—perhaps an unwelcome one—that our problems will not be over once nonconsensual surgeries end.

Semenya is a reminder that attaining bodily autonomy is not our only human rights issue. She's a reminder that some intersex people grow up to *look* in between, or gender nonconforming, and that we often face discrimination even though we weren't "fixed"—in fact, sometimes *because* we weren't.

In addition, Semenya's black, and in my experience the predominantly white American intersex movement hasn't incorporated perspectives of color.

Celebrity supermodel turned television host Tyra Banks *does*, however, and I get an e-mail from one of her show's producers telling me they're doing a segment about the Semenya situation and intersex issues and that they'd love to have me on it.

I don't know what Tyra's show is like, having never watched it, but the producer sounds intelligent and respectful. I also learn that the majority of the show's viewers fall into the nineteen- to twenty-four-year-old demographic. I've never done a television show watched specifically by young people, and I'd like to reach them, so I agree to do it.

"Wow, Tyra Banks, Miss Supermodel," my friend Marina says. "What are you going to wear?"

"I don't know," I reply.

For me, one of the most confusing parts of being an activist has been deciding how to present myself during interviews. Lots of folks say, "Just be yourself," which is a sentiment I typically agree with, but in my case "myself" varies greatly and sometimes entails looking like a "superhero cartoon character," to use one friend's description. While looking comically creative is "being myself" a lot of the time, I want my interviews to appeal to as many people as possible.

Also, visual appearance seems particularly important when you're an intersex person speaking out against cosmetic medical treatments that are performed precisely because being intersex is considered unattractive. I'm trying to counter that perception, so I feel like it's actually part of my responsibility to look as attractive as I can on these interviews. But how far can I take that while still remaining my authentic self? And attractive to *whom?* It's confusing, especially when your gender is fluid and your gender expression is multifaceted to begin with.

I start getting nervous. Not just about what to wear, but also because of Tyra being an ex-supermodel and the show's demographic being so young. I'm forty-one now, and I'm told I don't look it, but I am *feeling* different. I'm definitely not a kid anymore, but I'm not sure what I want this adult me to look like.

Moreover, many other adults I know are starting to "do things" to themselves, like my thirty-five-year-old friend. When I tell her she looks great, she confesses that she just had her "smile lines" filled in.

"Oh my god, I never even knew that was a thing," I say, "but I hung out with this friend that I hadn't seen for a few years recently, and he said I looked great except for some smile lines."

I hadn't thought about "doing something" about them when he said this, because I thought I looked fine, but now I'm about to be on *Tyra,* and this friend's had it done and she's not even in her forties yet, so I start wondering if maybe I should.

"Well," my friend offers, "I *could* give you my place's number..."

These are the events that lead me to make a very ill-timed decision, the results of which are so embarrassingly ridiculous that I couldn't share them with anyone at the time.

I take my friend's information and get the same collagen filler treatment that she did. But my cheeks, unlike hers, start swelling up immediately.

By the time I get home I look like a black-and-blue, deformed human chipmunk; and my flight to New York for the filming is on Monday, just three days away. I'm mortified that I'll have to cancel if I still look like this. So I proceed to spend the entire weekend icing my cheeks while hiding out in my room because I'm living, for the first time in ages, with a couple of girls I don't know well—definitely not well enough to tell them about *this*, especially since they won't remotely relate as they're only in their twenties.

Slowly but surely, the bruising starts to fade and the swelling goes down. By Sunday morning, I can cover the remaining discoloration pretty well with makeup, and by the afternoon, I no longer look like a chipmunk. I don't look like *me*, but people who don't know me won't know that, and the ones who do might just think I gained a lot of weight recently.

It's *far* from ideal, but in the end, this interview is not about me, so I decide to go through with it. I pack, cover up the bruising as much as possible, and make my way to the airport.

MANHATTAN, NEW YORK
NOVEMBER 2009

I don't have a good sense of what Tyra Banks's views are, which makes being on her show, in some ways, more nerve-racking than being on *Oprah*. Not to mention the fact that I have to ask the makeup artist to please be very careful that my bruising doesn't show up on camera.

Fortunately though, like with Oprah, I don't sense any negativity coming from Tyra. Or any discomfort with the fact that she's sitting next to an intersex person.

I'm also pleasantly surprised to hear her say, when introducing the segment, that being intersex is as common as having red hair. She's glancing at the notes the producers gave her, as hosts often do, so I'm guessing that one of them must have come up with the analogy using the statistics I shared with them.

Oh my god, that's brilliant, I think, *but is it true?*

OII and OII-USA use the 1.7 percent prevalence statistic for intersex people that comes from research at Brown University.[6] Unlike a commonly stated statistic of one out of every two thousand (0.05 percent), which refers only to some of the people with ambiguous genitalia, the 1.7 percent stat includes all the different variations that are considered intersex, or, in current medical terms, DSDs.[7] But I don't know if that's the same as the percentage of people that have red hair.

Tyra proceeds through some of the usual questions, such as, What was it like growing up intersex? Did your parents ever say anything? As she does, I notice that she's looking at me very carefully.

Suddenly, while touching her cheeks to demonstrate, she says, "I notice that you have a little shadow going on here. Can you grow a beard?"

Damn it! I think. *Just my fucking luck that it's Tyra Banks who's interviewing me—of course her model-assessing eyes don't miss a thing!*[8]

I am mortified. I have to decide, in a few seconds tops, which feels worse: pretending that I have a beard or admitting that I'm sporting a botched collagen-filler job.

"Um, y-yes... Well, no, actually..." I reply, trying to fudge my way through. "But I do have some upper-lip hair that comes in."

Luckily, the topic changes quickly, and the show moves on.

The rest of the interview is great. Tyra says I look like a contestant on *America's Next Top Model* in one of my pictures, which is sweet of her to say and extra nice to hear in my bruised-up, puffy-faced condition. She asks good questions, and my answers are informative and engaging, as far as I can tell, and also funny, apparently, because I make her and the audience laugh a few times. It makes up a little for the mortifying moment earlier.

When the interview is over, I look up "red hair prevalence" on my phone. Redheads are estimated to make up 1 to 2 percent of the population. That means the producer and Tyra were right: being intersex is indeed as common as having red hair.

Wow, we're that common, I think. *But we're still so unspoken about and closeted that most people have no idea there are so many of us living right among them.*

The show airs just a few days after I get back home, and my friend Catherine from Wesleyan calls me afterward to tell me it was great.

"There's just one thing though," she says. "I know we're getting older, but Hida, please don't fuck with your face. It's a really nice one."

I know what I did is understandable, but the irony doesn't escape me that I did something to change my appearance because I wanted to look better than usual as an intersex representative, and that when you overcompensate like that, it means you believe, at least to some degree, that you have to make up for something about you that isn't that cool. In this case, being intersex.

I'm disappointed—in myself.

SAN FRANCISCO, CALIFORNIA
JANUARY 2010

An article catches my attention in the *New York Times*:

A panel of medical experts convened by the International Olympic Committee recommended Wednesday that the issue of athletes whose sex seems ambiguous be treated as a medical concern and not one of fairness in competition.[9]

A medical concern? *Semenya is perfectly healthy—so healthy, in fact, that she's a gold medal–winning elite athlete. There's no medical* concern!

The article says that "athletes who identify themselves as female but have medical disorders that give them masculine characteristics should have their disorders diagnosed and treated, the group concluded after two days of meetings in Miami Beach."

"Identify" as female but have medical disorders that "need to be" diagnosed and treated? Oh god—it's basically the same rhetoric that we've been fighting all along, the kind that's used to justify infant "treatments." Except now it's being used against intersex adults too!

"Those who agree to be treated will be permitted to participate," said Dr. Maria New, a panel participant and an expert on sexual development disorders. "Those who do not agree to be treated on a case-by-case basis will not be permitted."

Disorder, disorder, disorder. The word spins around in my mind, making a mockery of my self-esteem. It's as if the *New York Times*, the "experts" at the meeting, and everyone who supported pathologizing me is saying, "Sure, you think you're okay, but you're oh so very wrong. You are not okay. You need to be treated."

I am reeling. I knew when DSD was imposed on intersex people that it would bleed over into mainstream use, even though ISNA kept saying that everyone was still free to identify as "intersex" too and that DSD was just a diagnostic label to be used in medical settings. Clearly they were wrong, because now, sure enough, I'm seeing myself described as a "medical disorder" in a national newspaper.

And now that we have been deemed a disorder and it's being used to hurt intersex adults like Semenya, where is ISNA? Or any of the advocacy organizations that adopted DSD after ISNA closed in 2008?

If the American intersex movement is not going to speak out for Semenya, then *I* should, I decide, more than I already have. I love my CNN.com essay, but the majority of it had been about my personal experience as an intersex person. I want to speak out about this more formally as a human rights issue that impacts the whole community. Basically, I want to address the discrimination that exists against intersex *adults* as well as infants.

FEBRUARY 2010

I'm on the phone with my old friend Jackie from Wesleyan, who went on to become a journalist for the *Washington Post*. In fact, she's the same Jackie I briefly dated who had referred to me as a hermaphrodite to her friend, who in turn relayed this information to *me* when we slept together a few months later.

"So what's new?" she asks.

"Well, I had an essay published last September on CNN.com," I say.

"That's great!" she screams.

"Thanks! I'm trying to get another one out and just sent a pitch to the *Nation*."

She proceeds to give me tips on how to get my piece published and says it'll help my chances if I represent an organization.

"Are there any you've been wanting to contact anyway? I would think you might want to, just to meet some of your peeps."

"Well, you know, there is this one group that looked interesting," I answer.

I'm thinking about OII, the Organization Intersex International.

They're the ones that posted the scathing critiques of DSD that kept me from losing my mind a couple of years ago. I go to their website.

I notice that there's an article from October 2007 called "Why We Do Not Use 'Disorder of Sex Development.'"[10] It takes me awhile to read because it's very thorough, and I want to digest everything it's saying. It covers everything I think is wrong with DSD and then some. It's brilliant, and it's authored by OII's founder, an intersex American named Curtis Hinkle. I decide to e-mail OII that afternoon.

Surprisingly, I hear back right away from Curtis himself, who says he's very familiar with me and my work.

"Hi, Hida!" he says when we speak shortly afterward on the phone. "It is *such* a pleasure to hear from you."

"Thank you—you too," I say.

I proceed to share how meaningful and helpful his posts were to me.

"Well, you know," he says, "your interview on *20/20* was one of the things that motivated me to start OII."

"Wow, *really*?"

"Yes! You had such a wonderful, positive attitude of acceptance and even pride about being intersex that it inspired me to step out myself."

"Wow, that's so wonderful! And then *your* work with OII helped me."

"Lovely the way that works, huh? That we were supporting each other all these years without even knowing it?"

"Yeah, it really is," I respond, marveling at the fact.

"You know, another thing I really liked about your interview is how shamelessly matter-of-fact you were about being gay and how you talked about intersex as an *identity*."

"Oh, thanks. You know, to me it's like, why wouldn't I? I'm Latina,

I'm left-handed, I'm a lesbian, and I identify as all those things, so why wouldn't I also identify as intersex? Since I *am* intersex."

"I know," he says, laughing. "I feel the same way, but I think you've probably noticed that not everyone else does."

We discuss how a lot of intersex folks talk about "having an intersex condition" but won't simply say they are intersex.

"And now this new label just exacerbates that," Curtis continues, "because you can't say, 'I *am* a DSD'; you have to say, 'I *have* a DSD'—"

"Like it's a disease or something!" I cut in. "It's so annoying."

"Horrible, just horrible," he agrees, "and so detrimental to building an equality-based approach to intersex people and addressing the discrimination we face as a people."

Curtis and I are clearly on the same page and it's very refreshing. Not only that, I learn that he speaks about thirteen languages, which has enabled him to turn OII into the world's first international intersex organization. I tell him that I'm interested in addressing Caster Semenya's situation, with the support of an advocacy organization behind me.

"Well, I'd be honored to have you join OII," he says, "and I think what's happening to Caster Semenya is terrible and would love for OII to address it."

I decide to write a petition to garner support for allowing Semenya to compete as is, as a woman. I've never written a petition before, but it seems like a good place to start. In the process of researching for it, I discover that another group in South Africa, the African Women's Development Fund, has already written one.[11]

The signatories seem to be mostly academics in South Africa, but I do notice that one of the names, Sally Gross, says "Intersex South Africa" after it. In the course of looking up Sally Gross, I find that, outside the US, there *are* intersex folks who care about Semenya's situation enough to do something.[12] These folks have spoken out in support against the terrible way Semenya has been treated, some as individuals and some as representatives of intersex organizations. There's someone named Sarah Graham in the UK; a Swiss intersex organization named Zwischengeschlecht, which means "between sexes"; and someone named Gina Wilson, president of OII's branch in Australia.

I see that Sally Gross of South Africa also published a few articles when the Semenya story broke, one of which contains some amazing news.

In 2006, South African intersex people had attained legal protection from discrimination on the grounds of sex by amending the definition of *sex* to include intersex. Incredibly, to me, it was a direct result of Sally's advocacy. The motivation was personal.

As Sally shared in an article titled "Intersex and the Law,"

In 1997, as a direct result of medical evidence that I am intersexed, I ceased to be a human being in South African law despite the Bill of Rights.[13]

This evidence had given Sally a great interest in where intersex people stood in terms of civil and human rights. Later, an American case had renewed this interest. According to the article, the court had ruled that intersex people could be discriminated against because in the eyes of the law, we don't exist—only males and females exist, and only things that exist are covered under the law's protection. Some people find that hard to fathom, because the simple fact that we're alive would seem to prove that we exist, but as the expression "the letter of the law" indicates, if something is not expressly spelled out, then it is not covered by the law.

Sally learned upon studying the existing laws in South Africa that, as with those in the US, they didn't provide protection from the discrimination of intersex people. South Africa's equality clause included protection from discrimination on the grounds of sex, but *sex* was defined as exclusively male or female. Therefore, if someone identified as intersex, rather than male or female, they *could*, by law, be discriminated against for being intersex. Even worse, as Sally explained,

> "human being" and "[natural] person" are also defined as having a sex in exclusively binary terms. The intersexed, somewhere in between, could thus be argued to be neither human beings nor natural persons. The potential consequences were terrifying. Intersex was an "analogical ground" of discrimination rather than a listed ground in the Equality Clause. Unlike discrimination on a listed ground, discrimination on an analogical ground is deemed fair until proven unfair. The burden of proof rests on the victims.

So Sally had taken it upon herself to try to amend the law to include intersex people. It was a process, but ultimately she realized that the easiest way to do it would be to amend the definitions of *sex* to include intersex people, as well as males and females. She drafted two definitions—"'sex' includes intersex" and "'intersex' means a congenital sexual differentiation which is atypical, to whatever degree"—and found an ally in the South African Human Rights Commission, which supported adding the new definitions into the definition of *sex*. In January 2006, the definitions were accepted into law, giving intersex South Africans legal protection from discrimination on a federal level, on the grounds of sex.

I am amazed and impressed that Sally was able to accomplish

this. However, Sally's personal story, which I read about in another article, is equally impressive, though it doesn't have such a happy ending.[14]

Sally, who is a white South African, was registered and grew up as male. As an adult, "he" was spiritual and had very little interest in sex, due to low testosterone levels, so he found a good fit in the Roman Catholic priesthood. However, when he shared his curiosity about his body's differences with his superiors, he was asked to move to a new town and live and work as a woman, and was eventually stripped of "her" clerical status.

I can't relate to the low sex drive and desire to be part of the Church, but Sally's experience and outlook as a child are otherwise so similar to mine that it's almost uncanny. As she shares, "I sensed there was something different about me but I didn't know what was up. I assumed people came in different shapes and sizes. There is a range of what fits different types. There is something called diversity."[15]

Also similar are Sally's attitudes about being intersex, once she found out. "I'm not a lab rat, I've resisted going inside my body to investigate because I prize myself as being a human being. I don't need to know the details."

I feel the same way. I make a mental note that I should try to contact her, and I get started on writing the petition.

When the petition is written, Curtis says it's time to introduce me to the OII board members and run it by them. I virtually "meet" Gina Wilson, the president of OII Australia, via e-mail. I can tell she's whip smart from the feedback she gives. We make a few changes as a group, post it on OII's website, and we all circulate it as much as possible.

The petition will go to the International Olympic Committee

(IOC), who will be deliberating the policies for intersex women athletes, and it makes two demands of the IOC: (1) Let intersex women athletes compete as is, without having to take medically unnecessary hormones; and (2) stop referring to intersex women as individuals with disorders of sex development (DSDs).

Pretty soon, the petition receives a few hundred signatures, including some from academics I admire who work in the field and are considered great intersex allies, like Dr. Suzanne Kessler and Dr. Anne Fausto-Sterling, who was on *Inside Edition* with me. Curtis also says some of the signatories from Europe are respected academics and human rights leaders. It's fantastic.

SEPTEMBER 2010

I get an e-mail from an intersex person named Hiker from Taiwan, telling me she'd like to meet me. She's getting a doctoral degree focusing on intersex issues and has received a grant to travel to the US to meet some of the pioneers in intersex activism. I readily say yes and offer to let Hiker stay with me in Oakland, where I've recently moved, when I learn that the hostel in San Francisco is rather expensive for her grant budget.

The first thing I think when I meet Hiker is that she is, perhaps, the most androgynous person I've ever met. Sometimes I feel like I'm talking to and looking at a man, and then something will shift and I feel like I'm with a girl. It's what people have said about me sometimes, and I'm happy to find that I really like this quality in someone else.

I take Hiker to Lake Merritt, Oakland's glistening man-made lake, and we talk about everything as we walk around its perimeter. Like me, she was raised as a girl and is legally female, but feels like both a man and a woman. Even more exciting is the fact that she's also connected to the spiritual aspects involved in unifying masculine and feminine energies.

"I've always loved the yin-yang symbol," I share, "and thought it's useful in thinking about being intersex."

Hiker agrees and shares her own experience as a Chinese intersex person. I learn that, in Chinese culture, masculinity was not traditionally viewed as macho and aggressive as it is in many Western societies. Instead, being intelligent was valued as the most positive trait in Chinese men.

I find learning about different cultural perspectives of masculinity and femininity fascinating. Even more fascinating to me, however, is that, despite our different backgrounds, Hiker and I have come to a similar place in our identities and have similar perspectives.

"The union of masculinity and femininity has been recognized as a spiritually evolved state by many spiritual disciplines," Hiker says, "and I agree that it is."

"I do too," I say. "I think that intersex people should be valued because we have an insight into this union."

The sun is setting over the lake, and the multitude of birds that make it their home are chirping and settling in for the night.

"I guess that's why I'm happy that I'm intersex," I continue, "and that I wouldn't be a regular man or woman if I could, even though I think that's easier."

"I feel this way too," Hiker says, and I know it's true, and it's very special.

I'm sad when it's time for Hiker to leave two days later. But more than that, I'm grateful for having finally had the chance to meet another intersex person face-to-face who is such a beautiful human being and who shares so many of my intellectual *and* spiritual perspectives. I'm also excited to know that Hiker is going to begin sharing her loving, equality-based perspective about intersex people, in Chinese, to a population on the other side of the world, by starting an OII affiliate there.

"HEY," I SAY TO Curtis the next time we speak, "my views about the IOC's stance have been based on what I saw reported in the *Times*, but we don't really know how accurate that is. So I was thinking, maybe we should just contact the IOC and have a conversation—ask them ourselves where they stand."

"You know, that's a fantastic idea," he says.

"Great, I'm glad you agree; I'll start writing a letter."

"Okay, but let me send it because I can translate it for the head of the medical commission into his native tongue, Swedish. I think it might be more effective that way."

"Wow—yeah, I think so too. Great!"

A couple of weeks later, Curtis calls me with an update.

"Hida, I have some great news. The IOC has invited OII to attend their next meeting in Switzerland to deliberate these policies."

"Oh my god, that's fantastic!" I say.

"Well, I'm glad you think so, because I'd like you to go," he says.

"Me? Why not you? You're the one they invited, right?"

"Well, they'd like a *representative* from OII there, and Hida, I'm no good at these things. I'm terrible at speaking in public. I'd really love it if you would go as OII's representative. What do you think?"

"Well, I guess I should think about it before I commit, but my first reaction is that I think I'd be honored."

LAUSANNE, SWITZERLAND
OCTOBER 2010

The IOC flies me out to Switzerland first-class, which is wonderful considering the long flight from San Francisco. The hotel itself isn't too fancy or ostentatious, which is good, but its elegant, sleek décor tips me off that it's expensive.

That night, the IOC hosts a mixer event, as it's the night before the meeting begins. Although I'd love to just unwind and mentally prepare myself for tomorrow in my room, I'm starving after my flight and there's food, and I also wouldn't mind meeting the other participants, so I go.

Most of them, I learn, are professionals—mainly doctors and lawyers—and after speaking with them I have an inkling that they make quite a bit of money from their jobs as well. I notice that the participants are also *all* white and almost all men. I'm bothered a bit by the lack of diversity in the room, especially because it can be difficult to make a plea for intersex rights to people who may never have experienced a similar degree of discrimination or disenfranchisement themselves.

Fortunately, I meet a journalist who tells me that she's worked with Maria Patiño, the Spanish hurdler who had fought the ruling that banned her from the Olympics back in 1986. She's obviously an ally and tells me that she's happy I'm here. The feeling is mutual.

The meeting itself is held in a conference facility near the hotel, where participants will give presentations on the subjects they've been invited to speak on. The first day starts off fairly well but then is a slow, downward spiral. For starters, some of the doctors, though well-meaning, keep referring to being intersex in stigmatizing ways, like the doctor who tells me in the elevator that he is "on my side" but then proceeds to call being intersex a "birth defect." It seems like he probably doesn't think it's an insulting thing to say because it's just a term that he's used to. I doubt, however, that he'd feel okay about his maleness being referred to that way.

What makes matters more uncomfortable is that while everyone there knows that I'm an intact intersex person—a very personal detail about me—I know next to nothing about them. Now, this is often the case, since I've chosen to come out publicly about my intersex traits in order to educate people about the subject, but the difference is I usually don't have to spend three days with the people I have come out to.

I'm glad to hear that many of the doctors are, like me, recommending that all intersex women be allowed to compete as is, which I wasn't expecting. The bad thing is, however, that I sense resistance to their arguments from some of the higher-ups in the IOC and the IAAF, the International Association of Athletics Federations. The IAAF governs all track-and-field events outside of the Olympic competitions and has a couple of representatives at the meeting, a doctor and a lawyer.

Also, even though it's apparent early on that there is no medical or scientific evidence to support the claim that intersex women have an "unfair physical advantage," some people still give presentations that demonstrate how very different intersex women are from other women. It's a clear attempt to create the impression that they should not be in the same category with other women.

The most maddening presentation, though, comes from one of the few men there who is not a doctor. Although he seems like a nice person, his presentation is a lengthy diatribe that says nothing much other than making the point that it falls to each nongovernmental body, sporting or otherwise, to make the kinds of rules they want and that they feel are right for them. It's the same logic responsible for whites-only golf courses.

I have a chance to make a few good rebuttals, and I even get applause from a few of the participants on one of them. However, I am also subjected to hearing "DSD" over and over again because doctors use it to describe us. It starts getting under my skin.

During a break on the second day of the meeting, one of the

doctors looks me up and down and says, "You know, other than having a slightly deep voice, you seem perfectly normal."

I can tell that she's trying to pay me a compliment, but her comment still makes me feel bad. She wasn't looking at me with *dislike* because of my difference, like people used to look at me and my family in my youth. She just seems to find the fact that I am different fascinating in a way that can be openly evaluated and commented upon to my face. Her statement makes me feel like she's commenting on an animal in the zoo.

As the meeting rolls on, I continue to feel objectified, like the "real-life intersex person" representing a "disorder of sex development," which these medical professionals have all worked on, read about, and/or deliberated extensively. And while I can tell that for some of the folks here, my being intersex is about as meaningful as the fact that I have brown eyes, it is more obvious that for others my being intersex is a *major* difference, something that sets me way apart from them.

The final session of the second, and last, day proves to be the hardest for me. In short, all the scientific evidence that intersex women with high testosterone levels can *not* be shown to have a competitive advantage is chucked out the window to support gender norms. And when I say the science is chucked out the window, I mean that one of the athletes in attendance at the meeting literally says that she doesn't care about science—*something* has to be done about athletes who look like men—and the other athlete there doesn't disagree with her.

Worse, I can tell, based on the reaction of the higher-ups at the meeting, that the athletes' views will likely decide the outcome. It makes sense, as nonintersex female athletes represent the largest group of people that will be affected by whatever regulations come out of this. So I'm not *outraged*, I'm just sad.

I'm sad that the athletes can't dig past their own prejudice to con-sider the evidence that has been so painstakingly presented by the doctors, that no matter how much "like a man" an intersex woman athlete might look, it doesn't mean she is more physically predis-posed to win. That's what the science is concluding, anyway, and isn't that supposedly what this is all about? Intersex women having an actual physical, scientific advantage?

I'm disappointed that the athletes here don't, at the very least, ask for more time to decide, given the scientific evidence in sup-port of intersex women athletes competing with their own naturally given bodies. But they don't do that, because they seem to want the opposite: for intersex women to be somehow "regulated"—that is, punished—because they are intersex.

The argument presented against intersex athletes pretends to be based on science, but in reality it's all about gender biases. It goes something like this:

1. Women who look like men might be men. We should test them.

2. Sports are divided between men and women, so if they are not women, they should not compete with us.

3. Even if women who look like men are not men, the ones with high testosterone levels must still have a physical advantage, so they should not compete in the women's category.

4. Although science doesn't support the theory that they have a physical advantage, they are still not "regular" women because some-times they look like men, which makes us uncomfortable because this is a "women's" competition. Therefore, they should not compete with us.

5. We're a private organization, and because of that we can exclude people our members don't like—probably not based on their

gender or gender expression, because there are laws against that, so we will pretend this is about science and medical issues, even though we know it's not.

As much as I know all too well how important enforcing gender roles is in our society, it's still a little strange to me that looks are such an important factor in these deliberations. Before I came to the meeting, I wanted to believe that the issue at stake would be based on science, but it's apparent now that it's really just based on a combination of sexism and discrimination against gender-nonconforming and/or intersex people. The realization reminds me of what I thought about Caster Semenya's case—that if she had made an effort to look like a pretty woman, which she *can* look like, she likely wouldn't have had this problem.

Granted, some athletes who are less masculine-looking than Semenya have also been found to be intersex over the years and banned as a result. Typically though, they were intersex women with CAIS, whose XY chromosomes were discovered during the period of mandatory chromosome testing for all female athletes. However, as previously stated, these intersex women had been allowed to compete since 1999, after Maria Patiño demonstrated that CAIS women had no functional testosterone.

Toward the end of the meeting, I realize that I'm not going to be able to convince the IOC and IAAF officials to ignore the athletes' demands for some kind of regulation, so I quickly switch gears, trying instead to convince everyone that whatever policies are decided upon must be mandatory for *all* women in order to be fair. But I can tell by the way the IOC and IAAF officials keep avoiding that issue that they're not going to do it. I suspect that, as with most things, it's because it will cost them more.

Instead, the IOC officials start a discussion about who, exactly, should be considered unqualified to compete as a woman. I was pre-pared for them to feel this way based on what had been reported about the first meeting they'd held in January. So I don't get upset. Instead, I keep trying to push them toward making their policies as fair as possible.

Since CAIS intersex women are allowed to compete because they have *no* functional testosterone, and transwomen who compete have to *lower* their testosterone, the conversation jumps to hormone levels as the best gauge for eligibility. However, several of the doctors think this is an inaccurate measure, given all the scientific evidence that natural testosterone functions very differently from steroids and that natural hormone levels vary greatly in male and female athletes. I completely agree, but the officials don't seem to want to listen to that reasoning.

One of the doctors picks a testosterone level that seems safely in the "male range," ten nanomoles per liter, and the sporting associ-ation officials suggest that any woman found to have that level or above must lower it in order to be eligible to compete as a woman. Many of us are completely opposed to this arbitrary choice, but it's a losing battle.

Then, the worst part comes: the discussion over what will "trig-ger" case-by-case testing. In other words, how will they know *who* should undergo testing—since it's not a mandatory test but based "upon suspicion"?

"That's easy," I hear the doctor sitting right next to me say. "They're ugly!"

This doctor, in particular, had already struck me as a pompous sexist based on his comments during previous presentations, so I'm not surprised by what he says, but I *am* saddened that the fate of so many intersex athletes is being determined by the likes of him—that indeed, all women athletes will now be pressured to look pretty in order to avoid coming under suspicion.

The only good thing that happens is that, because the attorneys and several prominent participants at the meeting had agreed with me that *disorders of sex development* is stigmatizing, they decide not to use the term to describe athletes in question. Since not *all* intersex women are at risk for being ineligible, we also decide that *intersex* shouldn't be used either. Instead, because it's only athletes who have high, functioning levels of testosterone—known as hyperandrogenism—who are in question, someone suggests referring to these athletes as "women with hyperandrogenism" in all future statements and policies, and we all agree.

Despite that bit of good news though, I'm extremely disappointed with the results. As much as I know there's a handful of people here who are disappointed along with me, I know it's not the same for them.

I leave the hotel the next morning feeling so dejected and vulnerable that I hop into the comfort of a taxi instead of dealing with the bus to get to the hostel I'll be staying at. It eats up $35 of my $120 spending limit for the next two days.

I spend the rest of the day marveling at how expensive Switzerland is—and feeling worried about having enough money to eat and still make it back to the airport to get home. Fortunately, the next morning a guy in the hostel's kitchen offers me some of his salmon.

"I made much more than I can eat," he says, "and I don't want it to go to waste."

I've been a vegetarian since 1990 and have eaten meat only a handful of times since then. But I casually say, "Sure, thanks," knowing that strong dose of protein will get me through the whole afternoon till dinner.

Lausanne is a beautiful city in many ways, but I'm relieved when my time there is over and I'm on the flight home. I had been so hopeful about what this meeting could accomplish, but it only made me feel terrible—so terrible that, in order to function, I need to push my feelings aside until I get home.

OAKLAND, CALIFORNIA
OCTOBER 2010

The day after I get back home, I go on a hike with my friend Rachel in Redwood Regional Park, which is just a short drive from my new digs in Oakland. There, in the safety of these old trees, I totally break down.

I start crying and saying things like, "I just want to disappear." I can tell the bad feelings are from the meeting but I'm surprised that they're hitting me so hard. I don't totally get why.

"Those fuckers' negative opinions just seeped right into you," Rachel says. "You've got to get rid of them. Just keep sobbing; purge that shit out of your system. This is the perfect place to do it."

She's right. And I do. I sob until my eyes are puffy, and when I finally finish, I feel better.

"Thank you so much for sitting with me through that," I say.

"I'm a New York brownie from Flushing, Queens, man, just like you. That shit don't scare us!"

I start giggling. Rachel is half-Indian and half-Filipino. She calls herself a brownie to describe her dark skin color, and I love that she calls me one too, despite my comparative paleness. She is also indeed from Flushing, just like me, but we'd met out here, through a mutual Burning Man friend.

"I can't believe you're already making me laugh when less than twenty minutes ago I wanted to be dead!" I say.

"If it felt *that* bad being around all that medically stigmatizing shit for just three days, just imagine what it's like for all the people who grew up with it *all* throughout their lives," Rachel says. "I think that's the *real* reason you had to feel this. So you would know more about what it's like and it would motivate you to fight it more than ever."

"Wow, I hadn't thought of it that way, but you're totally right."

NOVEMBER 2010

Not much happens in terms of my activism throughout the rest of the fall, not just because I desperately need a break from it, but also because I'm busy falling in love. I had gone on a date right before leaving for Switzerland with a girl named Simone whom I met a few years ago through a mutual lesbian friend, and we resume dating when I get back.

She tells me that she is probably polyamorous. Being "poly," as folks call it, is popular with the twenty- and thirtysomethings in town—it's *kind of* like being monogamous, in that you're in a relationship, only with several people at a time.

I can barely deal with being in one relationship, so I know that will *never* work for me. I don't want to think about obstacles though. I want to fall in love. And I do: quickly, recklessly, and blissfully. For about a month.

It starts around Thanksgiving, when I take her on a spur-of-the-moment trip to San Diego. We have an amazing time—so amazing that she tells me she wants to marry me.

Apparently though, she doesn't seem to get how poly relationships should work, because it's clear that she's interested in sleeping with this guy she'd introduced me to that she has been friends with for years, but when I ask her about it, she says she's not. It's a red flag that should make me want to walk away, but there's a kind of intensely addictive, destructive sexual connection in our relationship that I can't break away from.

FEBRUARY 2011

Curtis has been asking me if I'll start an American branch of OII for quite some time. He hadn't done so, mostly because he started OII in order to create a global intersex community. The problem is, I have no interest in, or experience with, running an organization.

However, I agree with Curtis that we need an OII perspective in the US, particularly in light of the hegemonic US control of the movement that resulted in DSD. Also, Curtis wants to retire soon, so he isn't going to do it.

I decide to go for it and start OII-USA.

SEPTEMBER 2011

Although we officially broke up in February, my relationship *actually* ends six mouths later, after a horrible scenario in which the woman she's started dating asks me if I'll do a seminude, group photo shoot for this gender-diverse project she's doing. I agree, and then Simone shows up, unexpectedly, with her friend—the guy that I had suspected she was interested in and that she had admitted she cheated on me with before we broke up. When I tell her I think it was a fucked-up thing to do, and that it was *deeply* upsetting that she'd shown up with him, she cuts off all contact with me.

It's a little embarrassing to admit that all of this happened, but as a very wise and incredible therapist I saw in the early nineties used to say, "The road to enlightenment is paved with a thousand humiliations."

Well, this must have been my lucky one thousandth time, because even though the experience nearly rips my heart out, I spend time recovering from the drama, and trauma, which I come to see was all about my father. That's the connection. She reminded me of him, my father, although I don't realize it until it's over. She has the same green eyes and the same ability and desire to use me as a way to feed her ego without any real love or regard for me, just like he had. Our breakup leaves me torn apart, devastated, but it's what I need to finally, *finally*, leave that old pain behind. Forever.

Meanwhile, Gina is changing things forever in Australia—and ultimately for intersex people everywhere—and I'm deeply grateful for her. As president of OII Australia, she's been working in coalition with four trans organizations to lobby the government for gender recognition for adults who do not want to be identified as male or female. On September 15 they succeed: Australia passes legislation offering a third gender marker, "X," to adult citizens who want it.

Kevin Rudd, Australia's former prime minister, is quoted in one article as saying, "This amendment makes life easier and significantly reduces the administrative burden for sex and gender diverse people who want a passport that reflects their gender and physical appearance."

And in the same article an Australian senator, Louise Pratt, who supported the legislation and whose partner is a transman, specifically talks about intersex people, saying that the X

is really quite important, because there are people who are indeed genetically ambiguous and were probably arbitrarily assigned as one sex or the other at birth. It's a really important recognition of people's human rights that if they choose to have their sex as "indeterminate," they can.[16]

Gina explains to me that the X was chosen because the International Civil Aviation Organization (ICAO), which is the agency that governs passports, already had an X gender marker available. The X has been available since 1945, when international organizations such as the Red Cross needed help resettling refugees and concentration camp survivors of World War II who had no identifying documents, or whose documents had been destroyed during the war. "X was made an allowable designator in view of the difficulties resettlement aid workers had with unfamiliar names and the sex usually associated with them," a post on OII Australia's website states. "We are legally able to take advantage of this facility despite the originators not having quite the same objectives in mind as we do."[17]

Gina says the X is beneficial because it allows anyone, not just intersex people, who feel they are neither male nor female to opt out of these gender designations. I agree that this is important given what we know about gender identity not being binary.

"Congratulations!" I shout when we have a Skype session. "Finally, something that *we* have lobbied for! Thank you!"

It's been obvious to me for a while that intersex people need to be legally recognized as a category, or class, of people in order to start fighting for legal protection from discrimination. And since intersex is a congenital sex variation, it's always seemed to me that our category should fall under sex, or "gender," as biological sex is also sometimes called in the law.

"So, do you think that having intersex people recognized as a third gender category will help lead to coverage in antidiscrimination legislation, like Sally got in South Africa?" I ask Gina.

"Yes, and in fact I've been working on that simultaneously," she shares. "We're pushing for protections to be on the grounds of 'intersex status' specifically so that our issues can't be lost or misinterpreted under the sex-discrimination umbrella."

"Yeah, I can see how that would be even more effective, and yet it seems like it would be harder to get passed," I respond.

"It is, but this is not a new project, Hida," Gina says. "I've been working on establishing good relationships with legislators, and educating them, for years, and I think we'll be able to enact antidiscrimination legislation within a year or so. I'll send you a link about it right now."

I open the article she sends on my old desktop computer. In it, Senator Pratt is quoted talking about antidiscrimination legislation:

> I would certainly hope that in the review of the anti-discrimination laws, the consolidation of the act that is happening at the moment, that both sexuality and gender come forward for recognition as grounds for discrimination…I'm certainly pushing that way and I'm quite hopeful.[18]

"So where she says 'gender' as grounds for discrimination," Gina explains, "that's where she's referring to our lobbying for antidiscrimination protection on the grounds of our intersex status, and she says she's hopeful, which is a very good sign."

"Wow, you are so kick-ass!" I shout. "That's such incredible news, Gina, and such incredible work you're doing. That's why I'm so annoyed about this American article!"

It's by an academic who writes a lot about intersex people. Some of her earlier work, such as a 1990s book about intersex people, is good; but in 2005 she coauthored the paper with Brittney that supported the use of the term *DSD*.

Shortly after the news broke about Australia's X, this person published an essay about it on her blog for *Psychology Today*. I even find the title, "Australia's Passport to Gender Confusion: Why I'm Not Thrilled with Australia's Re-gendered Passport System," disrespectful and condescending. It's revealing of the way she's positioned herself in relation to intersex people from the start: as someone who feels entitled to weigh in on what's best for us.

"Excuse me," I want to say to her, "are you intersex? Did you lobby for this legislation because it helps you live and travel with dignity? No? Then why, exactly, is your enthusiasm, or the lack thereof, important?"

In addition, she claims that the marker is mandatory for all inter-sex people, and ends with the words, "I really don't think we're help-ing anybody by marking people born with sex anomalies as 'X' men, grand as we might be imagining their superpowers to be."

After Skyping with Gina, I'm determined to not let this go unad-dressed. I go to work writing an engaging, under-750-word essay addressing every one of her claims. I research and cite it thoroughly, including quotes from Kevin Rudd, Australia's former prime min-ister of foreign affairs, the first recipient of the X, the UN high commissioner of the office for human rights, Navi Pillay, and, of course, Gina herself.

I even come up with a title I like to counter her disrespectful one: "X Marks Evolution: The Benefits of the 'Indeterminate Sex' Passport Designator." A few weeks later it's published in the very same bioethics blog that also ran her essay, so I know that their read-ers, at least, will get an accurate, respectful, *intersex* perspective on this important intersex human rights victory.[19] Thank you, Universe.

CHAPTER 16

City of Intersex Angels

VENICE BEACH, LOS ANGELES, CALIFORNIA
MAY 2012

I'M ALMOST TO ANGIE'S place in Venice Beach, where she moved to after working in New York for a number of years. Recently, I told Angie I was feeling bored and uninspired by the Bay, and she talked me into moving here—specifically, in with her.

"You'll love it," she said. "People are edgier, more like East Coasters."

That wasn't L.A.'s reputation, especially among SF hipster types, who often joked about how people in L.A. were stupid or superficial. As I thought about it though, I remembered that Bay Area folks had sometimes thought Angie's in-your-face Jersey demeanor was "too much." The L.A. artist/hipster crowd, on the other hand, adored her.

"Hmm, maybe you're right . . ." I responded.

"I *know* I'm right—get your ass down here!"

I arrive on the night of my forty-fourth birthday, and it looks like I've made it in time for a celebratory drink.

"Hey, girl! Welcome home!" Angie yells from the guesthouse I'll be renting.

"Hey!" I say, hugging her in the doorway.

"I was just moving your bed. You wanna give me a hand?"

An hour later I'm sitting with her and her boyfriend in the garden outside my new pad. It's almost midnight, but unlike the Bay Area, it's still warm enough to be in shorts and a tee shirt.

I love it instantly, and when I ride down to the beach on my motorcycle after settling in, I'm reminded that it's the best decision I've made in a while. I don't know if it's having the ocean so close or what, but I just feel happy and optimistic. Like anything is possible.

One weekend, Angie takes me to a party at an artists' warehouse where I meet a gorgeous Argentinian woman named Valentina. She's super cool, a leftist, and a Burning Man artist, and we start dating—exclusively. Soon after, I find a part-time job teaching ESL. It pays enough for the guest cottage while leaving me time to write, which I hadn't had in SF.

When I'm not writing or working, I have a blast with Angie, her brother, Devon, who has relocated here too and lives only a couple of blocks away, and a number of other friends whom I know from Wesleyan who live here now as well. Insta-girlfriend, insta-job, insta-friends, insta-life. Suddenly, I have everything I'd been wanting, including beautiful, warm weather.

My life seems to get even better when I meet with the television producer who wants to make a series about me and intersex activism. He contacted me shortly before I moved down here, and he's smart, sensitive, and so respectful that he wants me to be the coproducer so we'll "get it right." I'm all about intersex visibility, so it's obviously an exciting prospect.

The problem is, his specialty is television docudrama, aka reality TV. Not only does that make me cringe, but I don't think the networks will be interested in something as substantive as activism for reality TV. Nevertheless, we shoot a teaser video, as he calls it, write a pitch, and he and his team shop it.

"So, we have interest from one of the major networks," he tells me one day.

"Wow, really?"

"The only thing is," he says, pausing, "they like the activism stuff, but they'd also like to focus on your dating life, especially since you're somewhat single."

Things are good with Valentina, my girlfriend, but it's too soon to say whether it'll be serious.

"Oh geez, I was afraid of that," I tell him.

"Look, I know you said you weren't interested in that," he says, "so I'm totally cool with you saying no. Just think about it, I guess."

I talk to Devon about it as we stroll the Venice boardwalk. I like to get coffee here in the morning sometimes, before it gets hectic with the summer crowds.

"I mean, I *do* see why they'd be interested in that," I muse, "since people love watching reality shows about dating, but personally I *hate* it. It seems so stupid and voyeuristic. But the thing is, not everyone feels this way. A lot of folks actually like reality TV, so maybe it *would* be a good way to bring more visibility to the community—"

"So are you gonna sell out or *what?*" he jokingly asks, cutting me off.

"Well, I'm not really famous or anything, so you can't really call it selling out," I respond. "I guess it'd be more like 'selling in'...," which is a phrase I had once heard.

"Yeah, and you need the money! So I say do it—sell *in.*"

We laugh.

"Damn, if only I were shallow, or less intelligent, or one of these people that'll do anything to be on TV," I lament, "I'd be all over this!"

It's a hard decision to make, because (1) I know intersex people need visibility, *badly*; and (2) I'm forty-four, living in a tiny guest cottage, driving a beat-up '98 Ford Windstar, and still working a "day job"—so I could *really* use the money. Still, I ultimately decide to follow my gut, which says that having my personal life displayed on-screen for entertainment isn't for me, and isn't the kind of work that I want to, ideally, be creating.

I've begun to spend time with many people who are not only following, but manifesting, their dreams. One of my friends has just written a new sci-fi TV series. The other is working on his next film (and his first one made it to Sundance and got great reviews). I meet a girl at a party who tells me she just sold her second book, and she's in meetings about having it made into a series.

I start getting the feeling that I can pursue my dreams too. I'd had three more essays published since my first one on CNN.com in respectable, semiacademic venues before moving out here, and now I'm more inspired and motivated than ever.

I publish my first academic article—with Maria José Martínez-Patiño (the intersex woman responsible for ending the practice of *mandatory* gender-verification testing for all Olympic female athletes)—in the *American Journal of Bioethics*, on the issue of intersex women in sports.[1] Then I publish two more on the same topic: one is a letter to the editor in the *New York Times* and the other is an article I coauthor with an intersex colleague whose work I really like, Dr. Georgiann Davis, in *Ms.* magazine, which I've long been a fan of.

Then Claudia, my colleague at OII-USA, sends me a document she created called "Brief Guidelines for Intersex Allies." It needs a few substantive changes, and some editing, but I think it's fantastic.

We decide it would be great to publish it on Intersex Awareness Day (IAD). It's held on October 26 to commemorate the anniversary of the first known intersex protest, which took place at a medical clinic in Boston in 1996. I had known about it because it happened shortly after the intersex retreat I'd gone to, but unfortunately I'd been too broke to afford the plane fare from San Francisco.

Claudia is also organizing an event for IAD at NYU and invites me to present at it with her, just like I had two years ago when we first met. We had also presented at a venue named Bluestockings, and she wants to set that up again too.

"Okay, I'll write up a presentation, outline, and pitch and contact them," I offer.

It's been sixteen years since the 1996 protest that IAD commemorates, and I realize that sadly, not *that* much has changed. In fact, being intersex is now officially classified as a medical disorder, which wasn't the case back then. And because of that, there's a whole generation of young people that were taught and raised with the term *DSD* to describe themselves.

In fact, I'd spoken for hours with just such a person earlier this year when they left a post on an intersex Facebook group's page saying they felt so isolated that they wanted to kill themselves and desperately needed to talk to someone about being intersex. I called the number she left, and she told me how she felt totally alone and different from everyone around her. I listened and let her know I used to feel the same way.

I also noticed that she kept referring to herself as "disordered" or to her "disorder." Just hearing it was painful, especially because I'm old enough to remember a different time, a time when we referred to ourselves as "intersex," or even "hermaphrodites," and tried our best to feel proud about it.

After about twenty minutes I gently asked her why she was describing herself that way, and she replied, "Well, what else would

I call myself? That's the label my parents and doctors taught me to describe who I am."

When I explained that DSD had been imposed on the intersex community just six years ago, she was utterly stunned. She'd had no idea.

"So you're telling me that before 2006, we all called ourselves intersex?"

She vaguely remembered hearing of the word but didn't realize that it predated DSD.

"Yeah—those of us who were willing to be out about it did. The rest just referred to themselves as men or women with whatever particular intersex variation they had—CAIS, CAH, etcetera. And that's one of my big problems with DSD: we already had medical diagnostic labels that people who preferred identifying as men or women could use. We didn't need a new umbrella term, especially one that officially classifies us as a disorder."

"Wow...This is blowing my mind."

I took a deep breath and waited for her to soak it in.

"I mean, the truth is," she continued, "it had always felt terrible that they called the fact that I'm like this, that I'm different, a disorder. It made me immediately see myself as flawed, and I don't think I would have if they had just told me that I'm intersex."

A few weeks later she called to tell me that she was feeling much better. In fact, it was so freeing finding out that she's not actually disordered, but just a different type of human, that she'd even started coming out as intersex to folks in her grad program. One of them even asked her to give a presentation about it, and she's considering it.

I've been thinking about intersex issues for well over a decade now, but her turnaround still impresses me. It reminds me how powerful words are and what a fundamental difference labels can make. How they can be used to bring a whole community down or, in our case, try to make us disappear.

Society has been trying to make us disappear—not just with medical normalization but with language. I remember, for example, how some of the arguments for DSD had been about "labeling the condition," not the person, and how backward I thought that was. After all, labeling "the person" is considered bad only when what you're labeling them is put down by society.

For example, when being gay was so stigmatized that it was diagnosed as a "psychiatric disorder," until 1973, most folks didn't feel comfortable labeling themselves gay. They made the same arguments about not wanting the term *gay* to be a label for who they were, because their sexual orientation was really just one aspect of who they were. In fact, even when I was first coming out in the mid- to late eighties, I would hear older folks say things like, "I'm not 'gay,' I just happen to be a man who loves other men."

However, heterosexuals could say the same thing about being called "straight," but they didn't. They didn't have a problem with it.

Similarly, now lots of intersex people, especially the older ones, just want to talk about being people with a particular "condition" or "DSD." They're not comfortable claiming intersex as an identity the way they easily claim being "Jewish" or "a woman"—or even "gay" or "lesbian." The problem is, when people don't claim parts of who they are, those parts disappear—especially when those parts are something society doesn't want to admit exists.

That's it: we *exist*—that's what we need to put out there! It's so obvious, and yet, as I just described, it hasn't been happening. Other than me and a few handfuls of people who openly identify as intersex, the dialogue is still being dominated by a medicalized discourse about "having intersex conditions"—at least in the US.

I've always told the folks who contact me that they don't *have* to say they're intersex just because their bodies are classified that way, that how they want to identify is up to them. However, I'm also aware that saying you have a medical condition is not the same thing. Just ask anyone old enough to remember when they had to be identified as a "person with the psychiatric disorder" instead of being able to identify as gay. The former situation certainly didn't help the cause.

Fuck it! I think to myself. *Even if most folks aren't identifying as proud herms yet, I'm going to. I'm going to tell the world that we're a type of people, not just medical conditions.*

I get on my computer and write an e-mail to the folks at Bluestockings. I hear back from them within hours, telling me they're very excited about my presentation, "Hermaphrodites Exist: Intersex, the 'I' in LGBTI."

A month later, I fly to New York, Claudia and I publish "Brief Guidelines for Intersex Allies" right on time for Intersex Awareness Day 2012, and we rock our NYU and Bluestockings presentations. I make all the points I've been making for years, and I *also* directly address how we can combat erasure through LGBTI inclusion.

One of my dreams is that the institutionalized "medicalization" of intersex people will one day be deemed the human rights violation that it is by everyone involved, but right now, not even the intersex organizations in the US are doing that (besides my fledgling OII-USA). I see posts on social media by organizations that work with intersex youth and/or their parents talking about intersex people needing more fully informed consent, and I know these organizations are trying to "work within the system," but it feels weird. Like, would you feel better about baby girls being subjected to female genital mutilation (FGM) because their parents were "fully informed" about the risks? Wouldn't it be better to condemn the practice altogether?

I had written Secretary of State Hillary Clinton about doing just that last December and received a nice but noncommittal response from her office this past February.[2] Then, later that same month, after the International Day of Zero Tolerance for Female Genital Mutilation, I published an article in the *Global Herald* calling on Clinton to denounce IGM as well as FGM.[3] However, since I think that IGM is just as bad as FGM, shouldn't I be contacting people who deal specifically with human rights violations? Like maybe the UN's human rights office?

I decide to take it on. I figure I'll start by writing the best letter I can and then see how to get it to them. I also manage to apply for and receive a scholarship to attend the Second International Intersex Forum, in Stockholm.

STOCKHOLM, SWEDEN
DECEMBER 2012

Stockholm is fantastic. The organizers offer to help me get my letter to the powers that be. They also suggest that I present it to the other participants of the forum, who are representatives from the most active, prominent intersex advocacy organizations in the world.

The letter is titled "Open Letter: A Call for the Inclusion of Human Rights for Intersex People," and it is delivered to Navi Pillay, the UN's high commissioner for human rights, and to Charles Radcliffe, the chief of global issues at the Office of the High Commissioner for Human Rights (OHCHR). The letter calls for full LGBT*I* inclusion in antidiscrimination policies extended to the LGBT community and discusses human rights violations such as IGM and harmful in utero medical treatments and gender-verification testing of intersex women athletes.

The timing couldn't be more appropriate: it's December 10, Human Rights Day 2012. With all of the participants but one having signed in support, it's the first-ever global call for human rights by and for intersex people.

I can hardly believe that I've initiated it, but I also realize it makes sense that it would happen now. Now, I have finally started believing in myself and in life enough to aspire to that Margaret Mead quote I used to have on my fridge—the one that says, "Never doubt that a small group of thoughtful, committed citizens can change the world; indeed, it's the only thing that ever has."

I get to see a dear friend from Wesleyan who lives here now, Hiker from Taiwan, and Vincent of OII Francophônie, who I had the pleasure of meeting once in France. I also finally get to meet the other international members of OII that I've only been communicating with via e-mail, and they're all amazing: Julius of OII Uganda/SIPD; Ins, Dan, Thoralf, and Ev, of OII Germany; and Gina, of OII Australia, whom I have also been Skyping with for months.

With the exception of Sally Gross of South Africa, who unfortunately couldn't make it, Gina has achieved more for intersex people in terms of actual government change—which has such an enormous, long-term impact—than anyone else. Just like Sally, due to her brilliant work she has attained actual civil rights victories for intersex people in Australia. The first was getting the government to allow intersex people who desire it to be legally recognized as neither male nor female on their passports. Australia is the first first-world country to recognize a third gender category, and it's hugely important as it has made the rest of the first world begin to take notice that we exist.

Now, in Stockholm, Gina tells me that it's looking good for getting antidiscrimination legislation for intersex people passed by next year.

"And we did it all by working in coalition with allies and fellow members of the LGBTI community," she shares.

Unlike intersex activists like Brittney in the US and the organizations that followed ISNA's lead, OII Australia has been working in coalition with the greater LGBTI community there for years now, with fantastic results. They are now close to attaining legal gender recognition on *all* identification documents—not just passports—for intersex adults who want it. Once they do, it'll make it easier for intersex people to attain legal protection against discrimination by adding "intersex status" to "sexual orientation and gender identity" as a grounds for protection.

I've been pointing out our community's commonalities with the LGBT community for years—often noting that we suffer from discrimination like IGM because of society's desire to maintain heteronormative notions of gender and sexuality. However, despite this, many of the outspoken intersex Americans I know don't like being added to the LGBT acronym. It frustrates me that their simplistic "it's-not-a-sexual-orientation" arguments miss the point that regardless of whether or not we actually identify as queer, we're targets of discrimination if our differences are detected because it's presumed that we are. In effect, some of us are victims of homophobia from the minute we're born, which is why I often say that we're "born queer."

Given this, I think trying to pretend that being intersex isn't related to gay and lesbian issues is not only inaccurate but ineffective in terms of ending IGM. You can't stop discrimination without naming it and calling for an end to it, and the discrimination we are suffering from is based on homophobia. To me, it makes perfect sense to work in coalition with the other communities fighting homophobia. So it's affirming to see that working in coalition with LGBT people has indeed been very effective for intersex human rights in Australia.

It's even more affirming to get support and kudos for my activism from Gina.

"Sometimes I feel like I'm just so terrible at this stuff," I had said to Gina over Skype one day, before the meeting here in Stockholm. "I've only written one letter to a government official, I can barely keep my website updated, and I haven't even tried to change the law like you're doing. Honestly, I just don't know if I can, Gina. I'm so intimidated by it, for some reason, and I feel like I'm so bad at it. Like my brain just doesn't work that way."

"Yes, but Hida, you forget—I'm twenty years older than you, I'm retired, and I have a pension and a loving partner to support me. That makes this much easier for me to do."

"You're right," I said. "I did forget that." I smiled at her humility in pointing it out.

"And even still, without any of that, you've done so much, Hida. You've educated millions—do you realize that?—literally *millions* of people around the world about the fact that we exist and that it's perfectly all right to grow up and live as an intersex person without having been bloody 'normalized.' That's the kind of visibility that we so desperately need, and you are the *only* person on the planet in your position who is doing it consistently, and you have been for well over a decade now. The others who weren't mutilated are out there too—trust me. I see them all the time in the chat rooms—they're all just hiding. But you, I've known about you for ages all the way out here, across the pond, because of the enormous scale of your activism. It's a huge gift to the community, Hida, that can't be underestimated."

"Ah, Gina," I said. "You're gonna make me cry."

And then because I said it, I did. But they were tears of happiness.

"It feels so good to hear that—especially coming from *you*—after feeling kind of, I don't know, devalued for so many years out here."

"Well, you just keep ringing me and I'll keep telling you, because it's all true."

Learning about Sally's and Gina's work only furthers my belief that we must be acknowledged as a class of people—subjected to a specific type of discrimination because of who we are—in order to attain the legal protection from discrimination that will make it safe to be openly intersex. Only when that happens will parents of intersex kids feel safe letting them be who they are.

I HAVE A MELLOW Christmas and New Year's with Valentina, whom I'm still seeing. The passion we felt initially has started to wear off, and she's quite a hothead, so we get in a lot of stupid fights. I'm not sure where it'll go, but she's a wonderful person—fun, creative, and kind—and there's love there for sure.

Life is good living with Angie. In fact, it feels almost like Wesleyan again, having her just a few yards away. Her boyfriend lives with her here too, and he's only twenty-four, which adds to the college vibe.

I don't realize it at first, but having such a close-knit relationship with the people I live with is inspiring for my work—so inspiring that I decide to also create something that's needed for the intersex community but doesn't exist yet: a short pamphlet for parents who just found out their baby is intersex and need unbiased information. The host of one of my more recent radio interviews had asked if there was anything like that to help parents who suddenly found themselves in this position, uninformed. I felt sad to answer that there wasn't.

I told the host about the *DSD Guidelines*, but she disliked calling intersex people disordered as much as I do. It had to be something that used nonstigmatizing language. I saw that Curtis had published the *Handbook for Parents* on OII's website, but it was a rather long essay. She was asking for a pamphlet or one-sheet handout that could be easily read and distributed and that provided information—such as links to medical studies—about the serious health risks involved in "treating" intersex children with nonconsensual genital surgeries and hormone therapy.

Such a resource doesn't exist, and the thought of creating it is really intimidating, especially because I'm not into the medical focus, but Los Angeles has made me brave. I know the medical studies that demonstrate harm, *and* I happen to be dating a graphic designer who designs pamphlets like this all the time. So I start writing up my ideas.

Then, in March, Valentina and I have one fight too many and break up. Later that week, I'm let go from my day job teaching ESL, and it's entirely my own fault. I was doing great, already getting nines and tens, on a scale of one to ten, on the evaluations from my students, when most teachers take months to build up to that. But I made the mistake of advocating for my coworkers during my thirty-day evaluation meeting, telling my boss about things that people are unhappy with and how I think they can be improved.

"Well, I'm confident that we can find teachers who are a perfect fit for our environment," she said, staring at me blankly.

Oops.

When I get home, I start looking at job listings online. The pickings are slim and I start to get that sinking, semipanicked feeling—the one about hanging by a financial thread my whole adult life. I know it all too well. But then, suddenly, I decide to do things differently. I'm going to see if Angie will float me the rent so I can write like crazy until I have to start my next job. It's the only thing I really want to do, and it feels like now or never.

When Angie gets home though, she saves me from having to ask her by moaning about how much she's going to have to pay for this service to convert hard copies of her patients' files to online files. I leap at the opportunity to make some money and offer to do it for half the price. She agrees, and I'm back on track.

MAY 2013

I've finished all the text for my resource for parents, and I'm happy with how it comes out. I particularly like the "Tips for Communicating with Family and Friends" part, which goes through a Q & A of common things that new parents get asked when their baby is intersex, and how to deal with answering them.

I run the text by two doctors, one who is a pediatrician, for input. I want to make sure they find it professional and that none of the language I use is off-putting, because I want doctors to *want* to give this to parents.

I've also come up with a title—*Your Beautiful Child: Information for Parents*. Intersex babies have harmful things done to them based on the idea that they're undesirable, unattractive beings, so I want to give parents the opposite message.

Angie's roommate in the main house that shares the property with my cottage is a graphic designer, and he's agreed to design the pamphlet for free, which is a godsend since Valentina and I are no longer an item. It's been difficult editing the text down to fit into the pamphlet design, but I'm grateful to have the challenge.

We're almost done with it when I see some incredible news: the adoptive parents of an intersex child are suing the state of South Carolina and the doctors who operated on their son when he was a ward of the state![4] They are in a unique position to do so because, unlike most parents, they did not consent to the surgeries. I am thrilled to see that they feel no shame in openly referring to him as "intersex" in the press.

Finally, I have proof for something I've long believed: parents *can* love their intersex children. We don't have to call ourselves disordered or squeeze ourselves into the gender binary in order to be happy and loved.

Case in point, the genderqueer community is becoming more well-known. The word *genderqueer* describes folks who feel neither male nor female. Not only that, lots of genderqueer people are using gender-neutral pronouns (just as I tried to do almost twenty years ago) to indicate that they do not feel either male or female but some combination of both—even neither. Just like me.

I finally feel like I am not out here all on my own, having to explain something that nobody knows about. The world is catching up.

I'm elated and I'm grateful to each and every person in the genderqueer community, not just for keeping me company, but because I know that the emergence of people with nonbinary gender identities is an important step for the acceptance of all intersex people. After all, the big fear driving "corrective" treatments is that intersex babies won't grow up to be men or women. So if we have a whole community of people voluntarily saying that they are not men or women, and living voluntarily as neither, then that obviously throws a monkey wrench into the theory that it's impossible to be this way. It creates a viable community that parents can see and that encourages them to think, *Well, they might grow up to be men or women, and if they don't, then I guess they'll be genderqueer.*

Three days after the story of the lawsuit breaks, I publish *Your Beautiful Child: Information for Parents* on OII-USA's website. Seeing the words online makes my heart leap. Parents of intersex children have had terrible things said about their kids for so long. I'm proud to put something out there that sends them the opposite message.

Then one day, soon afterward, I receive a Facebook message

from the mother in the lawsuit. She introduces herself and says she wants to thank me for "making the world a safer place for her son to grow up as an Intersex person."

Oh. My. God.

I shout out to Angie, "You gotta see this!"

She runs over from her bedroom, which is right across the yard from the cottage I'm renting from her.

"Wow, that's fantastic! And so incredible what she said to you!"

I'm glad she's there for me to share this news with, because it's big. This mother has just made every scary, difficult moment that I've gone through after deciding to come out as intersex worth it.

I proceed to write several blog posts about various intersex issues and get tons of positive feedback.

I'm still bummed about my breakup with Valentina, but I can tell we'll be friends, so I decide—probably for the first time in my life—to just get right back on the dating horse, so to speak. I go on a date with a woman I meet on OkCupid. I don't find true love, but it inspires an idea for a fun essay about dating as an intersex person.

I title it "Intersex: The Final Coming-Out Frontier," and I like it so much that I send it to the *Advocate*, and they end up running it. I'm *thrilled*.

JULY 2013

I get word from Gina that the Australian government has released its new intersex-inclusive guidelines on the recognition of sex and gender. The guidelines state,

> The Australian Government recognises that individuals may identify and be recognised within the community as a gender other than the sex they were assigned at birth or

during infancy, or as a gender which is not exclusively male or female.[5]

Not only that, the government has also just amended its Sex Discrimination Act of 1984 "to introduce sexual orientation, gender identity and intersex status as attributes protected from discrimination."[6] It's absolutely amazing and a testament to what years of outreach and lobbying with our allies can do. As Gina explains in an interview outlining her years lobbying for the legislation as OII Australia's president, "As I started to become involved with political lobbying and human rights activism and to build this network, I found that our strongest allies were LGBT groups."[7]

OAKLAND, CALIFORNIA
SEPTEMBER 2013

"Dear Hida, I hope this e-mail finds you well."

I've been better. I'm back in Oakland—basically because it was easier, financially, to live here after Angie got a job on the East Coast and had to sell her house in Venice—and I'm bored. This e-mail, however, brings some much-needed excitement.

It's from Charles Radcliffe, the senior UN advisor on LGBT rights, whom I've been communicating with since I sent him my "Open Letter: A Call for the Inclusion of Human Rights for Intersex People" last year. He tells me they're doing an event at the UN in New York for Human Rights Day, and he asks if I'd like to be one of the presenters, along with Martina Navratilova, Jason Collins, and two other human rights activists.

Martina Navratilova?! I can't count how many times I watched her kick ass on the tennis court on TV, inspired by her talent as an openly gay athlete. She made it easier for me, and probably thousands of other baby dykes, to come out of the closet.

The event that the UN is hosting is called "Sport Comes Out against Homophobia." I've been asked because since we contacted them, they've been trying to include the *I* in LGBTI, and I'm a very visible "out" intersex human rights activist. Due to the numerous articles I've published on the topic and my involvement with the IOC, I'm also considered something of an expert on the issue of intersex women in sports.

The Third International Intersex Forum is coming up too. It's being held in the small Mediterranean island nation of Malta, which sounds lovely. Unfortunately, Gina won't be there, as she retires in September on the heels of the amazing human rights victories she has been instrumental in attaining.[8] I am, however, selected to be one of the three intersex co-organizers, which means having to go through and select participants from all the applicants and also do the actual organizing while I'm there.

Before the forum, which is being held from the end of November through the beginning of December, I'll be doing another Intersex Awareness Day event at the end of October with Claudia in New York. It feels like a lot, but at the same time I'm so excited that all these things are happening for intersex people. And I'm honored to participate in them.

I tell my mother about my upcoming trip to New York.

"Oh, that's wonderful, Hida Patricia! Your sister will be camping with her friends that weekend, so you and I will have lots of time together."

NEW YORK, NEW YORK
OCTOBER 2013

I make it to New York, and when I'm not at my presentations, I'm with my mom the whole time. I'm not sure if it's because we have the house all to ourselves, but we're able to talk for hours, like we never have before. It's wonderful.

We talk about things like her relationship with my father that, for whatever reason, I hadn't wanted or been able to ask about.

"I've always wondered how it started, Mom. Why did you marry him?" I ask.

"Well, I was pregnant with your brother before we got married," she says.

I had known this, but not the full story, I guess. "Did you really have to go through with marrying him though?"

"Yes," she says. "In those days it would have been completely unacceptable to have a baby and not a husband."

"Okay, I figured, but then why did you come here? And why did you stay with him?"

"Oh, I was so ashamed about what I did that I wanted to get away from my family so they didn't have to know that I was pregnant before we were married."

I pause. I'd never really known that was her actual emotional motivation for leaving everything she knew and moving to a place so far away, where she didn't even speak the language.

"Wow, Mom, I never knew. I just thought you were in love with him and hadn't realized yet what an abusive person he was…"

"No, I was never in love with him," she admits. "And when I got pregnant, he didn't want me to have your brother either, because he already knew he wanted to move to New York. But I wanted to have him. So I made your father marry me, and your brother, Hugh, was born in Colombia shortly after. I thought that once we got here I would leave him."

"So then what happened?" I press. "Why didn't you?"

"It seemed like he knew that I wanted to leave him and then he started getting very mean. He said that if I did, he would fight me in court to keep Hugh—that he would lie or say whatever he needed to in order to get what he wanted. So I was afraid to leave, and I stayed. A few years later I became pregnant with you."

"My god," I say. And then I realize something. "So if you had been able to leave him, you would have been happier, but then I would have never been born!"

"No!" she exclaims. "Don't say it like that, Hida Patricia. I wouldn't have been happier, because I *wouldn't* have had you! Or your sister."

I know she loves me, but I still feel like she would have been happier had she left my father earlier. It's a strange thing to consider. I feel so grateful, though oddly so, that she stayed, because in a way she sacrificed all her chances of having a joyful adult life in doing so.

"I'm sorry you all had to suffer so much though," she continues.

"Oh, Mom, I know you did the best you could, and I have so much respect for you. I always have. You are so strong and so smart—I mean, look at you. I always tell my friends how proud I am of you. You came here barely speaking English and with no money left after you decided to leave Dad, but you made your own career. You did so well that you bought this house with your own money, and in a nice neighborhood in New York City, one of the most expensive cities in the country—in the world! You've done better than I have, and I grew up here with all the advantages of speaking English and getting a good education."

She looks at me with an expression of deep appreciation for finally being seen as who she is, and valued for the same reasons she'd valued herself. It's probably the same look I had in my eyes when Gina told me how valuable my activism has been.

"Thank you, Hida Patricia," she says.

We have a wonderful, loving time for the rest of the two days I am there, with none of the usual estranged feelings and bickering. It's something we've never quite experienced, and it's so amazing I don't want it to end.

Fortunately, I'll be back in just a little over a month when I speak at the UN, and with the way things are going with my work, probably many times next year as well.

I can't wait.

VALLETTA, MALTA
NOVEMBER 29–DECEMBER 2, 2013

In Malta, my colleagues and I are amazingly productive. We get so much done, including drafting a statement about what our community wants that's geared toward anyone working on issues that impact intersex people. We call it the "Public Statement of the Third International Intersex Forum," and it's published on the ILGA-Europe (the European branch of the International Lesbian, Gay, Bisexual, Trans and Intersex Association) website, which is the hosting organization. I'm proud to say it uses quite a bit of language directly from *Your Beautiful Child*, the resource I created for OII-USA.

I am also pleasantly surprised that the minister for social dialogue, consumer affairs, and civil liberties of Malta, Helena Dalli, actually attends the forum one afternoon. One of the forum's non-intersex organizers, Silvan Agius, invited her because he's leaving ILGA-Europe to start a position with the Maltese government soon, and he knows her personally.

However, as wonderful as it is, my trip to Malta is also draining.

Somehow, even though I really try, I never get my body to adjust to the nine-hour time difference between Malta and California. I was pretty jet-lagged at my conferences in Stockholm and Switzerland too, but I wasn't organizing those events, so I didn't have to be up as early working and "on" the whole time like I am in Malta. I end up getting about five hours of sleep in three days, so by the end of the trip, I am a complete and utter wreck.

And although it certainly contributed to the situation, it wasn't *just* the sleep deprivation that wrecked me either. Rather, it was something much worse.

While engaged in a conversation one day at the forum, the participants and I began to discuss the issue of discrimination against female intersex athletes. As someone who has researched the issue, I'm familiar with the fact that women of color are disproportionately targeted by the sporting associations' policies against intersex athletes. However, when I began to make this point, a few people started demanding I turn over the mic.

I had been facilitating the discussion, and everyone but me had already had a chance to speak, but these folks acted like I was hogging the mic and insisted it was time for me to move on. Their adamancy coupled with my sleep deprivation and shock at being treated that way caused me to just give in to their demands.

After I handed over the mic though, I felt terrible—silenced. The only thing that reassured me was when I made eye contact with two participants who gave me a look that said, "Yes, we noticed. We see what's up."

But later on, a similar instance occurred. The minute the issue of race was mentioned—this time in relation to the fact that most American intersex organizations are led by white people, and the impact that has—one of the white participants cut me off. This time I was better prepared and pointed out that she was interrupting me, but in the process I never got to finish making my point. I guess I shouldn't have been surprised that addressing racism would be a touchy subject, but I didn't expect it to get totally swept under the rug—and by fellow activists, no less. It deeply upset me, especially because I was met with doubts and defensiveness when I brought it up privately with a couple of people.

Still, ultimately, I'm glad I attempted to bring these issues to the forefront of the forum, because I'm just as committed to combating racism as I am to combating the discrimination of intersex people. I'm also grateful to have met my fellow intersex siblings, the majority of whom *were* supportive of me and these issues and were wonderful.

I MAKE IT HOME to Oakland only to have to get on a plane to New York for Human Rights Day two days later. Although the UN invited me, another organization is sponsoring my visit, and they want me there a few days before my presentation so I can participate in the conference they're holding beforehand.

I decide to stay with a good friend in Manhattan because it's easier to get to the events from her place than from Queens. Once I'm settled, I call my mom with the update.

"Hi, Mom!" I say.

"Hi, Hida Patricia! How is everything? How was your flight?"

"Oh, pretty good, but they want me to go to all these events, and I'm so tired from my trip to Malta that I feel like I may get sick. I'm sorry, but I don't know if I'm going to be able to make it over there."

"Oh, it's okay," she says sympathetically. "I know it's not a vacation. It's a work trip and the train takes a long time to get here."

"Thanks for understanding, Mom."

"So when are you speaking?" she asks.

"On Wednesday."

"At the Naciones Unidas, right?"

"Yeah. I'm nervous, Mom. It's a big deal. I'm speaking on a panel with Martina Navratilova—remember her, the tennis player?"

"Yes, of course. Congratulations, Hida Patricia—that's wonderful."

"Thanks. I just hope I do a good job."

"Just relax until your presentation, and it will be great," she assures me.

"Okay, I will."

"And Hida Patricia?"

"Yes?"

"I'm very proud of you for what you are doing."

It's the first time she's ever said that about my activism, and it means everything to me.

CHAPTER 17

Practicing What I Preach

OAKLAND, CALIFORNIA
JANUARY 2014

HIDA?" MY SISTER'S VOICE is saying over the phone.

It's one in the morning, and I had been asleep when she called.

"Yeah, hey, what's going on?" I ask.

"It's Mom," she says, her voice starting to crack. "She's in the hospital undergoing surgery. She had a brain aneurysm..."

Three hours later I'm on a flight to New York.

Just short of three weeks later, my mother is dead.

Her brain was badly damaged by the hemorrhaging from the aneurysm, and she never came out of the coma she fell into.

It's the most surreal and horrific period of my life. It's horrific because she was only seventy-one and in great health, so I thought I had at least another fifteen years to enjoy our newfound closeness. It's surreal because of the details, like having to take her off life support and watching her body shrink down to nothing more than a breathing corpse; having her brothers and sisters cheerfully calling to wish her happy birthday, not knowing she'd died the day before it; feeling bad that my whole family is so estranged that they hadn't even known she was in a coma.

All of this transpired during one of the worst cold spells New York had seen in decades. As I drove my brother and sister to the hospital in Long Island and elsewhere, talked to the doctors, and attempted to talk to Mom while she was in a coma—because the doctors had said the part of her brain that enabled her to hear us *might* still be working—the weather seemed to mirror the desperate feeling in my soul, like the whole city had become a dangerously cold place without my mother's conscious presence.

I let my closest friends know what was happening. Jade offered to fly out and help me deal, and Beth offered to handle the funeral for me, if it came to that. It was touching but also depressing. My mom had fallen out of touch with most of her family and didn't have many friends, so we didn't even know who we'd invite to a funeral. Also, neither my mother nor my sister, Eden, who lived with her, had kept up the house, and I just couldn't bring Jade into the mess I had to organize.

My sister, who considered our mom her best friend, is completely distraught. She'd been the one who'd found her after the aneurysm, and she questions whether it would've been better if she hadn't— better if Mom had just died in her sleep at home instead of being rushed off to surgery that would eventually leave her in a coma. I do my best to comfort her and tell her that she did what any child would do, but I can understand why she feels the way she does.

My brother, who had always had a difficult relationship with our mom, is racked with guilt. She hadn't been able to protect him from our father. I guess I could say the same, in terms of not being protected, but I'd gone through so much therapy to heal those wounds that I didn't resent her.

Hugh did, and he hadn't always been nice to Mom, and now it haunted him. I encouraged him to tell her how he felt and to apologize if he wanted to, since the doctor told us she might be able to hear us. I opened the space for him to vent, telling him it wasn't his fault that their relationship was strained.

I also told my mom that it was okay if she needed to go, even though it was the last thing I wanted.

Then Hugh, Eden, and I just hung out with her, in her hospital room, day after day during visiting hours. We played Dolly Parton songs and other music that she loved, and talked to her, and when we were done with that for the day we'd watch *Weeds*. We got through almost all eight seasons, talking and laughing together like we hadn't since we were kids. I really hope she *could* hear us, because she would have loved to have heard that.

When I was younger, I often said that I could survive anything except my mother dying. Years later, after I'd healed a lot of my childhood wounds and felt so much stronger, I remember thinking it had been a strange thing to feel. But once it actually happens, seventeen days after she was first admitted to the hospital for surgery, I realize why I did.

I go through the necessary motions to get my siblings through the ordeal, not shedding a single tear while I do, because I know if I start, I won't be able to stop.

OAKLAND, CALIFORNIA
FEBRUARY 2014

As soon as I get back home to California, I fall apart. My mother's death unleashes a ceaseless ache deep within me and opens up a flood of painful memories about living in fear and longing.

I drink copiously to try to drown the pain but to no avail.

I remember my mother telling us that when she'd been a small child, she once became very sick—so sick the doctors and her family thought she might die, and she had to be quarantined in a little shack in the yard, away from her whole family. Besides one brave aunt who wasn't afraid of catching whatever she had—my mother always said, "They never figured out what it was"—only their animals could keep her company.

She told me and my siblings how scared and lonely she'd been during those quarantined days. Then, decades later, she had ended up isolated again, thousands of miles away from her family and stuck with a man who abused not only her, but her children as well.

On Valentine's Day, I see the news online that Sally Gross has passed away. We had wanted to meet, but now we never will. I will never get to thank her in person for the inspiration she gave me. It all feels like a nightmare.

I START SMOKING CIGARETTES and more weed than I knew was possible. I'm trying to drown out the remembrances of the pain that my mother endured throughout her life—and the pain I feel now that I will never see her again.

However, my feelings keep breaking through the fog.

I know there are other ways I could be dealing with this. I could seek support from my friends, for example. But the problem is, I'm too despondent to do that, let alone seek out some kind of grief counseling.

I've been through enough heartache and pain to know that the only way out is through. I also know that all my smoking and drinking are not going to hinder the process, though they often make my bad feelings worse.

I think I'm *supposed* to feel bad right now. I am mourning.

One day, I think about the fact that I wouldn't exist if she hadn't gone through this pain, if she'd been able to leave my dad when she'd wanted to, after my older brother was born—and the thought strikes me in a new way. Her situation always seemed so tragic, but now, through my foggy, tear-filled sorrow, I realize that the real tragedy is for her to have suffered so much for her children, only to have *them* end up being in pain.

I had thought about this loosely in the past, but this time it's a *feeling*, a feeling that sinks deep into the core of my emotional being, so deep that I suspect it has changed me forever—in a good way.

Why the hell did I go through all that if you're just going to sit here, depressed? I can almost hear her saying.

It's true—I shouldn't be depressed. Yet I am, and I'm starting to suspect that it's not just because she's dead.

IN THE MIDST OF my gloom, I receive an e-mail from Marilyn Milos, whom I know of from the human rights world. She's one of the founders of the anticircumcision—or "intactivist"—movement. In 1976, her nursing license was revoked by the state of California because she had mentioned the option of not circumcising a baby boy to his parents, and it drove her to become an activist. Decades later, she not only had her license reinstated, but she got a big award for excellence in nursing from *NurseWeek* magazine. Needless to say, her work had influenced millions of parents and millions of boys' lives.

Marilyn is an inspiration, and I had felt honored when she had reached out via e-mail a few years ago to tell me she was a fan of my work and message. Like Gina and others I've been lucky enough to meet over the years, she's an example of the incredible amount of positive change that you can make if you put the intention out there and dig in and do the work. Just like those folks, she is also inspirationally kind and humble and accomplished.

"Hida, I have so much respect and admiration for the work you're doing," she says when we have a chance to talk over the phone.

"Your courage to represent your community is phenomenal and so impressive."

"Wow, Marilyn, that means a lot coming from you," I say.

"Well, it's all true, so take it in!" she says, laughing.

Then she tells me about this year's Genital Autonomy conference, an international event that she's invited me to in the past. As the name implies, the focus of the conference is ending nonconsensual genital surgeries on infants and minors. In that vein, they've recently started to address IGM.

"It would be really amazing if you could come present at the conference, Hida, and this time we have the money to fly you there, since it's in the US."

I enthusiastically agree.

APRIL 2014

I have a new friend in Oakland, a professor named Marta, whom I sometimes go on hikes with in the redwoods, which I find very comforting. So when she texts to invite me to go up there with her and her dogs, I readily say yes.

After I get there and we start up the incline, I start talking with Marta about my mother.

"She gave up her whole life for us," I say. "She spent all her beautiful years with such a terrible man, and for what? I mean, I barely have a career…"

"But Hida, you've done so much great activism work! You're helping an entire community of people…"

"Yeah, I guess…"

"You guess?"

"I mean, yes, okay, thank you," I say, pausing, "but at the end of the day, I also wish I had a special person by my side as I did the work."

My voice cracks with the words. I feel the tears welling up. So I stop and take in the scenery.

These redwoods are the oldest things around. They have seen so much and they have grown so strong. They can hold my sorrow.

"You know, I do feel great about my activism," I continue, "especially having always been someone who wanted to help make the world a more loving place, you know? I've received so much great feedback from people about how it's helped them, some even telling me that hearing me speak actually helped them decide not to kill themselves—but the thing is, if I'm so wonderful, then why haven't I found someone who wants to spend their life with me?"

Somehow, although I haven't known Marta for long, I open myself completely to her. I let myself cry about what I truly long for in life with more sadness than I ever have before.

"I want love—I want it so bad," I say between sobs, "and I just don't know why it keeps eluding me..."

Marta seems unfazed by the intensity of my words and my tears. She just keeps walking by my side, listening. She is strong like these trees.

My heart feels torn apart, laid bare under the redwood canopy, and completely vulnerable.

I thank Marta profusely for listening, and when I get home, I have the strangest feeling come over me, like an epiphany, in the form of the following thought: *Maybe now that your mom is gone you are finally free to find love.*

It's such a strange thought to have, but somehow I sense in my gut that it's true. I'm still *not* truly happy, and it's not just because my mother's no longer with me. I'm still living in fear and longing when it comes to finding love—fear and longing, just like my mom, just like my childhood.

I've had so many different attitudes and approaches toward

finding a long-term relationship: wanting one, then being depressed when it didn't last, or thinking there was something wrong with me because it didn't, then thinking I was fine without it. But I know underlying all of these attitudes is the basic fear that finding love just won't happen to me.

As I think about this, I hear a voice in my head.

Hida Patricia, how will you ever find love in that manner—as a lesbian?

Oh my god—it's her! It's my mother's voice. Her voice has been stuck in my head all along, even though I thought, in my conscious, intellectual mind, that I'd rejected all that homophobic fear long ago.

I suddenly realize that my connection with my mother had kept her beliefs alive inside of me: her beliefs that I would never be able to find lasting love as a lesbian. *She's dead now though*, I think to myself, *and those beliefs died with her. She doesn't have them anymore, wherever she's evolved to, so I don't have to have them either.*

My mom lived a romantically loveless life, but I don't have to. She wouldn't want me to. I don't want to either.

It occurs to me that I've had it wrong all along, that instead of trying to convince myself that romantic love is a luxury that I don't need, I need to admit how much I want it. And I need to actually believe that I can have it—in the way that I believe the sun will rise tomorrow.

Then, I need to scream my desire out to the Universe as loudly as I can, and as purely as I can, which is exactly what I begin doing.

"I want love, I want love, I want love!" I scream out in the shower.

"Universe, please bring me love! I want it, *bad!*" I scream out on my next solo hike, when only the trees can hear me.

"Thank you in advance, Universe, for bringing me beautiful, long-lasting love. I know you will," I say before falling asleep, night after night after night.

*   *   *

I CONTINUE TO HEAR from intersex people, as well as many of the American organizations that advocate for us, who are using the term *DSD*. The term still has the power to upset me—not like it used to, but enough that I decide I finally have to say something about it again, publicly.

With the exception of the 2007 article that I published after my appearance on *Oprah*, in which I outlined the controversy over the term *DSD*, my approach was to not focus on the term or use it at all, instead promoting *intersex* visibility as much as possible. Then, once I joined OII, opposing DSD was already part of their mission, and I made it part of OII-USA's mission as well when I founded OII-USA. However, over the years, people have pressured me to change this position.

Some intersex people have said things like, "Oh, what's the big deal? It's just a label," which unsurprisingly elicits a long response from me. Others don't like DSD, either, but feel that it's a done deal that we just have to accept—a fait accompli. Still others ask me why I won't use DSD when a large portion of the youth population does. It's hard to know how true this is, because so many of us are not living openly, and many of us don't even know we're intersex until later. However, even if it *is*, I wonder if it's because, just like the youth I had spoken to a couple of years ago, they don't know about the history of DSD.

I understand that people use all sorts of stigmatizing terms and labels they've been taught, but there have always been those—the activists and others committed to equality—who have stepped out to reject prejudice and the language that conveys it. I find it distressing that this isn't happening more yet in the intersex community, that the medical establishment has had such an impact on our lives that some of us *voluntarily* use a label for ourselves, or others like us, that deems us disordered. But I also realize that it's the same as when I've seen women using language that denigrates women—and I've seen it a lot, starting with girls calling their period a "curse" or their vagina a "gash."

I have to remind myself that we're not the only ones who have been hurt so badly that we use words with implicitly negative meanings to describe ourselves. It's actually pretty common. But nevertheless, I feel like I also have to at least *try* to make people understand the importance of language—especially the people who I think, ultimately, feel the same way I do about intersex equality.

So I start talking on the phone and chatting online with some of the activists I know whom I've heard using DSD—or this new label that's also emerged: "intersex/DSD"—to describe community members. I tell them how I feel, even though it's not the most comfortable thing to do, even though I can tell that they think I'm criticizing them and not being inclusive of people who choose to use DSD. I try my best to make it clear that what I'm *really* criticizing and not accepting is the cultural, linguistic devaluation of intersex people.

I use a number of examples, like how useful it was for me, as a kid, to see black people confront racism and turn it on its head by proclaiming that "black is beautiful." I point out that even though not all black people felt that way when the slogan emerged—as the novel *The Bluest Eye* by Toni Morrison reveals—it was still very positive in terms of building black pride. And I talk, of course, about how the concept of "pride" has been used, with such positive results, by LGBT people, whereas the intersex community has often focused on the "shame" that we experience due to medicalization.

I tell them that I believe if we really want to be seen and treated as equal human beings, rather than people impaired by medical issues or birth defects, we have to lose the medical labels and focus. I do so even though I know I risk alienating myself from them, because a lot of the intersex people they know and work with use those labels and have that focus.

After expressing all this, I realize that I need to put these thoughts in writing so that they'll reach a bigger audience. I sit down at my computer, and I don't step away for days.

Editing the piece is the difficult part. For one, I want to pitch it to the *Advocate,* so I have to watch the word count. What's more difficult, though, is saying what I want to say without offending people, which isn't easy, as I'm critiquing the term that some intersex people like to use to describe themselves, and that some of those who advocate for people with intersex traits use to describe us as well.

When I'm finally done, I believe it's the most diplomatic, concisely worded, persuasive piece I've ever written. The *Advocate* editor likes it too. They run it with virtually no edits, not even the title, which they usually change.[1]

The day after it runs, I get an e-mail from an attorney at the Williams Institute, a legal think tank out of UCLA. She tells me she loved my essay and that, after reading it, the institute is rethinking the wording of a document they're creating. It's for statistical data-gathering purposes, and they have been using the language that other advocacy organizations are using, so intersex people are described throughout the document as "people with intersex conditions/DSDs." In the document, intersex people are also defined as individuals who have been "medically diagnosed with a DSD," which doesn't include me or any of the other intersex people like me who have never received a diagnosis.

Fortunately, the Williams Institute is interested in inclusive community representation, so after my input, the definition of *inter-sex* is amended to the following:

> Intersex people are born with (or develop naturally in puberty) genitals, reproductive organs, and/or chromosomal patterns that do not fit standard definitions of male or female (OII-USA, 2013).[2]

Also, we are described as "intersex people," right alongside the medical description of us that other intersex organizations prefer, throughout the entire document. I'm thrilled that as a result of my writing, a part of our community will not be excluded and that we will be referred to as *intersex people* instead of just people with medical conditions.

JUNE 2014

A few weeks later, I go on another hike with Marta. We walk for a bit in silence before she says, "Hey, by the way, are you still interested in dating?"

"Uh, *yeah*. Do you even have to ask?" I say, laughing.

"Okay, good," she continues, "because there's a woman I know that's starting to date again that I thought you might get along with..."

Two weeks after that, I'm on my way to meet this woman, whom I'll call C. We've exchanged a few getting-to-know-you e-mails and I've learned that she's a sign language interpreter (*cool*), she's only a year younger than me (good, I'm tired of the young'uns), she's a fellow Gemini (great, she won't bore me), she's a lesbian (hallelujah), *and* she's a mom (hmm, interesting). What I don't really know is what she looks like, because she's not in most of her Facebook pictures.

I see a woman standing at the corner as I approach the restaurant where we're meeting, and when she turns to face me, I think, *Oooo, pretty.* As the date progresses, I add, *Oooo, smart.* Then later, *Funny!* which is important to me.

Time flies on our date.

"So, I have something to admit," she says during dessert. "I watched a bunch of your videos."

"Oh my god, I guess that's one of the hazards of dating for me now," I say, laughing.

"Oh really?"

"Yeah, everyone looks people up on Google these days, and as you know, there's a lot that comes up for me."

"Is that weird?" she asks.

"Well," I say, giggling, "the funniest thing is that because I've talked about my, um, *anatomy,* I'll just say, as part of my activism, I feel like I kind of have to warn women that I'm not actually *that* big."

We both laugh.

"Really?" she asks.

"Yeah, because one of the last women I slept with actually said afterward, 'You know, you can call yourself whatever you want, but to me you're just a very large woman—I mean, not in your height but, you know...*there.*'"

She laughs. "That's pretty funny!"

"I know! But then I had to explain the whole thing to her—about how it's *not* a big deal to have a big clit, but it does make people like me different enough that doctors turn it into a big deal, and parents end up having their girls' clits cut off. Or cut *down,* I should say."

"Ugh. It's so awful," she says. "I had heard about it, but I honestly had no idea how common it was until watching your videos. It was so upsetting, especially as a mom."

"Oh really?"

"Yeah," she says seriously before pausing.

"Just so you know, I think the work you're doing is *so* important. I'm happy you're doing it and so impressed with your courage. I mean, from what I could tell, there's not a whole lot of people speaking out about this, and just from my own life I know that, even here in the oh-so-queer Bay Area, there are barely any intersex people that are 'out.'"

I'm really happy to hear this. I had told myself that I needed the next person I was with to really understand the significance and personal impact of my activism and my being out, and I wonder now if I've found her.

I can tell neither of us wants the date to end. When it finally has to—because she has to relieve her babysitter—I walk her to her car.

"Well, this is it," she says, stopping by a dark-gray Prius.

We stand looking at each other, the energy flying between our eyes.

I told myself, before meeting her, that I was going to go slow this time. I've had so many mistaken assessments, all because I got hooked on the sexual chemistry. So when I say slow, I mean like *no* contact of any orifices until I've had plenty of time to make sure we're at least somewhat compatible *out* of bed.

"Thanks for today," she says. "I had a really great time."

"Me too," I respond.

Then, before I know it, I lean over and kiss her. I pull away quickly, surprising myself.

"Oh wow—sorry. I told myself I wasn't going to do that yet."

"No need to apologize," she says, "but since you *did*, can I get a real kiss now?"

Butterflies fill my stomach and we kiss again.

Good thing there's a babysitter forcing this date to end. The fact that she has a kid helps us both keep from moving too fast in our relationship.

She had decided to have her son with her lesbian ex, and carried him herself. He's eight now, and she's dated only one other person, recently, since he was born.

"Honestly, I just didn't have a whole lot of extra energy or interest when he was little," she had explained, "and I also really don't like bringing people around to meet him until I have a good sense of who they are and how we're getting along."

This only makes me like her more. I'd seen mothers who put people they date ahead of their own kids and I had no respect for it.

I plan our second date, which involves a ferry ride over to San Francisco and an outdoor meal on the waterfront. After lunch we stroll along the Embarcadero. The date goes so well we decide to throw in a second waterfront meal, back home on the Oakland side.

The place we walk into is packed with a uniquely mixed crowd, which is my favorite thing about Oakland. There are black people and Asian people and Latinos and white people, all from different backgrounds, mingling comfortably together. I feel like it's the only place I've lived that's truly mixed: old white hippies sitting alongside young black teens sitting alongside working-class white families, as well as lesbians and yuppies and artist freaks and tech hipsters of all colors—everyone's all here, co-existing side by side.

My multiplicity can relax here in Oakland and, apparently, on this date. We snag the last spots by one of the outdoor fires.

"There's almost nothing I love more than sitting outside by a fire on a night like this," she says as she sinks into her chair.

It's the beginning of July, and unlike San Francisco, Oakland isn't as cold in the summer. The fire is all we need to keep toasty in our short sleeves, and our conversation dances back and forth easily, like the flames.

The following week I give a presentation at a graduate course in gender studies at UC Berkeley, and I speak with several of the students afterward, many of whom are older and close to my age. One of them—who is potentially the most adorable little gender-queer person I've ever met (and when I say little, I mean like five feet tall)—tells me that they work for a prominent trans organization I've heard of.

"We really liked what you had to say," they say, gesturing to a tall woman standing by her seat who had come out as trans during the Q & A.

She seems to be on an important phone call, but she sees us and nods.

"I'd love for us to have coffee or something sometime to discuss more, since we're all local…"

Their friend walks over, nodding in agreement.

I meet her about a month later for breakfast at a coffee shop in Berkeley, right near campus.

She reminds me of queer folks I used to know in New York, and our conversation flows easily. I find out that she's an attorney who lives with her partner and kids.

So, she's smart, beautiful, gainfully employed, and she lives here, I think, *where she can come out as trans if she wants to and not fear for her life.*

I'm so happy for her.

We talk about possibly working together in some capacity, though we both have a lot going on.

"Hida, in case we don't see each other for a while," she says as we stand up to leave, "I just want you to know that I think DSD was a travesty. Just terrible. I'm so sorry your community had to experience that."

"Thank you," I say, squeezing her arm to emphasize how much I mean it. "I appreciate it."

As I ride home I think about just how much overlap there is between our communities. Regardless of our specifics, what we have in common is that we are often considered nonnormative in terms of our gender. Obviously, if a trans person appears to be a perfectly "normal" man or woman, this isn't the case, but if that person comes out as trans, then their gender no longer falls under the "normative" description.

The same is true for intersex people. While we can hide under the semblance of being regular men or women, if we're somehow discovered to be intersex, that goes out the window. No matter how typically, or attractively, male or female we appear, we're still assessed to be something else.

I remember how much I'd bonded with trans folks in the early days of my coming out as intersex. They were my buddies in gender variance, especially because a lot of them hadn't fully transitioned (although most did later).

In those days, most of us inhabited this space where our outer appearance didn't match what was under our clothes. Or, in my case, if I was looking very in between, it *did* match, but that in and of itself was considered weird!

I think about how great it would have been if those connections between trans and intersex people had been a part of my activist scene early on, as well as my social life, if Brittney hadn't steered the ship away from that direction. Sadly, today, there are some prominent activists who have been doing the same thing, distancing themselves from association with the trans community. In addition, they are also claiming and *emphasizing*, without evidence, that intersex people mostly identify as men or women.

I think these kinds of claims are problematic because the only reason to assert that most intersex people identify mainly as men or women is to reassure the general public that we are still "normal," which positions genderqueer, or nonbinary, people as *abnormal*. Worse, asserting that most intersex individuals are gender normative obfuscates and marginalizes the existence of those of us who are gender nonconforming or nonbinary—who feel like both genders or, alternatively, neither. When people do this, it can also send the message that there's something undesirable about being nonbinary, and because this gender identity falls under the transgender umbrella, these assertions also border on being transphobic.

The term *transphobia* wasn't used much when I first came out as intersex because the trans movement was still relatively new then, so I wasn't used to thinking about things as being "transphobic," but now that I know the definition, I see that it applies perfectly to the way I was often viewed and treated by other people. Transphobia is basically negative attitudes toward people who don't conform to society's gender expectations, which is what I experienced from Brittney, but because the "genderqueer" and "nonbinary" communities didn't exist yet, I didn't consider myself trans and didn't realize I was experiencing transphobia. I just felt like I was different from most of the folks around me, and I couldn't understand why I was being devalued because of it. I had felt the same way in elementary school when my white classmates would call me a monkey because of my dark hair and eyes and darker skin tone.

Just as it would have helped me as a child to know that I was a target of racism, it would have helped me later, as an adult, to know that I was a target of transphobia. It would have made me feel less alone to know that others, many others, were being mistreated in the same way I was. However, I'm still glad to realize it now so that I can point it out if and when I see it happening to others.

In terms of some intersex people not wanting to be part of the LGBTQIA community (which now includes asexual people too) because we're not all gay, I'll just say that neither are all trans people, but it didn't stop them from being included. There was resistance at first—a lot of it—from both the trans and the LGB communities, but people ultimately realized that inclusion made sense because of how much crossover there is, and I think the same thing is true of intersex people. After all, lesbians and gay men have been portrayed as not being "real men" or "real women" for centuries and discriminated against because of that reason, and intersex people are not real men or women by the standard definitions.

Additionally, although some intersex people say that being "lumped into" the LGBT community will make our issues less visible, that didn't happen to trans people. Their distinctive medical issues involving getting access to hormones and surgeries didn't get lost when they joined the lesbian, gay, and bisexual movement. In fact, they got a lot more visibility and support around these issues.

So why would things have to be so different for us? At the end of the day, we're also heavily affected by gender and sexuality issues. In fact, I often say that intersex people are on the frontlines of homophobia and transphobia because if our differences are detected at birth, we're often mutilated in an effort to ensure that we'll grow up to be gender normative and heterosexual—efforts that are misguided, because lots of us who *were* mutilated still grow up to be L, G, B, or T adults.

BOULDER, COLORADO
JULY 2014

Soon, it's time for the Genital Autonomy conference. Dana Zzyym, a fellow intersex activist who works with me at OII-USA, will be attending, and I'm excited we'll finally get to meet in person.

Dana's not only intersex but also, like me, genderqueer or nonbinary. Dana self-describes using the pronouns *they/them/their*, which have become the most popularly used pronouns among genderqueer and nonbinary folks these days. Although I toyed with *ze* back in the nineties, I've recently begun using *s/he* and *he/r*. I consider these pronouns an homage to my female upbringing and my feminist commitment, though I'm not sure how long they'll last.

This is primarily due to the fact that because my gender identity has the potential to change, choosing a nonbinary pronoun, and asking everyone to say it in reference to me forever, feels like more of a commitment than I want to make—especially because at different times or sometimes all at once, I've felt like every pronoun.

My ideal solution would be a pronoun that doesn't gender people at all: like *per* for *person*. It might sound weird to some, but there are already languages that don't gender people with their pronouns (Cantonese, Mandarin, and Japanese, for example). Also, in terms of practicality, it would immediately eliminate hurt and confusion about using the "wrong" pronoun for someone.

I can't take credit for *per* though. It comes from the 1976 novel *Woman on the Edge of Time* by Marge Piercy, and I've heard that there is someone in Wisconsin who is using it. So we'll see.

There's an immediate sense of understanding when Dana and I finally meet. It often happens when intersex people come together. With Dana, however, there's also an immediate added comfort because we are both nonbinary.

Dana is neither male nor female and *feels* like neither a man nor a woman, and it's amazing being able to connect with them because of this. It's been years now since I came to realize that, although I know what it's like to live as a woman *and* as a man, in the core of my being I am neither. I am a herm, just like Dana. I'm a hermaphrodyke, to be exact: a herm who was raised as a woman and loves women.

I know from the social media posts, blogs, and articles I read, and from people who contact me, that there are many intersex folks who have nonbinary gender identities but aren't in the activism scene. Well, I can guess the reason. They probably feel unwelcome, just as I did, because the US intersex activism scene has been dominated by intersex folks who identify as men or women and make claims about "most intersex people being men or women" that make us nonbinary folks feel unwelcome.

These people have often been critical of those who feel, like I do, that "herm" is a gender. They are hugely resistant to intersex people speaking about herm or intersex gender identity. I find it kind of ironic because they have no problem speaking about their own gender identity as men or women. Also, I think if they don't want being intersex to be reduced to being a "medical condition," they should welcome our speaking about it as a gender, equal to "man" and "woman."

Dana shares how, like me, they have felt further marginalized by all this focus on intersex people growing up to be men or women.

"It's crazy, isn't it?" I say. "Because doctors are trying to make us into men or women, and now you have these adult intersex activists doing the same thing, linguistically."

"And how do they know how we all identify anyway?" Dana adds. "Half the people who have talked to me about it are deeply in the closet, so nobody knows *how* they identify."

"Yeah, it's true—there are no stats to back those claims, but even if there were, should it matter? I mean, most gay men are not drag queens, but some are, and leaders in the gay civil rights movement don't make a point to say, 'Most gay men do not cross-dress,' in their human rights work. They don't focus on distancing themselves from what mainstream society looks down upon. In fact, they do the opposite—they *confront* the fact that society looks down upon these things!"

"Yeah, and we know that has never been the approach in the intersex movement here, unfortunately. That's why I've always felt more comfortable in queer settings, to be honest."

"I know—me too! Except for when all the SF lesbians were trying to make me choose between being butch or femme," I share.

We both laugh. And we continue enjoying each other's company for days. It's wonderful.

In fact, there are so many wonderful people to meet at the conference in addition to Dana that I don't spend as much time preparing for my presentation as I want to. Then, when the day of my presentation arrives, I'm nervous—so nervous that I have to find a quiet room where I can sit by myself and breathe deeply in order to calm my palpitating heart.

Geez, Hida, you're nervous in front of this crowd? They're so nice! I think. But I guess it will always be this way, until the day when being intersex is just as accepted as being gay or lesbian is today. By that I mean so accepted that being intersex is no longer deemed a disorder, the medical efforts to "fix us" have ended, *and* there are enough of us who are "out" that *everyone* knows someone in their life who is intersex.

Despite my nerves, part of me knows that the times when I've been overprepared for my presentations, I didn't feel like they had as powerful an impact on the people who were listening.

So I write my key points down on index cards and meditate. I say my prayer to the Universe to use me as a vessel for the community's highest good, and I head out there.

As I face the crowd, I take one look down at the first point on my top card, and I never look down again.

I speak from the heart, and judging by how I feel as well as the looks on people's faces, I think it's one of my best presentations ever. At one point, when sharing a little about my experience, I end up saying that I am what doctors are trying to get rid of. It's powerful because it's so disconcertingly true—they are trying to get rid of intersex bodies—especially the *visibly* intersex ones.

I also talk about the fallacy that intersex people who haven't been "medically treated" won't be able to find love, and I use Jim Costich as an example. He's another intersex activist who appears in the documentary *Intersexion* with me. It came out two years ago and was directed by a New Zealand filmmaker who had previous films screened at the Cannes Film Festival. The film features Sally, Gina, Howard, and a host of other amazing intersex people. I think it's the best intersex documentary yet, and it's being shown twice here at the conference.

Like me, Jim was never subjected to IGM, and as he says in the film, he's "never been single for any appreciable amount of time." It's a fact that's even more noteworthy when you consider that he's a man, socially, and that there's much more stigma against men having undersized penises than there is against women having oversized clitorises.

I also use myself as an example for this point about our not finding love, and in the process I hear the words "currently, the woman I'm falling in love with…" come out of my mouth.

I'm stunned that I say it, since we've been dating for only about a month, and I'm scared for a moment that I'll live to regret it, that in a few months I'll have to tell Dana and Marilyn that I was wrong. But just as quickly as I said it, I banish the feeling away.

I have finally learned that this kind of fear—the unwarranted kind that appears simply because we've been taught that it should—only serves to chase our dreams away.

During the Q & A that is held after I've finished my presentation, a nurse asks me what she can do to help promote visibility and acceptance of intersex people. I'm about to give my usual answer about sharing educational resources and websites, but then I stop myself and say something that had never occurred to me before. I tell her and the large audience in front of me that if they really want to spread awareness and visibility, they can begin right this very moment by saying "male, female, *and* intersex" or "man, woman, *and* intersex person" every time the topic of sex or gender comes up.

I tell them that this small act alone will have a huge impact, because it will help eliminate society's denial of our existence. I remind them that every time we say "man or woman" or "male or female," we are participating in the centuries-old lie that intersex people don't exist. And I ask them to please stop participating in it, since it is this very lie that makes attempts to surgically eradicate us so much easier.

It seems amazing to me that I have never thought to ask people to do this before or seen anyone else do it. I guess it's because doing so is kind of a radical act, despite the fact that it's just acknowledging a scientific truth. I mean, if everyone suddenly started saying "men, women, and intersex individuals," it would quickly subvert the binary sex and gender system and make it easier for intersex people to be accepted and live as who we are.

This crowd is so great that several people come up to me after the Q & A and tell me that they're going to start doing it—and these are doctors, nurses, midwives, and other people whose professions deal with childbirth, so they'll have more than the usual opportunity to do so.

It is an incredible feeling, truly, to be so nervous and so exposed and then have it go so well. To know that my words will help intersex people of the future is why I do this, and I'm elated and grateful.

On the final day of the conference, Dana and I spend hours together, during which they tell me what an interesting but difficult life they have had. They were raised male and ended up becoming a navy officer. They also had relationships with heterosexual women, one who even told them that she preferred smaller-than-usual penises, as she'd never enjoyed the feeling of average to large ones.

The old saying "There's someone for everyone" really is true. It reminds me, yet again, how misguided the common medical opinions about androgynous genitalia are.

Sadly, however, the other procedures that were performed on Dana as a child to make them more male, unbeknownst to them, had made it so that having intercourse hurt. It hurt so bad that they ultimately had to seek medical help for the pain. In the process, they discovered that they had been born intersex, not male.

"Wow, what a mess. I'm so sorry," I say.

"Well, it feels like a lifetime ago at this point, but thanks."

Interestingly, Dana had already legally changed their name from their original masculine one to their current gender-neutral one before they discovered they were intersex.

"Part of me had never really felt male or like a man, even though I played the part well," they tell me. "In retrospect, I see that changing my name to Dana was part of my beginning to affirm who I really am."

The doctors recommended follow-up surgeries to ease the pain, and those left Dana's anatomy looking more female than male. So at that point, Dana legally changed their gender to female and attempted to live as a woman, but that didn't feel right either.

"I just finally came to a point where I realized that all my life I'd been trying to be things that I'm not—first, living as a man, then as a woman—when the reality is that I was intersex all along, and I should've just been left that way."

"God, it's amazing how much these so-called attempts to 'help us' just end up fucking with us ..." I marvel, yet again.

"Well, since then I've decided that I can't undo what they did, but I *can* be who I am *now*. That's why I want legal recognition as an intersex person."

Dana tells me that they want to get a passport that identifies their gender as nonbinary. I share that I had wanted to try to do the same thing in 2012, but after I looked into it I refrained because I would have needed to send in my existing passport, and that would have interfered with my going to the intersex forum in Stockholm.

"Well, for me it's different because I never had a passport," they say.

Dana didn't need a passport to travel as a navy officer, and they hadn't bothered to get one since then. So unlike the process I would have to go through, Dana's wouldn't be considered a change of gender.

"Oh, that's interesting ..." I say.

"Not only that, but my birth certificate says 'sex unknown,' and I have tons of letters from my VA doctors that state I am intersex."

"And the VA is one of the few US government agencies that acknowledges intersex people!" I exclaim.

I know that from when I researched the X passport issue in Australia, and the lightbulbs begin going off in my head. If Dana has a birth certificate that says "sex unknown" and letters from a government agency that verify they are intersex, then Dana has two pieces of valid ID that confirm they are neither male nor female, which means that—unlike me and almost all other intersex Americans— they actually have a very good case for getting a government ID that acknowledges their gender as nonbinary.

I was already impressed by Dana's strength and resilience at being able to be openly intersex and nonbinary after all they'd been through, but now they seem like my hero. They remind me of Gina from Australia, using their strength, intelligence, loving heart, and perseverance to not only survive their abuses but pave the way for others. I tell Dana that I will be happy to support them however possible in attaining their gender recognition.

OAKLAND, CALIFORNIA
AUGUST 2014

I've been noticing that the term *cisgender* has gained popularity, but I find it disappointing and even problematic. I first started hearing it in 2009, and it was used to refer to people whose gender identity corresponded with their birth sex. I had also heard that the term was initially created to provide an alternative to saying "non-trans" or "the opposite of trans."

The problematic part is that I'm a nonbinary person—an identity that falls under the transgender umbrella—yet I'm *also* cisgender because I was born intersex and my gender identity matches that. Being both trans and cis isn't supposed to be possible, but because the term *cisgender* is based on a binary sex system, it is.

Around 2011, I began to hear a different definition of *cisgender*, and it stated that *cisgender* referred to people whose gender identity matched the sex they were "assigned at birth." However, I was not assigned "intersex" at birth. Nobody in the US, or in most parts of the world, is. So according to *this* definition, nonbinary, intersex people like me are no longer cisgender. I think the intended goal of this revised definition was for the term to refer only to gender-*conforming* people, but otherwise it's still problematic to me. It's complicated, but in short, it's because in most of the world a sex assigned at birth can only be "male" or "female." Thus, using the phrase "sex assigned at birth" excludes "intersex" and consequently furthers intersex invisibility.

Additionally, in a society that tends to forget intersex people exist, the practice of defining those who don't identify as the sex they were assigned at birth (i.e., male or female) as *trans* implies that being intersex is something we grow up to be, rather than the way we are born. Doctors have been cutting us up for decades, but despite all of this prejudice, I like my nonbinary intersex body and the fact that I have a gender identity to "match" it, so it upsets me that cisgender rhetoric is trying to take this ability to have a mind/body match away from me and render it something that only typical males or females can experience.

The issue gets so under my skin that I take the time to write an essay about it, and I am thrilled when several gender studies professors tell me they like my ideas so much that they're teaching them.[3]

I support trans equality and rights, but the use of the term *cisgender* reinforces the very binary system that works against *my* equality as a nonbinary intersex person, and I don't think it has to be that way. I believe we can come up with terms that equally acknowledge and support us all.

SEPTEMBER 2014

Dana begins the process of applying for a passport and requesting an X as their gender marker. While at first glance the letter *I* would seem to make more sense, an X is actually more accurate because it stands for sex unspecified, which encompasses both intersex and genderqueer people who don't define themselves as male or female, or man or woman.

As Dana goes through the process, we continue to speak.

"No matter how it's done," Dana says during one of our conversations, "having some kind of legal recognition of intersex people—as a class of people—is critical for attaining legal protections in the long run, because the way the law works here, if you're not written into it, then by default, you're written out. You're not covered, and that's what's been happening to us all along. People say that these surgeries are a human rights abuse of intersex people, but doctors just turn around and say, 'Well, he's a man actually, with a disorder of blah, blah, blah.' It's like they know that we're there, but then they define us as men or women, so in the eyes of the law, we disappear."

I don't even have to tell Dana about Sally's and Gina's work; Dana has already studied the issue and totally gets it. I start writing letters of support for them, which I'm well suited to do because I learned all about the history and mechanics of the X from Gina, when I wrote my article about Australia's legislation on the passport X.

Meanwhile, MTV announces that a character on one of their television shows, *Faking It*, is going to come out as intersex in the season two premiere. I almost can't believe it: the first intersex character ever on a television show! I watch with bated breath and am pleased to see that they handle it very respectfully.

On the heels of the show's season two premiere, MTV also announces that they've released a video in conjunction with the nonprofit advocacy organization that they consulted about the character.[4] Before I even get to watch it though, I get some messages from intersex people telling me that they're upset the video says that "intersex or DSD" are the proper terms to use to describe us.

I watch it as soon as I have a chance. It features the actress who plays the intersex character and a young intersex woman, Emily Quinn. She's the first intersex person in a long time to publicly acknowledge that, like me, she still has her intersex traits intact (in her case, her undescended testes), and she speaks proudly and openly about it. It's wonderful.

I am loving the video until it gets to the part about labels. She says that some words aren't used to describe us anymore, and I imagine that she is referring to *hermaphrodite*, though I know that a lot of intersex people, including me and a whole slew of prominent intersex activists, *do* use the word—or the shortened version of it, *herm*—to describe ourselves.

I find it upsetting to hear, "The proper terms are *intersex* or *differences of sex development / DSD.*" While I think it's good that some intersex advocates and groups have started using the word *differences* instead of the word *disorders* to represent the first *D* in DSD, I still don't like hearing myself referred to as a medical diagnosis in this kind of nonmedical video. And I also find it problematic to state that "proper terms" exist for intersex people when our community is still very much debating this issue.

NOVEMBER 2014

I see the headline "AAMC Releases Medical Education Guidelines to Improve Health Care for People Who Are LGBT, Gender Nonconforming, or Born with Differences of Sex Development" on the Association of American Medical Colleges website. The article is about their new resource, which is "the first guidelines for training physicians to care for people who are lesbian, gay, bisexual, transgender (LGBT), gender nonconforming, or born with differences of sex development (DSD)."[5] As soon as I read this, I feel that disturbed, queasy feeling in my gut that I have often felt as an activist.

I click on a link in the article to the AAMC guidelines themselves and see that one of the editors of the new resource is the same academic who supported the pathologizing approach reflected in the term *DSD* and wrote the article criticizing Australia's passport

X. Even though it's her, I'm nevertheless shocked to see the words "Born with DSD" on the cover of the resource. Then I'm angered, because I know that the author knows there is a global intersex community that opposes DSD pathologization. I'd bet money that her response would be, "But I'm using *differences* of sex development, so the label is no longer pathologizing."

However, naming us by our differences from the norm doesn't foster equality. For example, how would it sound if LGBT people were referred to that way in the resource, making it the "Guidelines to Improve Health Care for People Who Have Gender Dysphoria, Atypical Gender Expression, or Are Born with Differences of Sexual Orientation, DSO"? It sounds terrible, because LGBT communities don't use diagnostic language to describe themselves; they use the social labels of their choice.

Describing us by our medical diagnosis in an LGBT resource makes this feel much worse. It's one thing for intersex people who don't want to be the *I* in LGBTQIA to call themselves people with DSDs, but everyone knows that when we *are* included in the community, it's as the *I*. So why are medical students being taught to call us DSDs in a resource that aims to improve health care for LGBTQIA people?

I find it maddening…and depressing. But how can I fight it when even well-known, well-funded advocacy organizations are using DSD and thus sending the message that we should be labeled with this term? It's too much to even think about for one second longer, much less do anything about, and my despondency makes me feel even worse.

DESPITE OUR EFFORTS, DANA'S application for a passport with an X gender marker is ultimately rejected. Dana, however, is not deterred. They take the information that the State Department sent them and the letters from OII-USA that I wrote in support and send them off with their own cover letters to all the legal and human rights organizations that they think will listen.

FEBRUARY 2015

"Hida, I have some good news," Dana says to me over the phone a few months later.

"Yeah?"

"I just got an e-mail from Lambda Legal telling me they're interested in taking my case."

Lambda Legal is the country's oldest, largest LGBT civil rights organization, and they have an excellent reputation and track record.

"Oh my god, that's fantastic! That's so awesome!"

I realize that I'm screaming.

"Okay, don't have a cow just yet. They only said they're thinking about it," Dana says.

"I know, I know, but it's still such good news! And I have a good feeling about it."

"Well, they said they need to talk to me, and maybe you too, because they liked your letter. Can I give them your info?"

"Of course!" I say.

Many fascinating, complicated phone conversations later, my good feeling turns out to be true. Lambda Legal is taking the case.

Just like I never thought I'd live to see marriage equality when I was growing up, I honestly never thought I'd live to see this day when I first started speaking about the need for intersex equality nearly twenty years ago. In fact, the best I hoped for was that, before I died, everyone would at least know who and what intersex people are. Now I see that they will not only know that, but we will be publicly recognized as equal citizens under the law. In fact, in South Africa and Australia we already are.

I know that no matter what happens with Dana's case, the ball is now rolling and it cannot be stopped. Now it's just a matter of time before the US government and all governments recognize intersex people's existence and equal citizenship. Once they do, discrimination against us will cease to be legal, and the injustices we're subjected to will begin becoming relics of an ignorant, hateful past.

MARCH 2015

I haven't had much contact with a lot of the folks in the greater intersex activism community since my mom died, because I've felt so hurt by the way some of them have treated me. It's less than a handful, but they're people that I deal with quite a bit, and I'm just too sensitive to handle it, because when they say things like that I should step down because I haven't been doing enough—or worse—it hurts. A lot. As far as I've seen, other activists aren't asked to prove what they've been accomplishing, but rather, are supported just for being willing to be "out" as intersex, and I wish I were treated the same—especially since I've tried to do a lot for this cause.

"Do you think it could have something to do with the fact that you weren't subjected to all those surgeries?" my friend Kelly asks me when I tell her about it over the phone.

She was my roommate for a few years in San Francisco, and we chat regularly to keep in touch.

"Maybe," I respond.

"Think about it," she continues. "There they are, unable to date or have orgasms because they've been mutilated, and then here you are, happy and talking about how having a big clit is a good thing for one's sex life."

She's referencing something I said in my CNN essay and in the documentary *Intersexion*.

"Yeah, you may be right," I reply.

I had realized way back in '96, at the intersex conference I went to in Northern California, that there were certain things I shouldn't talk about in front of folks who had been subjected to surgeries, unless I wanted to hurt their feelings. However, I had also been asked by the leader of those folks to speak publicly about the fact that I was happy I *wasn't* subjected to nonconsensual genital surgeries, and doing that entailed talking about liking my body and my sex life. It had basically become unavoidable, but I had decided it was okay because ultimately, if I'm saying that intersex people shouldn't be subjected to IGM, then it's really helpful if I'm actually happy that I wasn't. I mean, if I were miserable and talking about feeling ashamed of my body, it would only give doctors more reason to recommend nonconsensual genital surgeries.

Still, I think Kelly's probably onto something. I think even though it's good for the movement to have people like me speaking out, my experience of being intersex is so radically different from people who were subjected to IGM that it's probably a little painful for them to hear about it. It probably also makes it difficult for them to relate to me as a fellow intersex person.

I'm touched, however, that *other* people can relate to my message, like the group of academics that have invited me to give a keynote presentation this month at a conference in Madrid—X Workshop Internacional Ciencia, Technologia Y Genero: Visiones Y Versiones de Las Technologias Biomedicas—which roughly translates to the Tenth International Conference on Women, Technology and Gender: Visions and Versions of Biomedical Technologies. They tell me that they've noticed my essays, which have grown in number by now, and that they were thrilled to find an American intersex activist with my perspectives. I'm deeply honored, as previous keynote speakers have included the likes of

Thomas Laqueur, author of the seminal gender studies book *Making Sex*, which we'd read for one of my courses at Berkeley.

I'm also even more excited because C is coming with me. It's the first time in over a decade that I'm taking an international trip with a girlfriend, and it goes beautifully. I even give my presentation entirely in Spanish, which is special since it was the language of my youth but the one I'd had to separate from as an LGBTI person. I speak straight from the heart, and several people tell me it almost had them in tears.

C and I both fall in love with Madrid, and then Barcelona—where they've scheduled two more presentations for me—as well as everyone we meet. We also fall even more deeply in love with each other.

When we get back, I see something fantastic. One of the young intersex activists that I spoke with months ago about the dangers of using DSD has made a video, with several other young activists, talking about what it's like being intersex.[6] All of the activists in the video are fantastic, and perhaps best of all, they don't use DSD once! They refer to themselves exclusively as intersex, even though they're all involved with one of the organizations that still uses DSD. It's wonderful to witness, after nine years of being called a "disorder" by many of my own people. I am *so* grateful, and I circulate it immediately.

APRIL 2015

"Malta Becomes First Country to Outlaw Surgery on Intersex Babies," the headline reads.[7]

Holy shit! I think.

I learn that one of the nonintersex people who had organized the intersex forum in Malta, a fantastic ally named Silvan Agius, was instrumental in drafting the new legislation, the Gender Identity,

Gender Expression and Sex Characteristics (GIGESC) Act. It's the best LGBTQIA legislation the world has ever seen, not only criminalizing IGM but also recognizing and protecting trans and intersex persons in all spheres of life. Apparently, learning about intersex human rights abuses when she visited the forum had influenced Helena Dalli, the Maltese minister for social dialogue, consumer affairs, and civil liberties, and the country is small enough that it's easier to get federal legislation like this passed.

Wow. I never thought I'd see the day. I exhale a long sigh of relief and then breathe in a combination of gratitude and joy, the likes of which I've never felt before.

A FEW MONTHS LATER, I publish my first essay in a medical journal, the *Narrative Inquiry in Bioethics* (NIB). It's an issue aimed at giving doctors insight by featuring intersex people's narratives about their experiences with health care. As always, I share how happy I am that I was not subjected to nonconsensual surgeries or hormone therapy, but also the fact that most of my doctors had provided excellent care simply by treating me as they would any other patient. My hope is that doing so will inspire more doctors to do the same.

The essay is titled "Promoting Health and Social Progress by Accepting and Depathologizing Benign Intersex Traits," and it gives me the opportunity to share my views on the stigmatizing title of the AAMC's resource on improved health care for LGBT people and those "born with DSD." I explain that

> I think it's hurtful to our already marginalized community to be referred to as people with medical conditions when this is not how other communities are labeled. For example, the diagnostic term for being transgender is "gender dysphoria,"

but transgender people are not called "individuals with gender dysphoria."[8]

Perhaps best of all, I get to remind doctors that they are in a unique position to help make things better for intersex people by treating us with the same respect for bodily autonomy and self-determination that all humans are afforded. I truly hope that by reaching out in a nonconfrontational, respectful manner, some of the doctors who read the issue will be inspired to do so.

DENVER, COLORADO
OCTOBER 2015

Lambda Legal holds a press event to announce that they've just filed Dana's case, and it's held—beautifully, perfectly—on Intersex Awareness Day, October 26, 2015. C and I both fly to Denver to be there for it with Dana, who wears a pink tie with the word *queer* written subtly down the side for the event.

C likes Dana just as much as I do, and we all get on fantastically, so on top of being a breathtakingly historic experience, it's also actually fun. After hours of conversations over the phone, I meet Paul Castillo, the attorney who's representing Dana, for the first time, and his ethics and intellect are even more impressive in person.

I can't say what will happen, but I *can* say that I never thought we'd be this far along in our battle. However, two decades of activism have revealed that our abuses will not go away simply by pointing them out to our abusers. As Frederick Douglass so brilliantly noted one hundred and sixty years ago,

> Those who profess to favor freedom and yet deprecate agitation
> are men who want crops without plowing up the ground; they
> want rain without thunder and lightning. They want the ocean

without the awful roar of its many waters. This struggle may be a moral one, or it may be a physical one, and it may be both moral and physical, but it must be a struggle. Power concedes nothing without a demand. It never did and it never will.[9]

So it is for intersex people. We are going to have to do more than politely point out the injustices we suffer, and I'm thrilled that people like the Crawfords—the parents who are suing the state of South Carolina and the doctors who operated on their son—and Dana have had the conviction to take it to the courts.

So it has been, too, for me personally in my journey as an intersex activist. I never imagined that it would involve so many emotionally difficult experiences, sometimes at the hands of my own community members, but I know now that each tear I have shed has been an essential component of the river of progress that I have contributed to.

SANTA FE, NEW MEXICO
DECEMBER 2015

"Hida, do you want another cup of coffee?" I hear C's mother yell from the kitchen.

"Sure," I answer, getting up and coming in through the sliding glass doors.

"I thought you might," she says with a mischievous twinkle in her eye. "I'm going to have one too."

She is fun, C's mother, in the way that I think my own mother would have been if she hadn't been so weighted down by her marriage and her religion.

I'm here celebrating the Christmas holiday with C and her parents, who are just as lovely as she is. They're warm, funny, intelligent, caring people who are completely accepting of her being a lesbian.

Not only that, they know I'm intersex and want to hear all about my activism. They can tell their daughter's happy with me and they welcome me as part of the family—the loving, supportive family I didn't have.

After decades of being led by a childhood wound that I had ignored, denied, or only partially acknowledged, being led straight into romantic relationships that were never going to work, or into destroying the ones that *could*, I finally found the guts to dig all the way in and clean that wound out—and the patience to let it take its time to heal. I think that's why I'm finally here, and I hope that my mother can see me; see this.

I also wish I could tell her that one of my essays is getting published in a college textbook by Oxford University Press. She'd be so proud, and happy, that I'm finally getting somewhere, career-wise. And me, I'm thrilled to know that so many young people will be reading it, because it's all about how to discuss intersex people in a way that fosters acceptance.

Recently, I've also been thinking about my father more often. Namely, I've been thinking about him like I had at the hearing for intersex rights in 2004, when I explained how I had benefited in certain ways from his praise. Although he was controlling and had an ultimately selfish desire for his children to be successful, acknowledging that my father tried to instill arguably positive, strong values in his children makes me appreciate the complex people, relationships, and situations in my life. In fact, I think it's allowed me to have less adversarial, and more peaceful, relationships with other complex people and situations I encounter in life—and even with myself.

Now, nothing is leading me but my own desire, and it's been leading me to peace and joy. I don't talk about my relationship with C as much as I have talked about my love life in the past, because like all beautiful things, our love is beyond description. It just *is*. I don't have to say a word, because there's nothing to figure out or process about it. I just have to sit back and enjoy it, like the sun shining on my face on C's mother's patio.

I guess I just needed to believe that this could exist, and invite it in. I guess wounds really can heal after all. People can restore and love themselves, despite how different they are or how much they've been hurt and disparaged, and I wish it for everyone.

Being intersex hasn't always been easy, but it's been my greatest teacher, and the lessons have been worth every tortured moment. Now, for me, being intersex is the fusion, the effortless union, of yin and yang. It is a space all its own, where something revolutionarily loving, balanced, and harmonious is created. It actually exists, and it's where I live.

EPILOGUE

As I WRITE THIS, not everything is perfect in my life. On my trip to Santa Fe, for instance, I had a particularly uncomfortable experience with TSA agents at the airport.

"Hold on a moment," an agent said after I passed through the security checkpoint scanner. She stopped me to run a handheld scanner device back and forth over my pelvis.

Many people are aware that trans folks are often harassed when they have to go through security checkpoints, but they may not know how it works, or that intersex people are subjected to the same treatment—*if* we have intact, ambiguous genitalia. I think of it as harassment due to "traveling while trans or intersex": whenever someone approaches the scanning machine, the agents watching have to press a blue or pink button depending on what gender they assume the person to be, and problems arise for that person if their genitals, as seen through the scanner, don't match the genitals they "should have" based on the gender selected for them. For example, if a transwoman goes through the machine and the agent presses the pink button, but the genital scan reveals that she has a penis, she is deemed an "anomaly" that needs to be investigated. The same can happen the other way around for a transman when the scanner does *not* reveal a penis.

In my case, whether I'm noted as pink or blue when I go through the scanner, my genitals are flagged as a problem.

At the airport, when it happened this last time, I told the TSA agents around me that I'm intersex and have ambiguous genitals, but they didn't seem to have a clue what I was talking about. They only suggested I head with them to a private room, but I told them to do whatever they had to do right there. A female guard then pressed her fingers all around my crotch area in order to clear me—with C's son witnessing it and wondering why my privates were being publicly touched this way, when I hadn't done a thing and since that's not something people are supposed to do.

Once I returned from my trip, I shared my unpleasant experience at the airport with the lawyer at Lambda Legal who's representing Dana in their passport lawsuit.

"We just contacted the TSA about it recently," he told me, "and we included intersex as well as trans people in our complaint."

I'm grateful that they're on it, but it's just another reminder to me that intersex people's problems will not be over as soon as we ban nonconsensual genital surgeries. It's also a reminder of how much trans and intersex people's issues can overlap, much like the passing of the horrible bathroom laws in North Carolina and elsewhere.

These laws were clearly targeted at trans people but can impact intersex people just as badly. Recently, a new intersex friend of mine shared, for example, that they'd been so impacted by these laws that they had to legally change their gender. At birth, they were assigned the female gender because they have XX chromosomes and ovaries, and grew up looking female due to the feminizing hormones they were given to counteract their high testosterone levels. However, as an adult, the hormonal drugs started making them sick—so sick they ended up in a wheelchair. They finally decided to stop taking them, and once they did, they got healthy, they didn't need the wheelchair anymore, *and* they began looking like a man.

Their body was still considered biologically female though, so according to their state's bathroom laws, they were supposed to use women's restrooms. However, when they did, they looked like a man using the women's restroom, which is illegal according to that same law. So they went through the process to legally change their gender to male because it was the only way they could use a public restroom without being harassed and/or accused of breaking the law.

The TSA issue as well as the new antitrans and intersex bathroom laws have made me more aware than ever that I need to continue educating others about intersex people and the fact that you don't have to have been subjected to IGM in order to be discriminated against because you're intersex. In fact, in some cases, like mine and others', we face discrimination *because* we weren't medically "normalized" to fit into the male or female mold—and it's imperative that this be addressed, because there will only be more of us as the practice of IGM decreases.

My new intersex friend also tells me that, because they are gender nonconforming, they've connected more easily with the trans than the intersex community. I can certainly relate. I felt much more accepted and welcomed by the trans community, too, when I first came out as intersex. Today I realize that people can be *both* trans and intersex, and in fact I have several friends who are, but when I first starting working to end IGM I felt that focusing exclusively on being intersex would be more effective. So even though I talked about some of the same issues that trans people deal with, I didn't frame them that way.

Now I'm starting to realize that not only is this trans and intersex divide false in my own life, but it's also not necessarily the most effective strategy, though a lot of intersex activists still think it is. For starters, it's making our community appear smaller than it really is, which is detrimental to fighting for our rights.

In the past year, I've had two people who are openly trans come out to me, privately, as intersex. One of them I find rather shocking because I had no idea and I've known them for twenty years.

Wow, I think, *I wonder how many of us are out there, living openly as LGBT but secretly about this, right under everyone's noses?*

The newer acquaintance who came out to me tells me that he was born with genital variance but didn't feel like part of the intersex community because he wasn't subjected to IGM. When I remind him that I didn't experience IGM, either, but have been openly intersex for ages, he admits that it felt easier for him, emotionally, to be out as trans but not intersex.

It hurts a little to hear that, but I get it. It certainly hasn't always been easy coming out to people as intersex—and, specifically, my type of intersex—because when people hear I wasn't subjected to IGM, they automatically know that my genitals aren't what is considered "normal" for males or females. And while *I* feel no shame about that, I have often felt the shame from people with less open minds.

Even worse, though, is the fact that some intersex people have also been less friendly toward me because I didn't experience the trauma of IGM or medical "normalization." I didn't want to believe it at first, but as the years have gone by, I've had it confirmed. In fact, my new intersex friend tells me that, before getting to know me, he had seen me on *Oprah* and thought, *How the hell is she able to feel so good about being intersex, when I've been made to feel like I'm disordered by all these doctors?*

He shares that he had almost hated me because he was so full of envy, and I can understand why he felt that way. However, those kinds of reactions have sometimes left me feeling alienated within my own community. So I can also see why it would be easier for an intact intersex person who was raised female but then found themselves looking male (or vice versa) to identify as trans and become part of that community.

I've come to discover that sometimes when people like that have tried to come out as intersex and join the intersex community, they've been turned away with accusations that they're not really intersex. I've even received reports from intersex people who have tried to join other intersex organizations but were dismissed because, having escaped IGM, they don't have a medical diagnosis to "verify" that they're intersex.

I know it happens because certain community members have a fear that there are trans people pretending to be intersex and that it will be bad for the movement. I've been hearing about this fear since I came out as intersex twenty years ago, and I still hear it today. Recently, some intersex people I know have told me that people who weren't born intersex but are identifying as such are not working against, or even talking about, the irreversible harms of IGM. In fact, they say these people are jeopardizing efforts to address IGM by diverting the focus to other issues, and I agree that if that's true, it isn't great.

However, in the *long run*, given that intersex babies are operated on precisely because people think it's an undesirable way to be, it seems far from hurtful if adults who weren't born intersex nevertheless *want* to be identified as intersex. It demonstrates that it's actually something desirable (which personally I believe).

I also don't think anyone has the right to tell another person that they have to be born with certain sex characteristics in order to identify as the gender associated with those sex characteristics. In fact, intersex people are living proof that gender doesn't always match biological sex. People with CAIS, for example, are always assigned the female sex at birth, because they "look like" women, despite their male biology—so even the term *sex* does not always refer to actual biological sex, but gender! Therefore, at the risk of provoking the wrath of biological determinists, I feel compelled to point out that if both trans people and intersex people demonstrate that neither sex nor gender is determined by one's biological sex at birth, why does being intersex have to be determined this way?

More importantly, on a nonacademic, emotional level, I liked when my trans friend Christopher tried to include me in the trans community, even though I thought he was wrong. It felt good to have someone treat me with such a supportive, open-minded spirit. He didn't need me to "prove" that I was trans, and similarly, I don't need people to prove that they're intersex. I think that, in the end, our goal as a species should be for everyone to have a space where they feel safe, included, and loved (and interestingly, since my nonbinary gender identity is often included under the trans umbrella now, I guess Christopher was right!).

On another positive note, a couple of sets of parents contacted me in the past year to say that hearing me speak and seeing who I am helped them decide that it was okay not to operate on their intersex babies. It was great timing, because although things have gotten so much better since I was a child, the level of discriminatory, negative attitudes that I still experience and witness in the world around me is sometimes overwhelming. It's hard for me to dissociate from things like the frequent shootings of innocent people of color, or the ridiculously low prison sentences given to men who rape women.

Given this cultural climate, I guess I shouldn't be surprised or hurt by the fact that I still experience sexism, racism, and transphobia in the intersex movement—but I am. I also sometimes feel unsupported by certain community members who devalue my contributions—or worse, try to pass them off as their own! The combination of these things has almost driven me to step away from activism on a number of occasions. In fact, I found myself in that position right before those parents reached out to me.

However, their words reminded me of what really matters—and that I never got into intersex activism to be popular.

I got into it because I heard a group of ten adults talking about horrors and pain that no human being should have to experience, and I couldn't just go back to my normal life without doing whatever I could to try to stop the atrocities from continuing. I realize, too, that I would have never had that experience without Brittney, so ultimately, I'm grateful to her and thank her. She's an important piece of the puzzle of this beautiful human rights evolution that I've been able to participate in and experience.

I'm also grateful that one of the advocacy organizations that were still sometimes using the term *disorders of sex development* recently issued a public statement saying they oppose the use of *disorder* or any other terms that pathologize intersex people. After all these years, the American intersex movement is finally coming together! If it keeps up, I'll actually feel better about retiring, which I think about doing after two decades, now that I have a partner and a child in my life and want to take the next step in my career. I hadn't felt like I could do so before, because OII-USA was the only major national organization in the US denouncing DSD and pathologization, but now more and more intersex people are dropping DSD and promoting human rights language and perspectives.

Mainstream society is *finally* beginning to realize that all beings deserve to be treated equally, and it's a godsend. Tons of people are coming out as intersex and nonbinary—writing about it, making videos about it, and starting fantastic new projects or organizations—so many that I can hardly keep up. It's a thrilling "problem" to have. In fact, it's a dream come true.

Acknowledgments

Thank you to everyone who has read this book, especially those of you who encouraged me while patiently awaiting it. The path to this memoir, like my life, has been a long, turbulent, unexpected, nearly abandoned, and yet ultimately richly fulfilling and joyful one, and just like life, no one does it alone. There are many people I have to thank, and many of them in multiple ways, so there will be some overlap.

My deepest gratitude goes to those who believed in me in the early stages, many years ago, when becoming a writer was but an optimistic fantasy. Thank you to Sarah Colby, for reading some of my earliest prose and telling me I should pursue writing; to Dierdre DeFranceaux, for telling me I was an artist—just one who hadn't produced a lot of work yet; to Madalyn Aslan, whose handwritten birthday-card message, "One day you will write a book," has traveled with me from home to home for over a decade, inspiring me to persevere; and to Celia Jackson, for patiently being my self-proclaimed biggest fan for way longer than I care to admit. Thank you to Thea Hillman, for inviting me to read my early work at her readings; and to Justin Hampton Young, for encouraging me to find an agent and get legit. Thank you to Sarah Fran Wisby and Adam Sigel, for reminding me during more than one confused conversation to "just sit down and write." Thank you to Keelyn Heely, for taking me to my first writer's circle; and to Michelle Garcia and *The Advocate*, for helping me believe I'm a writer by running some of my first essays.

Thank you to the many who helped make this memoir a reality once the journey had actually begun. In addition to those listed above, I thank the following for never once displaying doubt that I would publish this one day, or being enthusiastically certain that I would: my late mother, Doris Matheus-Viloria (to whom this book is dedicated, in part), Ann Lane, Mary Hacsunda, Kelly Stuart, Lael Limber-Landis, Robin Racicot, Rana Lee Araneta, Gelareh Alam, Hannah Doress, John Farnsworth, Elizabeth Festa, Patricia Marino, Megan Willdorf, Mike Barclay, Eleanor Lacey, David Berkey, Sophia Berkey, Juliana Berkey, David Skolnick, Ariel Skolnick, Celia Jackson, Faera Taylor, Sarah Wakida, Caitlin Crandall, Llano Blue, Calen Draper Swift, Pierre Redon, Georgiann Davis, Samantha Ostergaard, Shanti Zinzi, Jon Lee, Jason Matzner, Lauren Kozak, Gina Carillo, Devin True, Logan Stewart, Heather Luttrell, Andrea Villafañe, Maria Nieto, Cathrael Hackler, and Kai Hackler-Brant. Special thanks to Terry Sendgraff, for telling me that my book would sell—with a conviction that made me actually believe it—when I was broke and terrified while shopping it.

Thank you to Heather Donohue for being an excellent writing teacher, and to all the ladies of the writers' group we formed after that fateful class, for your feedback on my early drafts. Thank you to my friend Maria Nieto, for encouraging me to shoot for the top once I had a finished product. Thank you, additionally, to Heather Donohue for reading the first manuscript of this memoir, and for her feedback, which gave me the courage to pursue publishing it; and to my friend Rana, the second reader, whose additional feedback gave me even more.

Thank you a million times over to my agent, Mollie Glick, for believing in this memoir and my ability to complete it; and to Stacy Creamer, who acquired it. Thank you also to Ali Wade Benjamin, for her fantastic feedback and encouragement as an early reader.

Thank you to everyone at Hachette Books, most especially my editor, Lauren Hummel, for her support and commitment upon inheriting this book. Her dedication in going over it, possibly as many times as I have, and her brilliantly detailed analysis through so many rounds made this final version what it is. Thank you also to Amanda Kain, for making it look so beautiful.

Thank you to my astoundingly beautiful friends, past and present, without whose love, acceptance, company, and support I would not be here today, most especially: Ann Lane, for making my childhood bearable and my young adulthood infinitely more enjoyable; Christa Stewart, for giving me hope; Shanti Zinzi, for sharing her spiritual wisdom and for telling me like it is; and Cynthia Hall, for being a kindred spirit and for being there through thick and thin.

I am indebted to the following friends for helping me get out of the hole I dug myself into (yes, I have been one of those writers) when beginning to pursue this project: Lael Limber-Landis, Yvette Pierce, Adam Sigel, and Jobi B. Wise. I am also deeply grateful to the friends who provided jobs, meals, a couch to sleep on, et cetera, along the way, most especially: Megan Willdorf, Celia Jackson, David Skolnick, Kelly Stuart, Laura Wiley, Eleanor Lacey, David Berkey, Michaela Halle, and, through the final push: Christopher Gault, Cynthia Hall, Terry Sendgraff and Aileen Moffitt, Annette Gagnon, and Cathrael Hackler.

Last, thank you to all the angels in my life. Thank you to those who inspired me to be who I am by paving the way, especially Grace Jones, Gina Wilson, and the late Prince Rogers Nelson. Thank you to the many incredible allies, especially Charles Radcliffe of the UN, and to the therapists and healers that I have been lucky enough to know and learn from, most especially Terry Hatcher. Thank you to all the television, radio, and film producers, directors, crews, and hosts, and to the editors and publications that have allowed me to educate the world about intersex issues and people, especially Oprah Winfrey, for introducing us to millions and thus helping countless of us, and our friends and families, meet each other and/or feel less alone.

Thank you to my siblings, Eden and Hugh Viloria, for keeping me company during those terribly dark days of my childhood, and to my father, Hugo Leonardo Viloria, who, despite causing many of those days, was also instrumental, along with my late mother, Doris, in my keeping the body I was born with and love. Thank you both, from the bottom of my heart, for allowing me to develop into the person, and gender, that I am, and to everyone over the years who has accepted me as such. Your love has made my life worth it, and this book a reality.

Notes

Chapter 6: The Grass Is Not Always Greener

1. Plato, *Symposium*, trans. Benjamin Jowett, accessed August 8, 2016, http://classics.mit.edu/Plato/symposium.html.
2. Sherry Velasco, *The Lieutenant Nun: Transgenderism, Lesbian Desire, & Catalina de Erauso* (Austin: University of Texas Press, 2000).
3. "110 Protesters to Face Charges at Wesleyan U.," *New York Times*, May 3, 1988, http://www.nytimes.com/1988/05/03/nyregion/110-protesters-to-face-charges-at-wesleyan-u.html.

Chapter 7: Finding the Vocabulary to Talk about Being Intersex

1. In December 1997, Bornstein uses *ze* again in her groundbreaking *My Gender Workbook*, and by '98 I hear people have started using *ze* in New York.
2. Christopher Lee is no longer with us, but he will be remembered as a fabulous, pioneering force for the trans community. I'm proud to pay a small tribute to him here and happy to have had the chance to know him and spend some time in his fiercely brave, caring, creative energy. RIP, Christopher—you rocked!
3. "Genderqueer" gender identity—which means not feeling like, or "identifying as," a man or a woman—hadn't taken off yet in 1997, even within radical gender-nonconforming communities in San Francisco, so I do not include it here.

Chapter 10: Nonbinary Blues

1. John Money, "Hermaphroditism: An Inquiry into the Nature of a Human Paradox" (PhD dissertation, Harvard University, 1952).

Chapter 11: Burning My Man

1. "2000 Art Theme: The Body," in "The Culture: Historical Archives," Burning Man, accessed August 8, 2016, http://burningman.org/culture/history/brc-history/event-archives/2000-2/00_theme/.

Chapter 13: The Lows of Being Out

1. A. D. Dreger, C. Chase, A. Sousa, P. A. Gruppuso, and J. Frader, "Changing the Nomenclature/Taxonomy for Intersex: A Scientific and Clinical Rationale," *Journal of Pediatric Endocrinology and Metabolism* 18, no. 8 (August 2005): 729–33, http://www.ncbi.nlm.nih.gov/pubmed/16200837.

Chapter 14: The Highs of Being Out

1. "Hida Viloria Tells Us What She Really Thinks," *SF Weekly*, accessed August 8, 2016, http://www.sfweekly.com/sanfrancisco/hida-viloria-tells-us-what-she-really-thinks/Content?oid=2164589.

Chapter 15: The Struggle at Home and Abroad

1. Christopher Clarey, "Gender Test after a Gold-Medal Finish," *New York Times*, August 19, 2009, http://www.nytimes.com/2009/08/20/sports/20runner.html?_r=0.
2. Luis Prada, "Testicles! Vaginas! Caster Semenya's Got 'Em All!," *Funny-Crave*, accessed August 8, 2016, http://funnycrave.com/testicles-vaginas-caster-semenya's-gotem-all/.
3. ANC Youth League, "Caster Semenya Is a Female—ANCYL," *politicsweb*, September 11, 2009, http://www.politicsweb.co.za/documents/caster-semenya-is-a-female--ancyl.
4. Ian Evans, "Wow, Look at Caster Go Now! Gender-Row Runner Gets Chance to Show She's All Woman in New Photoshoot," *Daily Mail*, accessed August 8, 2016, http://www.dailymail.co.uk/news/article-1212036/Sex-test-runners-makeover--Caster-Semenya-shows-shes-woman-YOU-magazine-photo-shoot-gender-row-Berlin-championships.html.
5. Hida Viloria, "Commentary: My Life as a 'Mighty Hermaphrodite,'" *Vital Signs*, CNN, http://www.cnn.com/2009/HEALTH/09/18/hida.viloria.intersex.athlete/.
6. Anne Fausto-Sterling, *Sexing the Body: Gender Politics and the Construction of Sexuality* (New York: Basic Books, 2000).

7. Hida Viloria, "How Common Is Intersex? An Explanation of the Stats," OII United States, April 1, 2015, http://oii-usa.org/2563/how-common-is -intersex-in-humans/.

8. Tyra Banks was also the host of another television show in which aspiring models competed before Tyra and other judges for the prize of being America's next top model, the show's name.

9. Gina Kolata, "I.O.C. Panel Calls for Treatment in Sex Ambiguity Cases," *New York Times*, January 20, 2010, http://www.nytimes.com/2010/01/21/ sports/olympics/21ioc.html?_r=2.

10. Curtis Hinkle, "Why We Do Not Use 'Disorder of Sex Development,'" OII Intersex Network, October 12, 2007, http://oiiinternational.com/697/ why-we-do-not-use-disorder-of-sex-development/.

11. "Statement by South African Feminists," African Women's Development Fund, accessed August 8, 2016, http://awdf.org/statement-by-south -african-feminists/.

12. I discovered many years later that there was another intersex American who also spoke out publicly in support of Caster—Professor Cary Gabriel Costello, PhD—and his blog posts revealed that he felt the same way I did.

13. Sally Gross, "Intersex and the Law," *Mail & Guardian*, accessed August 8, 2016, http://mg.co.za/article/2009-09-19-intersex-and-the-law.

14. Stephen Coan, "The Journey from Selwyn to Sally," News24, August 28, 2009, http://www.news24.com/Archives/Witness/The-journey-from-Selwyn -to-Sally-20150430.

15. Candice Bailey, "'I Prize Myself as Being a Human Being,'" *IOL*, September 19, 2009, http://www.iol.co.za/news/south-africa/i-prize-myself -as-being-a-human-being-459040.

16. "Third Sex Becomes Official: Australian Passports Now Have Three Gender Options—Male, Female and X," *Daily Mail*, September 15, 2011, http://www.dailymail.co.uk/news/article-2037662/Third-sex-official -Australian-passports-gender-options--male-female-x.html.

17. "On Australian Passports and 'X' for Sex," OII Australia, October 9, 2011, https://oii.org.au/14763/on-x-passports/.

18. Sarah Dingle, "Passport Gender Choice Made Easier," Australian Broadcasting Corporation News, September 14, 2011, http://www.abc.net.au/ news/2011-09-15/passport-gender-choice-made-easier/2899928.

19. Hida Viloria, "X Marks Evolution: The Benefits of the 'Indeterminate Sex' Passport Designator," *Hastings Bioethics Forum* (blog), The Hastings Center, December 7, 2011, http://www.thehastingscenter.org/x-marks -evolution-the-benefits-of-the-indeterminate-sex-passport-designator/.

Chapter 16: City of Intersex Angels

1. Hida Viloria and Maria José Martínez-Patiño, "Reexamining Rationales of 'Fairness': An Athlete and Insider's Perspective on the New Policies on Hyperandrogenism in Elite Female Athletes," *American Journal of Bioethics* 12, no.7 (June 2012), http://www.tandfonline.com/doi/abs/10.1080/152 65161.2012.680543.

2. Hida Viloria, "OII Receives Reply from US Department of State to OII Chairperson Hida Viloria's Letter Asking for Intersex Inclusion in LGBTI—Not LGBT-Only—Global Human Rights Efforts," OII United States, February 23, 2012, http://oii-usa.org/555/oii-receives-reply -department-state-oii-chairperson-hida-vilorias-letter-intersex-inclusion -lgbti-lgbtonly-global-human-rights-efforts/.

3. Hida Viloria, "Clinton's Pronouncements against Female Genital Mutilation Don't Go Far Enough," *Global Herald*, February 23, 2012, http://theglobalherald.com/clintons-pronouncements-against-female -genital-mutilation-dont-go-far-enough/27829/.

4. "Groundbreaking SPLC Lawsuit Accuses South Carolina, Doctors and Hospitals of Unnecessary Surgery on Infant," Southern Poverty Law Center, May 13, 2013, https://www.splcenter.org/news/2013/05/14/ groundbreaking-splc-lawsuit-accuses-south-carolina-doctors-and -hospitals-unnecessary.

5. Australian government, *Australian Government Guidelines on the Recognition of Sex and Gender,* July 2013 (updated November 2015), https:// www.ag.gov.au/Publications/Documents/AustralianGovernmentGuide linesontheRecognitionofSexandGender/AustralianGovernment GuidelinesontheRecognitionofSexandGender.pdf.

6. Emily Slaytor, "Sexual Orientation, Gender Identity and Intersex Status Now Protected under Federal Anti-discrimination Legislation," Hunt & Hunt Lawyers, accessed August 8, 2016, http://www.hunthunt.com.au/news -and-publications/sex-discrimination-act-1984-introduce-sexual-orientation -gender-identity-and-intersex-status?utm_source=Mondaq&utm_medium =syndication&utm_campaign=View-Original.

7. Gina Wilson, "Equal Rights for Intersex People: Testimony of an Intersex Person," *Equal Rights Review* 10 (2013): 133–39, http://www .equalrightstrust.org/ertdocumentbank/ERR10_testimony.pdf.

8. http://www.starobserver.com.au/news/changes-at-oii-as-trailblazer-gina -wilson-retires/109176.

Chapter 17: Practicing What I Preach

1. Hida Viloria, "Op-ed: What's in a Name: Intersex and Identity," *Advocate*, May 14, 2014, http://www.advocate.com/commentary/2014/05/14/op-ed-whats-name-intersex-and-identity.

2. The GenIUSS Group, *Best Practices for Asking Questions to Identify Transgender and Other Gender Minority Respondents on Population-Based Surveys*, ed. J. L. Herman (Los Angeles: Williams Institute, 2014), http://williamsinstitute.law.ucla.edu/wp-content/uploads/geniuss-report-sep-2014.pdf.

3. Hida Viloria, "Caught in the Gender Binary Blind Spot: Intersex Erasure in Cisgender Rhetoric," *Intersex and Out* (blog), August 18, 2014, http://hidaviloria.com/caught-in-the-gender-binary-blind-spot-intersex-erasure-in-cisgender-rhetoric/.

4. "9 Things You Need to Know about Being Intersex," MTV video, 1:46, September 23, 2014, http://www.mtv.com/video-clips/73crw5/faking-it-9-things-you-need-to-know-about-being-intersex.

5. Association of American Medical Colleges, "AAMC Releases Medical Education Guidelines to Improve Health Care for People Who Are LGBT, Gender Nonconforming, or Born with Differences of Sex Development," November 18, 2014, https://www.aamc.org/newsroom/newsreleases/414490/11182014.html.

6. Intersex Youth Advocacy Group, Legal Advocacy Group, "What It's Like to Be Intersex," YouTube video, 3:25, posted by "BuzzFeedYellow," March 28, 2015, https://www.youtube.com/watch?v=cAUDKEI4QKI.

7. Naith Payton, "Malta Becomes First Country to Outlaw Surgery on Intersex Babies," *PinkNews*, April 2, 2015, http://www.pinknews.co.uk/2015/04/02/malta-becomes-first-country-to-outlaw-surgery-on-intersex-babies/.

8. Hida Viloria, "Promoting Health and Social Progress by Accepting and Depathologizing Benign Intersex Traits," *Narrative Inquiry in Bioethics* 5, no. 2 (Summer 2015): 114–17, http://oii-usa.org/wp-content/uploads/Viloria-NIB-2015.pdf.

9. Frederick Douglass, "West India Emancipation" (speech, Canandaigua, New York, August 3, 1857), quoted on BlackPast.org, "(1857) Frederick Douglass, 'If There Is No Struggle, There Is No Progress,'" accessed August 8, 2016, http://www.blackpast.org/1857-frederick-douglass-if-there-no-struggle-there-no-progress.